First World War
and Army of Occupation
War Diary
France, Belgium and Germany

29 DIVISION
87 Infantry Brigade
King's Own Scottish Borderers
1st Battalion
1 March 1916 - 2 April 1919

WO95/2304/1

The Naval & Military Press Ltd
www.nmarchive.com
Published in association with The National Archives

Published by

The Naval & Military Press Ltd

Unit 10 Ridgewood Industrial Park,

Uckfield, East Sussex,

TN22 5QE England

Tel: +44 (0) 1825 749494

www.naval-military-press.com

www.nmarchive.com

This diary has been reprinted in facsimile from the original. Any imperfections are inevitably reproduced and the quality may fall short of modern type and cartographic standards.

© Crown Copyright
Images reproduced by permission of The National Archives, London, England, 2015.

Contents

Document type	Place/Title	Date From	Date To
Heading	WO95/2304/1		
Heading	29th Division 87th Infy Bde 1st Bn K.O.S. Bdrs Mar 1916-Apr 1919		
Heading	29th Division. 87th Infantry Brigade. Marseilles From Egypt 17.3.16 1st Battalion King's Own Scottish Borderers March 1916 Dec 18		
Heading	1 K.O.S.B. Vol I BEF 29		
War Diary	Suez	01/03/1916	11/03/1916
War Diary	Port Said	11/03/1916	16/03/1916
War Diary	Marseilles	17/03/1916	18/03/1916
War Diary	Domart	21/03/1916	30/03/1916
War Diary	Amplier	31/03/1916	31/03/1916
Heading	29th Division 87th Infantry Brigade. 1st Battalion King's Own Scottish Borderers April 1916		
War Diary	Amplier	01/04/1916	02/04/1916
War Diary	Mailly Mallet	03/04/1916	03/04/1916
War Diary	Firing Line	04/04/1916	13/04/1916
War Diary	Louvencourt	14/04/1916	30/04/1916
Heading	29th Division. 87th Infantry Brigade. 1st Battalion King's Own Scottish Borderers. May 1916		
War Diary	Firing Line	01/05/1916	03/05/1916
War Diary	Englebelmer	04/05/1916	13/05/1916
War Diary	Firing Line	14/05/1916	17/05/1916
War Diary	Mailly Wood	18/05/1916	25/05/1916
War Diary	Mailly	26/05/1916	30/05/1916
War Diary	Mailly Wood	31/05/1916	31/05/1916
Map			
Heading	29th Division. 87th Infantry Brigade. 1st Battalion King's Own Scottish Borderers. June 1916		
War Diary	Mailly Wood	01/06/1916	04/06/1916
War Diary	Englebemer	05/06/1916	06/06/1916
War Diary	Firing Line	07/06/1916	15/06/1916
War Diary	Louvencourt	15/06/1916	22/06/1916
War Diary	Acheux Wood	23/06/1916	30/06/1916
Heading	29th Division. 87th Infantry Brigade. 1st Battalion King's Own Scottish Borderers July 1916		
Heading	War Diary Of 1st Bn. K.O.S.B. July 1916		
War Diary	Firing Line	01/07/1916	01/07/1916
War Diary	Firing Line Hamel	02/07/1916	08/07/1916
War Diary	Acheux Wood	09/07/1916	16/07/1916
War Diary	Firing Line	17/07/1916	22/07/1916
War Diary	Mailly Wood	22/07/1916	23/07/1916
War Diary	Bus-Les-Artois	24/07/1916	24/07/1916
War Diary	Amplier	25/07/1916	26/07/1916
War Diary	Proven	27/07/1916	30/07/1916
War Diary	Ypres	31/07/1916	31/07/1916
War Diary	Firing Line	01/07/1916	01/07/1916
Heading	29th Division. 87th Infantry Brigade. 1st Battalion King's Own Scottish Borderers August 1916		

Heading	War Diary Of 1st Bn The King's Own Scottish Borderers. From 1-8-16 To 31-8-16 Volume 8		
War Diary	Ypres-Firing Line	01/08/1916	04/08/1916
War Diary	Firing Line	05/08/1916	05/08/1916
War Diary	Firing Line-Ypres	06/08/1916	06/08/1916
War Diary	Ypres	07/08/1916	07/08/1916
War Diary	Ypres-"B" Camp Brandhoek	08/08/1916	08/08/1916
War Diary	B Camp Brandhoek	09/08/1916	16/08/1916
War Diary	B Camp Ypres	17/08/1916	17/08/1916
War Diary	Ypres Firing Line	18/08/1916	18/08/1916
War Diary	Firing Line	20/08/1916	29/08/1916
War Diary	Ypres	30/08/1916	31/08/1916
Map	Plan Shewing Trenches Of 29th Divnl Area.		
Heading	29th Division. 87th Infantry Brigade. 1st Battalion King's Own Scottish Borderers September 1916		
Heading	War Diary 1st Bn. The King's Own Scottish Borderers. From 1st September 1916 To 30th September 1916 Volume No 9		
War Diary	Ypres	01/09/1916	07/09/1916
War Diary	Ypres "B" Camp Brandhoek	08/09/1916	11/09/1916
War Diary	B Camp Brandhoek	12/09/1916	17/09/1916
War Diary	B Camp Brandhoek-Ypres	18/09/1916	18/09/1916
War Diary	Firing Line	19/09/1916	23/09/1916
War Diary	Firing Line-Ypres	24/09/1916	24/09/1916
War Diary	Ypres	25/09/1916	28/09/1916
War Diary	Ypres-Firing Line	29/09/1916	30/09/1916
Map	Plan Shewing Trenches Of 29th Divnl Area		
Heading	Defence		
Heading	29th Division. 87th Infantry Brigade. 1st Battalion King's Own Scottish Borderers October 1916		
Heading	War Diary 1st Battn The King's Own Scottish Borderers. From 1st October 1916 To 31st October 1916 Volume 10		
War Diary	Firing Line Ypres	01/10/1916	04/10/1916
War Diary	M Camp Near Poperinghe	05/10/1916	06/10/1916
War Diary	M Camp Poperinghe To Cardonette	07/10/1916	07/10/1916
War Diary	Cardonnette	08/10/1916	09/10/1916
War Diary	Cardonette-Buire-Sur-Ancre	10/10/1916	10/10/1916
War Diary	Buire-Sur-Ancre	11/10/1916	13/10/1916
War Diary	Fricourt	13/10/1916	18/10/1916
War Diary	Bernafay Wood	19/10/1916	19/10/1916
War Diary	Bull's Road Trench	20/10/1916	20/10/1916
War Diary	Firing Line	21/10/1916	25/10/1916
War Diary	Bull's Road Trench	26/10/1916	26/10/1916
War Diary	Bernafay Wood	27/10/1916	28/10/1916
War Diary	Mametz Village Camp	29/10/1916	29/10/1916
War Diary	Fricourt	30/10/1916	31/10/1916
Map	Plan Shewing Trenches In 29th Div Area		
Heading	29th Division. 87th Infantry Brigade. 1st Battalion King's Own Scottish Borderers November 1916		
Heading	War Diary 1st King's Own Scottish Borderers From 1st November 1916 To 30th November 1916 Volume XI		
War Diary	Fricourt Camp	01/11/1916	02/11/1916
War Diary	Araines	03/11/1916	14/11/1916
War Diary	Citadel Camp Nr. Fricourt	15/11/1916	15/11/1916
War Diary	Firing Line Nr. Le Boeffs	16/11/1916	18/11/1916

War Diary	Firing Line	19/11/1916	20/11/1916
War Diary	Carnoy Camp North	21/11/1916	23/11/1916
War Diary	Guillemont Camp	24/11/1916	25/11/1916
War Diary	Firing Line Near Lesboeufs	26/11/1916	27/11/1916
War Diary	Firing Line Near Lesboeufs and Carnoy Camp	28/11/1916	28/11/1916
War Diary	Carnoy Camp	28/11/1916	30/11/1916
Heading	29th Division 87th Infantry Brigade. 1st Battalion King's Own Scottish Borderers December 1916		
Heading	War Diary 1st King's Own Scottish Borderers From 1st December 1916 To 31st December 1916 Volume 12		
War Diary	Carnoy Camp	01/12/1916	02/12/1916
War Diary	Guillemont	03/12/1916	03/12/1916
War Diary	Firing Line Nr Morval	04/12/1916	06/12/1916
War Diary	Carnoy Camp	07/12/1916	08/12/1916
War Diary	Mericourt	09/12/1916	11/12/1916
War Diary	Corbie	12/12/1916	12/12/1916
War Diary	Le Mesge	13/12/1916	31/12/1916
Heading	War Diary 1st Kings Own Scottish Borderers From 1st January 1917 To 31st January 1917 Volume 13		
War Diary	Le Mesge	01/01/1917	12/01/1917
War Diary	Bresle	13/01/1917	13/01/1917
War Diary	Guillemont Camp	14/01/1917	14/01/1917
War Diary	Firing Line	15/01/1917	16/01/1917
War Diary	Carnoy Camp	17/01/1917	19/01/1917
War Diary	Guillemont Camp	20/01/1917	20/01/1917
War Diary	Firing Line	21/01/1917	21/01/1917
War Diary	Guillemont Camp	22/01/1917	22/01/1917
War Diary	Firing Line	23/01/1917	24/01/1917
War Diary	Carnoy Camp	25/01/1917	26/01/1917
War Diary	Guillemont Camp	27/01/1917	27/01/1917
War Diary	Firing Line	28/01/1917	30/01/1917
War Diary	Carnoy Camp	31/01/1917	31/01/1917
Map	Plan of Trenches. M. 1B. Scale 1:10,000. 29th Div. Area.		
Heading	War Diary Of 1st Batt. The King's Own Scottish Borderers. 1st February 1917 To 28th February 1917 Volume No. 31 Vol 14		
War Diary	Carnoy Camp	01/02/1917	01/02/1917
War Diary	Guillemont Camp	02/02/1917	02/02/1917
War Diary	Firing Line	03/02/1917	04/02/1917
War Diary	Carnoy Camp	05/02/1917	07/02/1917
War Diary	Meaulte	08/02/1917	17/02/1917
War Diary	Bronfay Camp	18/02/1917	18/02/1917
War Diary	Support Line	19/02/1917	19/02/1917
War Diary	Firing Line	20/02/1917	22/02/1917
War Diary	Bronfay Camp	23/02/1917	23/02/1917
War Diary	Support Line	24/02/1917	24/02/1917
War Diary	Firing Line	25/02/1917	26/02/1917
War Diary	Hardecourt	27/02/1917	27/02/1917
War Diary	Bronfay	28/02/1917	28/02/1917
Heading	War Diary Of 1st Battn The King's Own Scottish Borderers From March 1st 1917 To March 31st 1917 Volume 32 Vol 15		
War Diary	Bronfay	01/03/1917	01/03/1917
War Diary	Ville	02/03/1917	02/03/1917
War Diary	La Neuville	03/03/1917	19/03/1917

War Diary	Le Mesge	20/03/1917	28/03/1917
War Diary	Flesselles	29/03/1917	29/03/1917
War Diary	Bonneville	30/03/1917	31/03/1917
Heading	1st Bn. King's Own Scottish Borders War Diary Month Of April 1917 Volume No. 33 Vol 16		
Miscellaneous	18887/8 Officer i/c Historical Section, Committee Of Imperial Defence, Public Record Officer, Chancery Lane, London. W.C.2.	25/10/1917	25/10/1917
War Diary	Hem	01/04/1917	01/04/1917
War Diary	Lucheux	02/04/1917	04/04/1917
War Diary	Lienvillers	05/04/1917	06/04/1917
War Diary	Grand Rullecourt	07/04/1917	07/04/1917
War Diary	Monchiet	08/04/1917	11/04/1917
War Diary	Arras	12/04/1917	12/04/1917
War Diary	The Brown Line	13/04/1917	13/04/1917
War Diary	Firing Line	14/04/1917	18/04/1917
War Diary	Brown Line	19/04/1917	19/04/1917
War Diary	Arras	20/04/1917	21/04/1917
War Diary	Firing Line (Monchy Le Preux)	22/04/1917	23/04/1917
War Diary	Support Line	24/04/1917	24/04/1917
War Diary	Duissans	25/04/1917	25/04/1917
War Diary	Lattre St Quentin	26/04/1917	26/04/1917
War Diary	St. Amand	27/04/1917	30/04/1917
War Diary	Hem	01/04/1917	01/04/1917
War Diary	Lucheux	02/04/1917	04/04/1917
War Diary	Lienvillers	05/04/1917	06/04/1917
War Diary	Grand Rullecourt	07/04/1917	07/04/1917
War Diary	Monchiet	08/04/1917	11/04/1917
War Diary	Arras	12/04/1917	12/04/1917
War Diary	The Brown Line	13/04/1917	13/04/1917
War Diary	Firing Line	14/04/1917	18/04/1917
War Diary	Brown Line	19/04/1917	19/04/1917
War Diary	Arras	20/04/1917	21/04/1917
War Diary	Firing Line	22/04/1917	22/04/1917
War Diary	Firing Line Monchy Le Preux	23/04/1917	23/04/1917
War Diary	Support Line	24/04/1917	24/04/1917
War Diary	Duissans	25/04/1917	25/04/1917
War Diary	Lattre St Quentin	26/04/1917	26/04/1917
War Diary	St. Amand	27/04/1917	30/04/1917
Miscellaneous	Instructions For Officers Going Into The Front Line To Night.	21/04/1917	21/04/1917
Operation(al) Order(s)	Operation Order No. 5 By Lieut. Colonel A.J. Welch, Commdg. 1st. Batt. The King's Own Scottish Borderers. In The Field 22nd. April. 1917	22/04/1917	22/04/1917
Map	Trench Map.		
Map	Probable Distribution Of Enemy's Forces		
Heading	War Diary		
Map	Situation Map		
Map	Guemappe		
Map	Western Front 4		
Map	Situation Map		
Map	Western Front 4		
Map	Barrage Map		
Heading	War Diary Of 1st Battn. The Kings Own Scottish Borderers. From 1st May 1917 To 31st May 1917 (Volume 34) Vol 17		

War Diary	Wanquetin	01/05/1917	01/05/1917
War Diary	Arras	02/05/1917	02/05/1917
War Diary	Support Line	03/05/1917	03/05/1917
War Diary	Arras	04/05/1917	06/05/1917
War Diary	Duissans	07/05/1917	13/05/1917
War Diary	Firing Line (Monchy Le Preux)	14/05/1917	14/05/1917
War Diary	Firing Line	14/05/1917	17/05/1917
War Diary	Brown Line	18/05/1917	19/05/1917
War Diary	Monchy Le Preux	20/05/1917	20/05/1917
War Diary	Arras	21/05/1917	29/05/1917
War Diary	Brown Line	30/05/1917	30/05/1917
War Diary	Firing Line (Monchy Le Preux)	31/05/1917	31/05/1917
War Diary	Firing Line	31/05/1917	31/05/1917
Heading	War Diary Of 1st Battn. The King's Own Scottish Borderers From June 1st 1917 To June 30th 1917 Volume No. 35 Vol 18		
War Diary	Firing Line Monchy Le Preux	01/06/1917	02/06/1917
War Diary	Arras	03/06/1917	04/06/1917
War Diary	Autheux	05/06/1917	26/06/1917
War Diary	Hopoutre	27/06/1917	27/06/1917
War Diary	Krombeke	28/06/1917	28/06/1917
War Diary	Line	29/06/1917	30/06/1917
Map	Trench Map No. 1 Scale 1.10,000		
Heading	War Diary 1st King's Own Scottish Borderers From 1st July 1917 To 31st July 1917 Volume 36 Vol 19		
War Diary	Support Line (Canal Bank)	01/07/1917	04/07/1917
War Diary	Line	05/07/1917	06/07/1917
War Diary	Crombeke	07/07/1917	12/07/1917
War Diary	Caribou Camp	13/07/1917	16/07/1917
War Diary	Caribou	17/07/1917	19/07/1917
War Diary	Caribou Camp	19/07/1917	25/07/1917
War Diary	Capt at X.27.b (Sheet 19) Proven Area	26/07/1917	29/07/1917
War Diary	Camp 16 Forest Camp Area	30/07/1917	30/07/1917
Heading	War Diary Of 1st Batt. The King's Own Scottish Borderers From August 1st 1917 To August 31st 1917 Volume No. 37 Vol 20		
War Diary	Camp 16 Forest Area	01/08/1917	02/08/1917
War Diary	Putney Camp (Proven Area)	03/08/1917	03/08/1917
War Diary	Putney Camp	04/08/1917	07/08/1917
War Diary	Forest Area (Camp. 5)	08/08/1917	10/08/1917
War Diary	Abingley Camp (B.7.c)	11/08/1917	12/08/1917
War Diary	Widjendrift Left Sub	13/08/1917	17/08/1917
War Diary	B.9.c.	18/08/1917	24/08/1917
War Diary	Langemarck Station	25/08/1917	29/08/1917
War Diary	Paddock Wood Camp	30/08/1917	31/08/1917
Miscellaneous	Narrative Of Action Of 16th August 1917	16/08/1917	16/08/1917
Heading	War Diary Of 1st Battn The King's Own Scottish Borderers. From 1st September 1917 To 30th September 1917 Volume No. 38 Vol 21		
War Diary	Paddock Wood Camp	01/09/1917	08/09/1917
War Diary	Herzeele	09/09/1917	12/09/1917
War Diary	Paddock Wood Camp	13/09/1917	20/09/1917
War Diary	Dublin Camp	21/09/1917	30/09/1917
Map	Broembeek		
Heading	Illustrations to Accompany Notes on The Interpretation of Aeroplane Photographs Series B.		

War Diary	War Diary Of 1st Battn The King's Own Scottish Borderers From 1st October. 1917 To 31st October 1917 Volume 39. Vol 22			
War Diary	White Mill Camp	01/10/1917	02/10/1917	
War Diary	Line	03/10/1917	05/10/1917	
War Diary	White Mill Camp	06/10/1917	07/10/1917	
War Diary	Dragon Wood Camp	08/10/1917	09/10/1917	
War Diary	Pitchcott Camp	10/10/1917	15/10/1917	
War Diary	Bailleulval	16/10/1917	31/10/1917	
Map				
Heading	November 1917 19 5th Div			
War Diary	Bailleulval	01/11/1917	17/11/1917	
War Diary	Haut Allaines	18/11/1917	18/11/1917	
War Diary	Dessart Wood	19/11/1917	20/11/1917	
War Diary	Marcoing (Line)	21/11/1917	26/11/1917	
War Diary	Marcoing	27/11/1917	30/11/1917	
Heading	War Diary Of 1st Battalion King's Own Scottish Borderers From 1st December 1917 To 31st December 1917 Folio 41 Vol 24			
War Diary	Line (Marcoing)	01/12/1917	07/12/1917	
War Diary	Beaudricourt	08/12/1917	17/12/1917	
War Diary	Fillievres	18/12/1917	18/12/1917	
War Diary	Wambercourt Cavron St. Martin	19/12/1917	19/12/1917	
War Diary	Herly	20/12/1917	31/12/1917	
War Diary	Assinghem	01/01/1918	01/01/1918	
War Diary	Le Nieppe	02/01/1918	02/01/1918	
War Diary	Rietveld	03/01/1918	03/01/1918	
War Diary	Privett Camp	04/01/1918	05/01/1918	
War Diary	Canal Bank (Boesinghe)	06/01/1918	18/01/1918	
War Diary	Red Rose Camp	19/01/1918	26/01/1918	
War Diary	English Fm Camp	27/01/1918	03/02/1918	
War Diary	Firing Line	04/02/1918	09/02/1918	
War Diary	B Area (Watou)	10/02/1918	26/02/1918	
War Diary	Poperinghe	27/02/1918	05/03/1918	
War Diary	English FM. California Camps	06/03/1918	06/03/1918	
War Diary	Firing Line	07/03/1918	09/03/1918	
War Diary	Junction Camp	10/03/1918	12/03/1918	
War Diary	Firing Line	13/03/1918	18/03/1918	
War Diary	Hasler Camp	19/03/1918	22/03/1918	
War Diary	B Camp Brandhoek	23/03/1918	30/03/1918	
War Diary	Firing Line	31/03/1918	31/03/1918	
Heading	87th Brigade. 29th Division. 1st Battalion King's Own Scottish Borderers April 1918			
War Diary	Firing Line	01/04/1918	02/04/1918	
War Diary	Junction & California Camps	03/04/1918	05/04/1918	
War Diary	Firing Line	06/04/1918	08/04/1918	
War Diary	Road Camp	09/04/1918	09/04/1918	
War Diary	Neuf Berquin	10/04/1918	10/04/1918	
War Diary	Firing Line	11/04/1918	13/04/1918	
War Diary	Borre	14/04/1918	14/04/1918	
War Diary	Sylvestre Cappel	15/04/1918	16/04/1918	
War Diary	Borre	17/04/1918	17/04/1918	
War Diary	Sylvestre Cappel	18/04/1918	20/04/1918	
War Diary	La Brearde	21/04/1918	27/04/1918	
War Diary	Firing Line	28/04/1918	30/04/1918	
Map	Diagram of XV Corps Defence Works			

War Diary	Firing Line	01/05/1918	05/05/1918
War Diary	Le Grande Hasard	06/05/1918	13/05/1918
War Diary	Firing Line	14/05/1918	20/05/1918
War Diary	Petit Sec Bois	21/05/1918	27/05/1918
War Diary	Hazebrouck	28/05/1918	31/05/1918
Miscellaneous	Account of Raid Carried Out By The 1st King's Own Scottish Borderers On The Morning Of The 27th May 1918	27/05/1918	27/05/1918
Map			
War Diary	Hazebrouck	01/06/1918	04/06/1918
War Diary	Firing Line	05/06/1918	11/06/1918
War Diary	Morbecque	12/06/1918	14/06/1918
War Diary	Firing Line	15/06/1918	17/06/1918
War Diary	Hazebrouck	18/06/1918	19/06/1918
War Diary	Firing Line	20/06/1918	21/06/1918
War Diary	Eeck Hout Casteel	22/06/1918	22/06/1918
War Diary	Racquinghem	23/06/1918	14/07/1918
War Diary	Hazebrouck	14/07/1918	15/07/1918
War Diary	Reserve Line	16/07/1918	17/07/1918
War Diary	Hazebrouck	17/07/1918	18/07/1918
War Diary	C Camp.	18/07/1918	22/07/1918
War Diary	Hondeghem	22/07/1918	24/07/1918
War Diary	St. Marie Cappel	25/07/1918	03/08/1918
War Diary	Hazebrouck	03/08/1918	14/08/1918
War Diary	Firing Line	15/08/1918	19/08/1918
War Diary	Reserve Line	20/08/1918	20/08/1918
War Diary	Hazebrouck	20/08/1918	26/08/1918
War Diary	Support Line	26/08/1918	27/08/1918
War Diary	Firing Line	27/08/1918	31/08/1918
Map	T.S.260 Corps Topo Section 6.8.18		
Miscellaneous	29th Division Intelligence Summary From 6 a.m. 18th to 6 a.m 19th August 1918	19/08/1918	19/08/1918
Map	Ref. Sheets 27. SE And 368 NE		
War Diary	Reserve Line	01/09/1918	02/09/1918
War Diary	Firing Line	03/09/1918	03/09/1918
War Diary	Reserve Line	04/09/1918	10/09/1918
War Diary	Nevada Farm	11/09/1918	12/09/1918
War Diary	Wallon Cappel	13/09/1918	16/09/1918
War Diary	St Jan Ter Biezen	17/09/1918	19/09/1918
War Diary	Firing Line	20/09/1918	22/09/1918
War Diary	Support Line	23/09/1918	24/09/1918
War Diary	Road Camp	25/09/1918	26/09/1918
War Diary	Poperinghe	27/09/1918	27/09/1918
War Diary	Firing Line	28/09/1918	30/09/1918
Operation(al) Order(s)	Operation Order No. 40 By Major C.H. M.G. Commanding 1st Battn. The K.O.S.B. In The Field 26.9.18	26/09/1918	26/09/1918
Map	Second British Corps.		
War Diary	Line	01/10/1918	03/10/1918
War Diary	Veldhoek Line	04/10/1918	04/10/1918
War Diary	Westhoek	05/10/1918	07/10/1918
War Diary	Ypres	08/10/1918	10/10/1918
War Diary	Westhoek	11/10/1918	11/10/1918
War Diary	Firing Line	12/10/1918	16/10/1918
War Diary	Heule (G.10.C.)	17/10/1918	20/10/1918
War Diary	Line	21/10/1918	22/10/1918

War Diary	Rappart	23/10/1918	23/10/1918
War Diary	Harlebeke	24/10/1918	27/10/1918
War Diary	Mouscron Area	28/10/1918	28/10/1918
War Diary	St. Andre	29/10/1918	31/10/1918
Miscellaneous	Operations Of 87th Infantry Brigade From 28th September, 1918 To 16th October, 1918	16/10/1918	16/10/1918
Miscellaneous	Operation Order No By Major C.H. Crawshaw M.C. Commanding 1/KOSB		
Operation(al) Order(s)	1st. Batt. The K.O.S.B.-Order No. 73	12/12/1918	12/12/1918
War Diary	St. Andre	01/11/1918	07/11/1918
War Diary	Tourcoing	08/11/1918	08/11/1918
War Diary	Support Area	09/11/1918	10/11/1918
War Diary	Celles	11/11/1918	13/11/1918
War Diary	St. Sauveur	13/11/1918	17/11/1918
War Diary	Stoquoi	18/11/1918	18/11/1918
War Diary	Soignies Area	19/11/1918	19/11/1918
War Diary	Petit Roeulx-Les-Braine	19/11/1918	21/11/1918
War Diary	Ittre	22/11/1918	23/11/1918
War Diary	Bousval	24/11/1918	25/11/1918
War Diary	Orbais	26/11/1918	27/11/1918
War Diary	Bierwart	27/11/1918	28/11/1918
War Diary	Ferre	29/11/1918	29/11/1918
War Diary	Mont	30/11/1918	30/11/1918
Miscellaneous	Base Instructions.		
Miscellaneous	K.O.S.B Centre of General		
Map			
Miscellaneous	H Qrs. 87th Bde.		
War Diary	La Reid	01/12/1918	01/12/1918
War Diary	Francorchamps	01/12/1918	04/12/1918
War Diary	Weywertz	05/12/1918	05/12/1918
War Diary	Montjoie	05/12/1918	06/12/1918
War Diary	Thum	07/12/1918	07/12/1918
War Diary	Muddersheim	08/12/1918	08/12/1918
War Diary	Gymnich	09/12/1918	09/12/1918
War Diary	Kriel Area	09/12/1918	13/12/1918
War Diary	Berg Gladbach	13/12/1918	15/12/1918
War Diary	Burscheid	16/12/1918	16/12/1918
War Diary	Burg Castle	16/12/1918	24/12/1918
Heading	Southern (Late 29th) Div 87th Infy Bde 1st B K.O.S.B. Jan-Apr 1919 To UK		
War Diary	Burg Castle	01/01/1919	28/02/1919
Miscellaneous	DAG GHQ 3rd Echelon	03/04/1919	03/04/1919
War Diary	Burg Castle	01/03/1919	17/03/1919
War Diary	Mulheim	18/03/1919	31/03/1919
War Diary	Dunkirk	01/04/1919	02/04/1919

wqs12304 11

29TH DIVISION
87TH INFY BDE

1ST BN K.O.S.BDRS
MAR 1916 - DEC APR 1919

29th Division.

87th Infantry Brigade.

Arrived MARSEILLES from EGYPT 17.3.16.

1st BATTALION

KING'S OWN SCOTTISH BORDERERS

MARCH 1916

29

1 KOSB

Vol I II
~~III IV~~
BEF

Army Form C. 2118.

WAR DIARY
INTELLIGENCE SUMMARY.
(Erase heading not required.)

Place	Date	Hour	Summary of Events and Information	Remarks and references to Appendices
SUEZ	MARCH 1st		Battalion Training	To hospital nil
"	2nd		Battalion Training	To hospital 5¢o
"	3rd		Battalion Training	to hospital "
"	4th		reformed Battalion 1st King Transfer to P¢ Said thereafter dropt 22 others to embark for France.	
"	5th		Battalion Training	to hospital — one
"	6th		Service	to hospital nil
"	7th		Battalion Training	to hospital H.O. Moore on his return
"	8th		Battalion Training New two drove water tensit and Taken to use short fat	
"			Battalion Training	to hospital one. Lost A.J.M. Stone yearned battalion
"	9th		draft of 23 of the ranks joined Battalion Training	to hospital one
"	10th		A, B & half C lookay and headquarters embarked at Suez on board H.M.T.S. Wandilla. Total 24 Officers 596 other ranks. sailed at night for Port Said arrived there next morning. 10 hospital three	
"	11th		Remainder of C & D Coys left by train for Port Said at 11.00 arriving 17.00 and embarked on H.M.T. Megantic. Total 10 Officers	

367 other ranks. To hospital nil.

Army Form C. 2118.

No 97

WAR DIARY
or
INTELLIGENCE SUMMARY.

(Erase heading not required.)

Instructions regarding War Diaries and Intelligence Summaries are contained in F. S. Regs., Part II. and the Staff Manual respectively. Title pages will be prepared in manuscript.

Place	Date	Hour	Summary of Events and Information	Remarks and references to Appendices
	March			
Port Said	11th		H.M.T.S. Megantic sailed	
	12th		H.M.T.S. Manuella sailed	
	13th		At sea	
	14th		At sea	
	15th		At sea	
	16th		At sea	
Marseilles	17th		H.M.T.S. Megantic arrived, party disembarked and entrained for Pont Remy, arrived there night of 19th and marched to Dorbast arriving there morning of 20th and went into billets	
			H.M.T.S. Manuella at sea	
"	19th		H.M.T.S. Manuella arrived, party disembarked and entrained for Pont Remy, arrived there night of 20th and marched to Dorbast, arriving there morning of 21st and went into billets. To hospital 7.	
Dorbast	21st		Battalion rested. 1 officer to hospital, nil	
"	22nd		Battalion route march to hospital 12.	
"	23rd		Battalion route march. To hospital 1.	
"	24th		Battalion route march. To hospital one.	

Army Form C. 2118.

WAR DIARY
or
INTELLIGENCE SUMMARY.
(Erase heading not required.)

Instructions regarding War Diaries and Intelligence Summaries are contained in F. S. Regs., Part II and the Staff Manual respectively. Title pages will be prepared in manuscript.

No 8

Place	Date	Hour	Summary of Events and Information	Remarks and references to Appendices
Domart	March 25th		Battalion route march to hospital n°6.	
"	26th		Divine Service to hospital 3.	
"	27th		Battalion took march to hospital n.	
"	28th		Battalion route march to hospital n°1.	
"	29th		Battalion route march to hospital n°1.	
"	30th		Battalion marched to Amplier to hospital two. Sent to hospital 2.	
Amplier	31st		Battalion rested and had medical inspection.	

Written up by L. H. Chipman Capt + Adjutant 1st K.O.S. Borderers.

29th Division.
87th Infantry Brigade.

1st BATTALION

KING'S OWN SCOTTISH BORDERERS

APRIL 1 9 1 6

WAR DIARY or INTELLIGENCE SUMMARY

Army Form C. 2118.

Place	Date	Hour	Summary of Events and Information	Remarks and references to Appendices
Amphlies	May 1st		Battalion on fatigue unloading ambulances. To hospital 6.	
"	2nd		Battalion arrived. Mostly Muster at evening. Pier about 1830 and moved into billets. To hospital 2.	
Monthly Huella 2nd			Battalion refitted and prepared to leave line and take over position occupied by 15th W. Yorkshire Regt.	
"			Reynolds Regiment by Batteries S.S. MOTORS R.D.G.A D.S.O.B also supplied by 230. C Coy in support in trenches St. D Coy in reserve at Aveluy nullah. To hospital 4.	
Firing line	3rd		Very quiet day, reported no enemy movement of trenches. Casualties.	
"	5th		Only overworked for staff to hospital. Patrol went out for 12 hours at night. Very quiet day. B Coy moves into front line. "D" Coy moves into support trenches A. being relieved at Aveluy nullah by a Coy of 1st R. Inniskilling. Casualties one wounded.	
"	6th		Very quiet day. troops on improvement of trenches. 2/Lt. A°Neil relieved by 2/Lt. Got 4 hospital out.	
"	7th		Very quiet day. Sep. 5,6,7,8 [ ] dispatched and reinforcements built at Sgt Kearn. 8 to hospital sick.	

Army Form C. 2118.

WAR DIARY
or
INTELLIGENCE SUMMARY.
(Erase heading not required.)

N0100

Place	Date	Hour	Summary of Events and Information	Remarks and references to Appendices
Loung Line	8th		Very quiet day, work carried out repairing trenches. Sick to hospital Nil.	
"	9th		Very quiet day. "B" Coy commenced new harrows on coy frontage.	
"	10th		Very quiet day, work carried out repairing trenches. Sick to hospital Nil. A Patrol of 2 Officers & 50 men went out from 0230 to 0345.	
"	11th		Very quiet day work carried out repairing trenches. Sick to hospital Nil.	
"	12th		Very quiet day work carried out repairing trenches. Sick to hospital Nil.	
"	13th		Very quiet day work carried out repairing trenches. Battn relieved by 1st Lancashire Fusiliers relief completed by 2330. Battn moved into billets at Louvencourt. Casualties one man wounded. Sick to hospital two.	
Louvencourt	14th		Battn rested. Sick to hospital Nil.	
"	15th		Battn training two Companies bathing. Lecture to Battn on gas with demonstration. Sick to hospital Nil.	
"	16th		Divine Service. Sick to hospital Nil.	
"	17th		Battn training. Courses started for specialists. One boy on fatigue. Sick to hospital 5.	

Army Form C. 2118.

N° 104

WAR DIARY
or
INTELLIGENCE SUMMARY.
(Erase heading not required.)

Instructions regarding War Diaries and Intelligence Summaries are contained in F. S. Regs., Part II. and the Staff Manual respectively. Title pages will be prepared in manuscript.

Place	Date	Hour	Summary of Events and Information	Remarks and references to Appendices
LOUVENCOURT	April 18th		Battn. training. Lecture to Officers & N.C.O's on wiring. Demonstration on Flammenwerfer. Two boys bathing. One boy on fatigue. Sick to Hospital 2 A.B.S.	
"	19th		Officers to England to resume medical studies. Sick to hospital Pul. Battn. training. Lecture to Officers & N.C.O's on discipline. One boy on fatigue. Sick to hospital 4.	
"	20th		Battn. route march. Sick to hospital Pul. One boy on fatigue	
"	21st		Battn. training. One boy on fatigue. Sick to hospital 6. & to J.H.D.	
"	22nd		Hunts to Brigade Mathews Bad boy	
"	23rd		Battn. training. One boy on fatigue. Sick to hospital 2.	
"	24th		Divine Service. Sick to hospital 13.	
"	25th		Battn. lecturing recruit wiring. Sick to hospital 2. One boy on fatigue. Battn. training. Lieut-General Sir A. Hunter-Weston, commanding 8th Army & Officers inspected Officers, N.C.O's and men who took part in the landing on Gallipoli peninsula, and gave them a stirring address. Total number on parade Two Officers, one hundred and twenty other ranks. Sick to hospital Pul. One boy on fatigue	

WAR DIARY
or
INTELLIGENCE SUMMARY.
(Erase heading not required.)

Army Form C. 2118.

Place	Date	Hour	Summary of Events and Information	Remarks and references to Appendices
LOUVENCOURT	APRIL 1916 26/4			
	27th		Batt. training. Lecture on Bayonet fighting. 1 Boy on fatigue. Sick to hospital 1.	
			Batt. training. Lecture on Bayonet fighting by Major Blampied Shots thro'	
			Quarters. 1 Boy on fatigue. Sick to hospital 4.	
	28th	1830	Batt. Training. 1 Boy on fatigue. Batt. moved off to the firing line via	
			MAILLEY-MAILLET and relieved the 16th Middlesex Regiment on the sector	
			of the Divisional area. Relief completed by 2030. Sick to hospital out.	
	29th		Very quiet day. Work carried out, repairing of trenches, & digging shell proof	
			dug outs.	
		1130	Our artillery commenced heavy bombardment of enemy's trenches, opposite	
			our front, to enable a raiding party to gain access to the German	
			trenches. Enemy retaliated upon our line, damaging it considerably.	
	30th	0100	Bombardment ceased. Casualties. Killed 2/Lt H S J Hunter and 3/NAT	
			Hoy and five men. Wounded forty four men. Sick to hospital 3.	
			Written up by :-	
			Capt F B Miller Lieut	
			Bdy 1st KOSB	

29th Division.

87th Infantry Brigade.

- -----

1st BATTALION

KKNG&S OWN SCOTTISH BORDERERS.

M A Y   1 9 1 6

Army Form C 2118.

WAR DIARY
INTELLIGENCE SUMMARY.
(Erase heading not required.)

Instructions regarding War Diaries and Intelligence Summaries are contained in F. S. Regs., Part II. and the Staff Manual respectively. Title pages will be prepared in manuscript.

Place	Date	Hour	Summary of Events and Information	Remarks and references to Appendices
MAY 1916 FIRING LINE	1st		Battn occupied firing line from Q 4/2 – Q 4/12 with two Coys, 1 Coy occupied Tenderloin and 1 Coy in Br Allen Trench and Cardiff Street (ref map attached)	Appendices
"	2nd		Very quiet day. Continued repairing trenches, and building dug outs. Sick to hospital nil	Casualties
"			Very quiet day. Continued repairing trenches, and building dug outs.	Casualties
"			Nil. Sick to hospital 5.	
"	3rd		Very quiet day. Continued repairing trenches, and building dug outs.	
"		2000	Battn relieved by 4th Bn Worcs R. Regt. The first Coy arrived at 2000 and were followed at 1/2 hour intervals. The relief was completed by 2300.	
"			The Battn on being relieved moved into Billets at ENGLEBELMER. Casualties	
			Nil. Sick to hospital 3.	
ENGLEBELMER	4th		Battn employed in deepening and repairing trenches. Sick to hospital 5.	
"	5th		Battn employed in deepening and repairing trenches. Sick to hospital nil.	
"	6th		Battn employed in deepening and repairing trenches. Sick to hospital nil.	
"	7th		Divine Service was held. 160 men employed by R.E. Sick to hospital 1.	
"	8th		Battn employed in deepening and repairing trenches. Sick to hospital 1. 2nd R Revd.	
"	9th		Battn employed in deepening and repairing trenches. Casualties 4. 2 wounded	

Army Form C. 2118.

WAR DIARY
or
INTELLIGENCE SUMMARY.
(Erase heading not required.)

Place	Date	Hour	Summary of Events and Information	Remarks and references to Appendices
MAY 1916 ENGELBELMER				
"	10th		Sent to hospital 2 slightly wounded at duty, all shell wounds. Sick to hospital 1.	
"	11th		Battn employed on deepening and repairing trenches. Sick to hospital 5.	
"	12th		Battn employed on deepening and repairing trenches. Sick to hospital 2.	
"	13th		Battn employed on deepening and repairing trenches. Sick to hospital nil.	
		15.00	Battn moved up to firing line. Starting from ENGELBELMER at 1500 till 1800. The boys moved off at show intervals to relieve the 1st R.I.F. The Battn took over the front line from Q⁷/₁₁ – Q⁶/₁₇ (copy map attached) Disposition from right to left. In firing line A.B and D Coys. C Coy took over the reserve line KNIGHTSBRIDGE BARRACKS. The relief was completed at 1900. Sick to hospital 3. Casualties Capt. J.K.A. Campbell, Lieut. E. Robertson, Lieut W.W. Mills wounded, also a stray lot of B Coy	
FIRING LINE	14th		Very quiet day. Battn employed on drawing, deepening and repairing trenches and building dug outs. Casualties Nil. Sick to hospital Nil.	
"	15th		Very quiet day. Battn continued drawing, deepening and repairing trenches	

No 105
Army Form C. 2118.

WAR DIARY
or
INTELLIGENCE SUMMARY.
(Erase heading not required.)

Instructions regarding War Diaries and Intelligence Summaries are contained in F. S. Regs., Part II. and the Staff Manual respectively. Title pages will be prepared in manuscript.

Place	Date	Hour	Summary of Events and Information	Remarks and references to Appendices
MAY 1916 FIRING LINE				
"		2300	and building dug-outs. At about 2300 the enemy started bombarding our trenches slightly on our left, but very little damage was done. Casualties 4 wounded. All their wounded sick to hospital nil.	
"	16th		Very quiet day. The Battⁿ continued improving the trenches. O patrol of 1 officer and 5 men left our trenches at 2030 by sap head at Q16½ to examine a path which led through enemy's wire. No enemy patrols were seen, but the path had recently been used. Nil The patrol returned at 2300. Casualties Nil Sick to hospital Nil.	W.M.Kenyon Capt 1st KOSB
"	17th		Quiet day. The Battⁿ continued improving trenches. Casualties Nil. Sick to Hospital Nil.	
MAILLY WOOD	18th		Battⁿ relieved by 2nd Hampshire Reg^t. Relief began at 1400 completed by 1715. Bⁿ in camp at MAILLY WOOD Casualties Nil. Sick to Hospital Nil	

Army Form C. 2118.

WAR DIARY
or
INTELLIGENCE SUMMARY.
(Erase heading not required.)

Instructions regarding War Diaries and Intelligence Summaries are contained in F. S. Regs., Part II. and the Staff Manual respectively. Title pages will be prepared in manuscript.

Place	Date	Hour	Summary of Events and Information	Remarks and references to Appendices
MAILLY WOOD	MAY 19th		Two parties working at cable trenches at night. Casualties NIL Sick to Hospital. NIL. Lt Col A T Welch took over Command of 183 wire draft of Sturn Lillyson	
"	May 20th		One working party by day and one by night on cable trenches in the vicinity of Q.15.C.9.1 (Rt Sect 57d S.E.) ½ Bn to ACHEUX for bathing. Casualties NIL Sick to Hospital 2 Officers dismist/other Ranks Christn	
"	May 21st		Divine Service was held. ½ Bn to ACHEUX for bathing. Casualties NIL Sick to Hospital NIL	
"	May 22nd	1900	Working party of 450 OR. on cable trenches at Q.15.C.9.1. Colonel sick to Hospital NIL	
"	May 23rd	1900	Working party of 5 officers 543 OR on cable trenches at Q.15 C.9.5.	
"	"	1400	Cable Party tired v.v. Best night big aerial fight scrap with aeroplanes. Casualties not known in the strength of the 183	
"	May 24th	1900	Working party of 5 officers 460 men to AUCHENVILLERS STATION for work on signal cables Casualties nil Sick to Hospital 4	
"	" 25th	0800	Working party of 2 officers and 100 men to Q.8.D.3.2 for work on cable trenches. also 1 officer and 30 men at 14.30. Casualties	
"	"	1900	Working party of 5 officers and 316 men to AUCHENVILLERS STATION for work on cable trenches. Casualties Nil Sick to Hospital 1	

Army Form C. 2118.

N°107

WAR DIARY
or
INTELLIGENCE SUMMARY.
(Erase heading not required.)

Instructions regarding War Diaries and Intelligence Summaries are contained in F. S. Regs., Part II. and the Staff Manual respectively. Title pages will be prepared in manuscript.

Place	Date	Hour	Summary of Events and Information	Remarks and references to Appendices
MAILLY	26th May	0930	1 Officer & 64 men working on Cable trenches at Q.8.d.21	
		1030	5 Officers and 407 men working on cable trenches at AUCHENVILLERS STATION.	
		1900	A draft of 108 men arrived from 9th Entrenching Bn. Casualties NIL SICK to Hospital NIL	
	27 May	1430	5 Officers and 480 men working on cable trenches at AUCHENVILLERS STATION Casualties NIL SICK to Hospital NIL	
	28 May	2030	6 Officers and 556 men working on Cable trenches at AUCHENVILLERS STATION. Casualties NIL SICK to Hospital: 2 Lieut Gas & 1 man.	
	29 May	1400	2 N.C.Os & 72 men working under West Riding Field Coy R.E. at Q.8.D.21	
		2030	5 Officers & 538 men working on Cable trenches at AUCHENVILLERS STATION. Casualties NIL SICK to Hospital NIL	
	30 May	1400	2 N.C.Os & 72 men working under West Riding Field Coy R.E. at Q.8.d.3.1	
		1900	5 Officers & 536 men working on Cable Trenches at Q.22.c.2.8. Casualties NIL SICK to Hospital NIL.	

Army Form C. 2118.

WAR DIARY
or
INTELLIGENCE SUMMARY.
(Erase heading not required.)

Instructions regarding War Diaries and Intelligence Summaries are contained in F. S. Regs., Part II. and the Staff Manual respectively. Title pages will be prepared in manuscript.

Place	Date	Hour	Summary of Events and Information	Remarks and references to Appendices
MAILLY WOOD	MAY 31st	0900	5 Officers and 250 men working party at WHITTINGTON AVENUE under arrangements by G.O.C. 67th Bde.	
		0730	1 Officer + 50 men working party at DIVISIONAL range under arrangements by G.O.C. 67th Bde.	
		0845	1 Officer + 37 men working party, rendezvous at CAPE JOURDAIN for work on cable trenches.	
		0830	4 Officers and 200 men working party on cable trenches at Q22 c & o.	
		1330	3 Officers and 70 men working party on cable trenches in the vicinity of WHITTINGTON & GABION AVENUES. CASUALTIES NIL SICK TO HOSPITAL 3.	

Written up by
JKB Campbell Capt A/Adj
1/KOJB.
31/5/16

29th Division.
87th Infantry Brigade.

1st BATTALION

KING'S OWN SCOTTISH BORDERERS.

JULY 1916
June.

WAR DIARY
INTELLIGENCE SUMMARY

Army Form C. 2118
No. 109
Vol 6

Place	Date	Hour	Summary of Events and Information	Remarks and references to Appendices
MAILLY WOOD	1st June 1916	0730	1 Officer and 30 men on working party at Divisional Range.	
		0830	1 Officer and 50 men on working party and working at CAFE JOURDAIN. This party proceeded to work a cable trench running parallel with BROADWAY. During the morning they were fired at by enemy Mountain Battery and shelled, no man being wounded.	
		1900	3 Officers and 200 men working on cable trenches at P.22.a.0.8. Relieved by another party of same numbers at 23.30. Casualties 1 man wounded SICK to Hospital. NIL	
"	2nd June	0130	5 Officers and 250 men working on WHITTINGTON AVENUE	
		0830	1 Officer and 30 men working party at Café Jourdain under O.C. Signals 29th Div	
		1900	5 Officers and 250 men working a cable trenches at P.22.a.08	
		1930	2 Officers and 100 men working on WHITTINGTON AVENUE. Casualties nil. Sick to Hospital 1.?"	
"	3rd June	0745	1 Officer and 6 men working under R.A. Officer at THURLES DUMP.	
		0830	1 Officer and 30 men at CAFE JOURDAIN under O.C. Signals 29th Div	
		1330	5 Officers and 200 men working at Whittington Avenue. Casualties NIL Sick to Hospital NIL	

Army Form C. 2118.
No 110

WAR DIARY
INTELLIGENCE SUMMARY.
(Erase heading not required.)

Instructions regarding War Diaries and Intelligence Summaries are contained in F. S. Regs., Part II. and the Staff Manual respectively. Title pages will be prepared in manuscript.

Place	Date	Hour	Summary of Events and Information	Remarks and references to Appendices
	June 1916			
MAILLY WOOD	4 June	0730	1 Officer and 50 men under R.A. Officer at THURLES DUMP.	
		0930–1130	Divine Service held for Church of England, Presbyterians and Roman Catholics	
ENGLEBEMER		1930	"B" proceeded to billets in ENGLEBEMER. MAILLY WOOD evacuated 1515.	
	5 June		1 Officer and 100 men completing Signal Cables under of S. job 29th Div at Q.22.a.20. Casualties NIL Sick to Hospital 1	
"			Working parties throughout the day numbering in all 5 officers and 274 men working and repairing WITHINGTON, GABION, and TIPPERARY AVENUE. 6 small parties working by day under KENT R.E. No working parties by night.	
"	6 June (crossed out)		Casualties NIL Sick to Hospital. NIL	
"	6 June		Working parties continued on WITHINGTON and TIPPERARY AVENUE Also working Parties under KENT R.E. Two parties each of 120 men working with 2/SWB, and 1st Royal Inniskilling Fusiliers. Total number working by day 10 officers 550 men. Working party of 2 officers and 100 men on WITHINGTON AVENUE. Casualties NIL Sick to Hospital 2	
FIRING LINE	7 June		"A" B and D Companies in working parties as follows: "A" Coy on WITHINGTON – GABION AVENUES and FRENCH TRENCH. "B" Company at KNIGHTSBRIDGE BARRACKS. D Company	

1577 Wt. W10791/7773 500,000 1/15 D. D. & L. A.D.S.S./Forms/C. 2118.

Army Form C. 2118.

N°1/1

WAR DIARY
—or—
INTELLIGENCE SUMMARY

(Erase heading not required.)

Instructions regarding War Diaries and Intelligence Summaries are contained in F. S. Regs., Part II. and the Staff Manual respectively. Title Pages will be prepared in manuscript.

Place	Date	Hour	Summary of Events and Information	Remarks and references to Appendices
FIRING LINE	7th June		On working party in KNIGHTSBRIDGE Barracks and on Deep Dug outs in Hyde Park Corner after working parties closed. Relief commenced. Firing line taken over from 1st Royal Innuskilling Fusiliers at 14.20.	
		1915	Relief complete. B's took up line from BUCKINGHAM PALACE ROAD in Q17 & 36 to Q16 & 47 from Right to left in firing line A, B and C Coys. D in Reserve	
			D Company in KNIGHTSBRIDGE BARRACKS. Quiet night Casualties nil. Sick to Hospital nil.	
"	8th June		Quiet day B's employed cleaning drawing trenches and defensive Jumping out steps in Bird Street, St James St, Buckingham Palace Rd, Bridge St, Wellington Barracks. One Right of trench were	
			In the afternoon enemy fired on front line trenches wounding three men. Just of fit Casualties 3 men wounded from shell fire. Sick to Hospital nil.	
"	9th June		Quiet day Work continued as on 8th June. Throughout the afternoon enemy trench Mortar firing on REDAN. Also intermittently throughout night. Otherwise night quiet. Casualties nil Sick to Hospital 8.	
	10th June		Quiet day. Enemy Trench Mortar firing on Redan in the afternoon. We retained at us the 9th June. At 2300 Enemy commenced bombardment on front line trenches chiefly on the right of our at Peter Robert and round about 0100. Not much damage to trenches but MARY REDAN suffered a great deal. Casualties Killed 7 wounded (including my self). Sick to Hospital nil.	

Army Form C. 2118.

WAR DIARY
INTELLIGENCE SUMMARY

(Erase heading not required.)

Instructions regarding War Diaries and Intelligence Summaries are contained in F. S. Regs., Part II and the Staff Manual respectively. Title Pages will be prepared in manuscript.

Place	Date	Hour	Summary of Events and Information	Remarks and references to Appendices
Firing line	11th June		Quiet day. Trenches repaired. Bridging work continued & putting out strip continued long ones. At night wiring party putting wire in front of Chaing Cross Rnd. also built up MARY REDN. & Standings. Casualties NIL. Sick to Hospital NIL.	
"	12th June		Quiet day. In the afternoon enemy shelled "A" Company one man being wounded. Bridging work & putting out strips being continued. St James' Street revetted & the top built up. At night front of St James' Street wired. Weather very wet. Casualties 1 wounded. Sick to Hospital 3.	
"	13th June		Work continued as on the 12th. Gaps cut in wire between second and first lines. Desultory shelling during the afternoon. Quiet night. Casualties 1 wounded. Sick to Hospital 11.	
"	14th June		Quiet day. Work on Bridges & putting out strips completed. Numbers put up completed in front of Bridges &Gaps. Weather very wet. Trenches cleaned and drained. Casualties NIL. Sick to Hospital 1. 2/Lieut. R. Reid 1/KOSB rejoined from sick leave.	
"	15th June		Quiet day. Bn relieved after dinners by 2nd Hampshire Regiment. Relief complete by 2030. Bn marched into Billets at LOUVENCOURT. Captain & Bt. Major G. Hill, KOSB rejoined his arrival and is taken on the strength of the Bn. Casualties NIL. Sick to Hospital NIL.	
LOUVENCOURT				

Army Form C. 2118.

WAR DIARY
or
INTELLIGENCE SUMMARY
(Erase heading not required.)

Place	Date	Hour	Summary of Events and Information	Remarks and references to Appendices
LOUVEY COURT	16th June		Bn. doing Bde duties and working parties. Companies training under Company arrangements. Draft of 15 men arrived from the Base. Casualties nil. Sick to Hospital nil. 2 invalids met to Bath.	
"	17th June		Companies training in the morning and Bde. marching in the afternoon. Casualties nil. Sick to Hospital 2. Lieut W.M. Clark 7/K.O.S.B reported for duty & is taken on the strength of the Bn.	
"	18th June		Practice Bde attack in the morning. Divine Service held for Presbyterians and Church of England. Bn. doing Bde Duties and working parties. Casualties nil. Sick to Hospital 4.	
"	19th June		Company training before breakfast. Practice Bde attack 1100. Company training in the afternoon. 2nd Lieut. Kirk Sloan & McClelland 9/K.O.S.B reported for duty and are taken on the strength of the Bn. Casualties nil. Sick to Hospital 1.	
"	20th June		Practice Bde attack in the morning. Training by Companies in the afternoon. Casualties nil. Sick to Hospital nil.	
"	21st June		2/Lt Glennie reported for duty & is taken on the strength of the Bn. Afternoon inspection by Major General De Lisle, Commanding 29th Division. Casualties nil. Sick to Hospital 4.	

Army Form C. 2118.

WAR DIARY
or
INTELLIGENCE SUMMARY
(Erase heading not required.)

Instructions regarding War Diaries and Intelligence Summaries are contained in F. S. Regs., Part II. and the Staff Manual respectively. Title Pages will be prepared in manuscript.

No. 1/14

Place	Date	Hour	Summary of Events and Information	Remarks and references to Appendices
LOUVENCOURT	22nd June		Br finding Bde Duties and working parties. Divisional Tactical Scheme in the morning. Casualties nil. Sick to Hospital nil.	
AT MAILLY WOOD	23rd June		Bn moved to MAILLY WOOD & march as a Bn at 1800 from LOUVENCOURT. Move completed 2200 when last load of Transport arrived. Casualties nil. Sick to Hospital nil. Bn in Bde Reserve.	
"	24th June		Bombardment of enemy's line commenced. In the afternoon while detonating bombs an accident took place one man being wounded. Casualties 9 wounded. Sick to Hospital 2.	
"	25th June		Bombardment of enemy's line continued. Divine Service held at 1100. Lieut. J.K. Ballantyne and 2/Lieut. R.B. Honey 7th & Bn K.O.S.B. having reported their arrival are taken on the strength of the Bn from this date. Casualties NIL. Sick to Hospital NIL.	
"	26th June		Bombardment of enemy's line continued. Nothing to report. Casualties NIL. Sick to Hospital nil.	
"	27th June		Bombardment of enemy's line continued. Companies at the disposal of Company Commanders, for tactical features suitable for attack. Casualties NIL. Sick to Hospital NIL.	

Army Form C. 2118.

WAR DIARY
~~or~~ INTELLIGENCE SUMMARY

(Erase heading not required.)

Instructions regarding War Diaries and Intelligence Summaries are contained in F.S. Regs., Part II. and the Staff Manual respectively. Title Pages will be prepared in manuscript.

Place	Date	Hour	Summary of Events and Information	Remarks and references to Appendices
ACHEUX WOOD	28th June	1500	Bombardment of enemy's line continued. Bn. preparing to march out. Telegram received furthering offensive operations 48 hours. Casualties NIL Sick to Hospital NIL	
"	29th June	1700	Bombardment of enemy's line continued. Very heavy Bombardment about 1700. Companies at disposal of O.C. Companies. Also companies attending bathing parade. Casualties 1 Killed 1 Wounded (attached 87th T.M Battery ENGLEBEMER) Sick to Hospital NIL	
"	30th June	1815	Quiet day. Bn. preparing to move up into trenches. The 10th Reserve under Major G. Hilton paraded and proceeded to ENGLEBEMER	
		2100	Bn. paraded and moved off in the following order: "C" Company, Platoon 1/2 Monmouth Regt, D Company, A Company, Brigade 87th Machine Gun Company, B Company, 1 Section 87.2 T.M Battery. Route followed was ROTTEN ROW, EDGE MAILLYWOOD, entered ENGLEBEMER, GABION AVENUE. Trenches reached without any casualties. CASUALTIES NIL Sick to Hospital NIL	

Written at by
J.H.B Campbell Capt.
for Adjutant 1/10/13

29th Division.
87th Infantry Brigade

1st BATTALION

KING'S OWN SCOTTISH BORDERERS

~~JUNE~~ 1916
July.

87/29

War Diary

of

1st Bn. K.O.S.B.

July 1916

WAR DIARY / INTELLIGENCE SUMMARY

Army Form C. 2118.

(Erase heading not required.)

Instructions regarding War Diaries and Intelligence Summaries are contained in F.S. Regs., Part II. and the Staff Manual respectively. Title Pages will be prepared in manuscript.

July 1916

Place	Date	Hour	Summary of Events and Information	Remarks and references to Appendices
FIRING LINE (WOOD)	July 1	0200	Bn in the line as previously arranged. "D" Company in BROOK STREET, "B" Company and T.M. Section in PICCADILLY. "A" Company and Machine Gun Section in ST. JAMES STREET. "C" Company and a Platoon 1/3 Monmouth Regiment in BUCKINGHAM PALACE ROAD.	
			2/Lt GOW "C" Company killed whilst getting his Platoon into position and 2 men "C" Company wounded. Bn Head Qrs in Dugout at Junction PICCADILLY, BOND STREET.	
		0733	1 Royal Inniskilling Fusiliers commenced attack from front line trenches. Bn to advance when last wave of 1/R.I.F. reached German wire.	LOUVENCOURT
		0740	1/R.I. held up by Machine gun fire.	
		0752	1/K.O.S.B. attack not progressing. Bn moved out under heavy machine gun fire.	
		0810	Our attack not progressing. Bn moved out to intense enemy machine gun fire. Attack on left seemed to be equally unsuccessful.	
		0831	Advance still going on but being constantly checked.	
		0838	Enemy heavily shelled MARY REDAN.	
		0845	The attack ceased.	
		0900	Capt Ainslie sent a message to say he was collecting all wounded and unwounded men in trenches N of MARY REDAN.	
		0940	Newfoundland Regiment and Essex Regiment advanced, the Newfoundland Regt on left and the Essex in support. 1st Bn attack failed.	
		1030	1st Reserve under Major G. Wills arrived and took up their position in front-line trenches.	
		1137	Our front line and support trenches very heavily shelled by enemy.	
		1600	Orders received for the 1st Bn and Bn Reserve to re-organize at FORT JACKSON on relief.	
		1730	Bn relieved by 1 Essex Regiment attacked and re-organized in FORT JACKSON	
		2300	10 Officers and 20 men digging a grave at KNIGHTSBRIDGE. Heavy bombardment by enemy on front line trenches at night but undisturbed at FORT JACKSON	

Army Form C. 2118.

WAR DIARY
or
INTELLIGENCE SUMMARY
(Erase heading not required.)

July 1916

Place	Date	Hour	Summary of Events and Information	Remarks and references to Appendices
FIRING LINE. HAMEL	July 2nd	1000	Bn moved from FORT JACKSON via KNIGHTSBRIDGE, CONSTITUTIONAL HILL and Front line to HAMEL and took over line occupied by 108th Bde. Front line occupied from River ANCRE exclusive at LANCASHIRE POST Q 24 A 3.7 to JEAN STREET exclusive to Q 23 B 57. A.D. Company on right, C.D. Company on left. B Company in reserve, CROWS NEST held by one Platoon of "A" Company and 2 Lewis Guns. Casualties KILLED 1 WOUNDED 4 Sick to Hospital NIL. IN KENTISH CAVES. Parties out bringing in dead and wounded of 108th Bde.	
FIRING LINE HAMEL	July 3rd		Work on trenches continued all day. Trenches very bad and falling in. Weather very bad. An attack expected at night - bent nothing happened. Activity near THIEPVAL WOOD. Casualties KILLED NIL WOUNDED 3 Sick to Hospital NIL.	
FIRING LINE HAMEL	July 4th		Work still continued on trenches. Spare arms and equipment sent thro' k Banyule Dump. Weather still very bad. Casualties KILLED 1 Wounded NIL Sick to Hospital NIL	
FIRING LINE HAMEL	July 5th		Quiet day and night. B Company relieved "C" Company at 1730 and C Company went into reserve. Covering parties provided for RE. working party and for 1/2 Monmouth Regiment who were digging new trench in front of firing line. Casualties NIL Sick to Hospital NIL. Enemy fired trench mortars shells during the afternoon but without casualties and damage.	

July 1916.

WAR DIARY
or
INTELLIGENCE SUMMARY

Army Form C. 2118.

Place	Date	Hour	Summary of Events and Information	Remarks and references to Appendices
FIRING LINE HAMEL	July 6		Work continued on trenches. Weather still very wet. Thiepval Kirk Moan & McLellman passed from Divisional Stunt ACHEUX. A draft of 121 O.R. arrived from the base and were posted to "C" and "D" Companies. Casualties 1 wounded sick to Hospital nil	
FIRING LINE HAMEL	July 7	1800	Weather still very wet. Great activity to the right of THIEPVAL WOOD. 1800 took over the part of the line occupied by 1st S.W.B. 13 Company extending its left flank to JEAN STREET inclusive and D Company occupying from JEAN STREET to S.A.P. in front of LOUVERCY STREET Q25B29. Covering parties supplied to working party 1/2 Monmouth Regiment. Casualties KILLED 1 WOUNDED 4 Sick to Hospital nil	
FIRING LINE HAMEL	July 8		Headquarters shelled at 0130, 0800 & 1130 & 1400. Relieved by 1st Lancashire Fusiliers Relief complete 2100. Bn marched into huts at ACHEUX WOOD arriving 0200 on 9th. Casualties 2 Killed R.S. Robertson wounded KILLED 2. WOUNDED 4 Sick to Hospital nil	
ACHEUX WOOD	July 9	1700	Quiet day all troops cleaning up. Inspection of draft by C.O. at 1700. Casualties nil Sick to Hospital nil.	
	July 10	1100	Bn inspected by the Corps Commander Lieut General A. Hunter-Weston K.C.B. D.S.O. Company Parades in the afternoon. Casualties nil Sick to Hospital nil	

WAR DIARY / INTELLIGENCE SUMMARY

Army Form C. 2118.

July 1916

Place	Date	Hour	Summary of Events and Information	Remarks and references to Appendices
ACHEUX WOOD	July 11		Company Parades. Lewis Gunners dispatched & Bombing Classes. 200 men of Bn. bathed in the afternoon. Casualties: Sick to Hospital nil.	
"	July 12		Company Parades. Lewis Gunners & Bombers & Bombing classes. Reading Party being trained under Captain Knote. 200 men bathed. Bn. route march with 1st Line Transport. Ban. took LOUVENCOURT.	
		14.20	LEALVILLERS. Casualties nil. Sick to Hospital nil.	
"	July 13		Company parades and training continued. Casualties nil. Sick to Hospital 2 [?]	
"	July 14		Company parades and training continued. Lewis Gunners shooting on the range & Bombers practising on Bombing ground. Casualties nil. Sick to Hospital nil.	
"	July 15		Company parades and training continued. Casualties 1 man killed. Sick to Hospital 1.	
"	July 16		Parade twice in the morning. Casualties nil. Sick to Hospital 3.	

WAR DIARY / INTELLIGENCE SUMMARY

Army Form C. 2118.

July 1916

Place	Date	Hour	Summary of Events and Information	Remarks and references to Appendices
Firing line	July 17		Leading Company started from ACHEUX WOOD at 1400. Bn. relieved 1st Essex Regiment. Line occupied from LONG ACRE on the right exclusive to the left B, C and D in firing line. A Company in Reserve. Bn. Headquarters in FETHARD STREET. Artillery activity by us at night. No retaliation in our sector. Casualties 1 killed, 3 wounded. Sick to Hospital nil. 1 man front.	
"	July 18th		Cleaning and repairing trenches by day. Bn. H.Q. changed from FETHARD ST to ST JOHN'S ROAD. Lieuts. Dolbey, Maxwell, Henning, and Maxwell with F.O.R. arrived. Covering parties provided for working parts of 1st Royal Inniskilling Fusiliers and 1st Border Regt. working on Advanced Firing Line. Parties from "B" and "D" Companies making and erecting fire step in Advanced firing line. Burial and wiring parties out. Quiet night. Casualties nil. Sick to Hospital nil. 1 refused.	
"	July 19th		Work on trenches continued. Fine day continued by day on Advanced firing line. Working parties of 1st Royal Inniskillings & Border Regiment as before. Enemy turning Trench mortar shelling on our support line between 2000 - 2300, otherwise quiet night. Casualties nil. Sick to Hospital 1.	

WAR DIARY / INTELLIGENCE SUMMARY

Army Form C. 2118.

July 1916

Place	Date	Hour	Summary of Events and Information	Remarks and references to Appendices
FIRING LINE	July 20		Work continued on trenches. Between 1800-1900 enemy shelled PICCADILLY and FETHARD ST. Burial and salvage parties out at night. Work continued by 1st R.I.F. and 2nd Border Regt on advanced firing line. Activity on the night in the direction of THIEPVAL at night but quiet on our front. Casualties 1 wounded sick to Hospital nil 1 man to United Kingdom.	
"	July 21st	2320 - 0200	Work continued on trenches. Normal day. Working parties out at night as on previous days. The night enemy bombarded our front line and to our right. Chiefly on the right of our sub sector but "B" Company on the right experienced a good deal of the bombardment. 1st R.I.F. working party reconnoitre in advanced firing line and only had 1 casualty. Casualties 1 wounded sick to Hospital 1. 2/Lt Farrell & 2/Lt Brown arrived.	
"	July 22nd		Work on trenches continued. Relieved by 1st R.I.F. Relief complete 1915. Working party of 150 off in trenches to dig new communication trench to the advanced firing line and work on trithem end of advanced firing line. 1 Platoon from "C" Coy garrisoning FORT ANLEY and 1 Platoon "C" Coy garrisoning FORT WITHINGTON. Remainder Bn to tents in MAILLY WOOD. Casualties nil	
MAILLY WOOD			Scale to two/total 2	

Army Form C. 2118.

WAR DIARY
INTELLIGENCE SUMMARY
(Erase heading not required.)

July 1916.

Instructions regarding War Diaries and Intelligence Summaries are contained in F.S. Regs., Part II and the Staff Manual respectively. Title Pages will be prepared in manuscript.

Place	Date	Hour	Summary of Events and Information	Remarks and references to Appendices
MAILLY WOOD	July 23rd		Companies at the disposal of O.C. Companies. Working party of 150 men working on the new communication trench and southern portion of new advanced firing line. Casualties nil. Sick to Hospital nil.	
BUS-LES-ARTOIS	July 24th		Brigade relieved by 74th Brigade. Bn relieved by 13th Bn Cheshire Regt. Platoon garrisoning FORT WITHINGTON relieved by Platoon from 13th Bn Cheshire Regt. Platoon garrisoning FORT MILEY relieved by Platoon from 9th Bn Loyal North Lancashire Regt. Bn marched by companies to BUS-LES-ARTOIS. Casualties nil. Sick to Hospital nil. 3 men reported.	
AMPLIER	July 25	0915	Bn marched to AMPLIER arriving at 1200. Bn accommodated in huts. Casualties nil. Sick to Hospital nil.	
"	July 26th		Bathing parade for 100 men in the morning. Companies at the disposal of O.C. Companies. Casualties nil. Sick to Hospital nil. 2nd Lieut Bell left for United Kingdom.	
PROVEN	July 27th		Bn left AMPLIER 1230. Entrained at DOULLENS and left 1534. Arrived HAZEBROUCK 2030. Arrived PROVEN 2230. Bn marched to "K" Camp between	

July 1916

87
29

1 KOSB
Vol 7

14 T
9 sheets

WAR DIARY
—or—
INTELLIGENCE SUMMARY
(Erase heading not required.)

Army Form C. 2118.

Instructions regarding War Diaries and Intelligence Summaries are contained in F. S. Regs., Part II. and the Staff Manual respectively. Title Pages will be prepared in manuscript.

Place	Date	Hour	Summary of Events and Information	Remarks and references to Appendices
PROVEN	July 27th (continued)		PROVEN and POPERINGHE arriving 2400. Transport arrived 0200. Casualties nil. Sick to Hospital nil.	
"	July 28th		Bn moved to "M" Campalment & rode from "K" Camp. "A", "B" and "C" Companies bathing in the afternoon. Casualties nil. Sick to Hospital nil.	
"	July 29th	1100 0945	Company parades 0900, 1100 and 2400. Inspection of Transport by C.O. Lewis Gunners and Bombers on parade under their respective officers. Casualties nil. Sick to Hospital 2.	
"	July 30th		Church Parade services in the morning. Casualties nil. Sick to Hospital 1.	
YPRES	July 31st		Company Parades 0900 and 1100. Bn paraded 1930 and marched to entraining point near POPERINGHE. Train left 2030 arrived at the ASYLUM YPRES 2115. Bn relieved 9th Suffolk Regiment. Bn Hd Qrs and 'B' Coy in the PRISON. 'A' Coy in and east in front of PRISON. 'D' Coy in Dug out in DRY SWITCH 'C' Coy at the MAGAZINE. Rgt Shields, 9 Gallery and A.H. Corner arrived. Casualties nil. Sick to Hospital 1. 1 man rejoined from Hospital. Written up by J.K.R. Campbell Major 1/KOSB 31.7.16	

WAR DIARY
INTELLIGENCE SUMMARY
(Erase heading not required.)

Army Form C. 2118.

1st KOSB
July 1/16

Place	Date	Hour	Summary of Events and Information	Remarks and references to Appendices
ARMY LINE	July 1		Casualties Officers <u>Killed</u> Capt A.J.M. Shaw 11th KRRC att'd/KOSB 2/Lieut R. Reid 9th KOSB 2/Lieut J.L. Gow 9th KOSB 2/Lieut R. Stewart 9th KOSB 2/Lieut I.A.J. Scott 3rd KOSB 2/Lieut J.H. Glennie 1st KOSB 2/Lieut W. Dickie 9th KOSB 2/Lieut F. Paterson 9th KOSB 2/Lieut H.P.B. Porter 7th KOSB 2/Lieut P.T. Pont Y. Coys 2/Lieut J.A.S. Graham-Clarke 1/KOSB <u>Wounded</u> Capt G.E. Malcolm 11th Royal Highlanders att'd/KOSB Lieut A. Kennedy 1st Herts Rifles surveys Major G. Helm 1st KOSB Tempy Captain E. Robertson 3rd KOSB 2/Lieut R.B. Harvey 7th KOSB 2/Lieut H.F. Dixon 3rd KOSB 2/Lieut D.B. Bontein 3rd KOSB 2/Lieut C.A. Morton 9th KOSB 2/Lieut D. McLaren 9th KOSB Killed Officers 11 O.R. 88 Wounded Officers 9 O.R. 406 Missing Officers NIL O.R. 59 Total: Officers 20 OR 546	

29th Division.

87th Infantry Brigade.

- -----

1st BATTALION

KING'S OWN SCOTTISH BORDERERS

AUGUST 1 9 1 6

Appendix attached; - Trench Map

87/29.

Vol 8

15
10 sheets

CONFIDENTIAL.

WAR DIARY

of

1st Bn. The King's Own Scottish Borderers.

from 1-8-16 to 31-8-16.

Volume:- 7

A W Welch
Lieut. Col.
Comm dg 1st. K.O. Sco. Borderers.

In the Field
1-9-16

Army Form C. 2118.

August 1915
No 175

WAR DIARY
or
INTELLIGENCE SUMMARY.
(Erase heading not required.)

Instructions regarding War Diaries and Intelligence Summaries are contained in F.S. Regs., Part II. and the Staff Manual respectively. Title pages will be prepared in manuscript.

Place	Date	Hour	Summary of Events and Information	Remarks and references to Appendices
YPRES — FIRING LINE	Aug 1.	7/15	"D" Company left the PRISON YPRES. Rest of the Bⁿ followed by ½ Companies at five minutes interval. Bⁿ occupied right sub sector of Brigade Area. "A" and "D" Companies occupied from right of ASA to FENCHURCH STREET. "A" and "D" Confined in firing line. "C" Company in support, with one platoon at S.8 and 1 Platoon and 2 sections each at X4 and X5. "B" Company in reserve in COMGREVE WALK. Bⁿ took over line from 1ˢᵗ LEICESTERSHIRE Regt. Relief completed 23.50. Quiet night. Casualties nil. Sick to Hospital nil.	
"	Aug 2		Quiet day. Work at night. Building up front line, support and reserve lines. Quiet night and during both in front line. Building up parapet. Revetting Traverses. Casualties nil. Sick to Hospital nil. on front line	
"	Aug 3		Enemy active with MINNENWERFER during the morning. Work continued at night as before. Party from 1ˢᵗ R.I.R on work in stand. Quiet night. Casualties nil. Sick to Hospital nil.	
"	Aug 4		Enemy again active with MINNENWERFER on front line. Work continued at night as before. Casualties 2 wounded (since died of wounds) 1 Sick to Hospital taken to U.K. for ammunition work. Quiet night.	

Army Form C. 2118.

N°/26

WAR DIARY
— OR —
INTELLIGENCE SUMMARY.
(Erase heading not required.)

Instructions regarding War Diaries and Intelligence Summaries are contained in F.S. Regs., Part II. and the Staff Manual respectively. Title pages will be prepared in manuscript.

Place	Date	Hour	Summary of Events and Information	Remarks and references to Appendices
FIRING LINE	5 Aug		Enemy very active with MINNEWERFERS on A.8. in the morning. Work continued in Trenches. Quiet night. Casualties 1/Sergt. DOBBEY wounded (at duty) 1 man wounded 1 man to United Kingdom under age.	
" - YPRES	6 Aug		Quiet day. Bⁿ relieved by 1ˢᵗ Royal Innuskilling Fusiliers at night and went into Batn Reserve. 1 killed at YPRES north Hd. Qrs at PRISON. Relief complete 10.10. Casualties Wounded 1 Sick to hospital 1.	
YPRES	7 Aug		Working party of 3 Officers and 160 men working in front line on communication trench STRAND and FLEET STREET. 1 Officer and 50 men making drain in rear of firing line. About 24.00 enemy sent over gas and heterogeneity shells among working party in the STRAND and FLEET STREET. (Caused party to cease work at 01.15.) Casualties Lieuts W. GORDON, T.K. BALLANTYNE, and 2/Lieut J. BROWN and 8 men suffering from effects of gas. 1 man rejoined from hospital. Bⁿ relieved in N.W. YPRES by 2ⁿᵈ 18ᵗʰ Royal Fusiliers. Bⁿ entrained at	
YPRES — "B" CAMP BRANDHOEK	8 Aug		2330 and arrived "B" Camp BRANDHOEK 24.00 just before leaving YPRES enemy put over gas at right St. Jacob St- Bⁿ entrained without sustaining Casualties. Casualties 1 killed 1 wounded and 2 suffering effects of gas all attached to 87ᵗʰ Batty which was firing adjacent to Bⁿ. Bⁿ forming part of Divisional Reserve.	

1577 Wt. W10791/1773 500,000 1/15 D. D. & L. A.D.S.S./Forms/C. 2118.

Army Form C. 2118.

WAR DIARY
INTELLIGENCE SUMMARY
(Erase heading not required.)

August 1916.

Place	Date	Hour	Summary of Events and Information	Remarks and references to Appendices
"B" CAMP BRANDHOEK	9th Aug		Continued at the disposal of O.C. Companies. Kit inspection etc. Casualties nil. Sick to Hospital nil.	
"	10th Aug		Bathing parade for all companies at POPERINGHE Baths in the morning. Company parades in the afternoon. M.G. Class for Lewis Gunners and Bombers under Lewis Gun Officer and Bombing Officer. Casualties and Sick to Hospital nil	
"	11th Aug	1730	Raiding Party paraded for training. Training continued. Casualties, 1 man attached Trench Mortar Battery wounded suffering from effects of gas. Sick to Hospital nil. 2/Lieut T.I.R. Higgins and 2/Lieut J.McG. Robertson reported their arrival and were taken on the strength of the Bn.	
		2130.	Night operations for Raiding Party.	
"	12th Aug		Church Parade service in the morning. Casualties nil. Sick to Hospital nil	
"	13th Aug		Training continued in the morning and afternoon.	
		1720	Inspection of Camp by the Corps Commander. Casualties nil. 1 man sick to Hospital.	
"	14th Aug		Working party of 2 officers and 86 O.R. on work at "C" Camp in the morning and of 2 officers and 120 O.R. at "B" Camp in the afternoon. Training continued with available remaining men. Casualties nil. Sick to Hospital nil	

2449 Wt. W14957/M90 750,000 1/16 J.B.C. & A. Forms/C.2118/12.

WAR DIARY
INTELLIGENCE SUMMARY
(Erase heading not required.)

Army Form C.2118.

No/28

August 1916

Place	Date	Hour	Summary of Events and Information	Remarks and references to Appendices
"B" Camp BRANDHOEK	15th Aug		Training continued. Route March by Companies in the morning. C.O. Inspection of Camp. Night Operations for Ration party. Casualties nil. Sick to hospital nil.	
" "	16th Aug	0900	Lecture to officers and NCOs by Divisional Gas Officer. Battery parade for all Companies at POPERINGHE train in the morning. Training continued in the afternoon. Casualties nil. Sick to Hospital nil.	
"B" Camp - YPRES	17th Aug	2145	Tactical School for officers in the evening under C.O. Companies at the disposal of Coy Companies in the morning. Bn left by train from BRANDHOEK to YPRES and relieved 1/4th Lancashire Fusiliers and 1/1d Co in Gaol. Coy in "X" occupying same billets as before. Casualties nil. Sick to hospital nil.	
YPRES FIRING LINE	18th Aug		Bn relieved 2nd Bn Royal Fusiliers in firing line. Same line occupied as on August 12. Front line "B" Company on the right. "A" Company on the left. Support "D" Company in "X" line. "C" Company in reserve in CONGREVE WALK. Relief complete 2330. Casualties nil. 1 man sick to hospital.	

WAR DIARY or INTELLIGENCE SUMMARY

Army Form C. 2118.

August 1916

No 129

(Erase heading not required.)

Place	Date	Hour	Summary of Events and Information	Remarks and references to Appendices
FIRING LINE	Aug 20		Work begun on GARDEN OF EDEN. Other working parties at front line; drawn from LATE at Bn.H.Q. & BELLE WAERDEBEKE continued. S.P. entrenched. Trench WARWICK FARM. Officers patrol out from "B" Company at night. No result. Two dead Germans found in wire tonight in and turned. Identified as belonging to 234 R.I.R. Enemy machine guns active at night. Casualties nil. Sick to Hospital nil	
"	Aug 21. 15.00		Bombardment of enemy front line by our artillery. Our front line initially withdrew during bombardment to "X" line and COSGREVE WALK. The time towards but afterwards "A & B" suffered from MINNINWERFER fire. Work continued at night. Casualties 1 man killed, "M" period 4 men wounded. Sick to Hospital nil.	
"	Aug 22		Quiet day. Work continued. Patrol from "A" Company out reconnoitring in front of KAISERBILL. Casualties nil. Sick to Hospital nil. 1 man referred from Hospital.	
"	Aug 23. 15.30		Bombardment by our 2" Trench Mortar. Retaliation small. Work continued. Patrol from "B" Company reconnoitring MOUND. Casualties 1 men wounded. 1 man sick to Hospital	
"	Aug 24. 06.00 07.30		Inspection of lines by G.O.C. Division. Two Germans seen in trench but escaped on being fired on. Suffered to have been left from enemy patrol of previous night. Work continued. Borrow drains being dug in rear of each line. Captain J.B.W. Pennyman arrived and took over duties of Senior Major. T/Major J.K.B. Coppell wanted to Captain 2 wounded Sick to Hospital nil.	

Army Form C. 2118.

August 1916

No 130

WAR DIARY
INTELLIGENCE SUMMARY

(Erase heading not required.)

Instructions regarding War Diaries and Intelligence Summaries are contained in F. S. Regs., Part II. and the Staff Manual respectively. Title Pages will be prepared in manuscript.

Place	Date	Hour	Summary of Events and Information	Remarks and references to Appendices
FIRING LINE	Aug 25th		Quiet day. Work continued on barbed wiring parties at night. Three officers arrived 2/Lieut R Taylor - 2/Lieut N H Roberts and 2/Lieut G S Ross (Casualties nil Sick to hospital nil) 2/Lieut Nora sick to Field Ambulance (not evacuated) One man reported for triplets	
"	Aug 26th		Quiet day. Artillery strafe. Patrol from A Company attempting to get (enemy identification) Casualties 3 wounded. Sick to hospital nil.	
"	Aug 27th		Quiet day. Work continued. Casualties a 2/Lieut of 9 O.R arrived. Patrol out from "B" Coy. Casualties nil Sick to hospital.	
"	Aug 28th 0700		Inspection of lines by G.O.C. VIII Corps. Work continued. Patrol out from A Coy. Casualties nil sick to hospital.	
"	Aug 29		Rained heavily all afternoon. Bn. relieved by 1st Bn Royal Inniskilling Bn. marched to billets in YPRES. Bn HQ at the PRISON. Casualties 1 killed 2 wounded Sick to hospital nil.	
YPRES	Aug 30		Working party of 10 Officers + 250 men clearing the STRAND by day + 5 Officers and 125 men by night. 2/Lieut W.R Douglas arrived. Casualties nil Sick to hospital nil.	

Army Form C. 2118.

WO/31

WAR DIARY
or
INTELLIGENCE SUMMARY

(Erase heading not required.)

August 1916

Instructions regarding War Diaries and Intelligence Summaries are contained in F. S. Regs., Part II. and the Staff Manual respectively. Title Pages will be prepared in manuscript.

Place	Date	Hour	Summary of Events and Information	Remarks and references to Appendices
YPRES	31 Aug		W.O.R.T. party 2 officers and 25 men working by day draining STRAND FLEET ST. 1 Officer and 75 men working by night on STRAND STREET ST. 1 Officer and 20 men on T.C. & supplies and some C.B.S. Casualties nil. Sick to hospital nil. Written at by JA.S. Campbell Cotton Lieut Adjutant 1/5 yorks 1.9.16	

2449 Wt. W14957/M90 750,000 1/16 J.B.C. & A. Forms/C.2118/12.

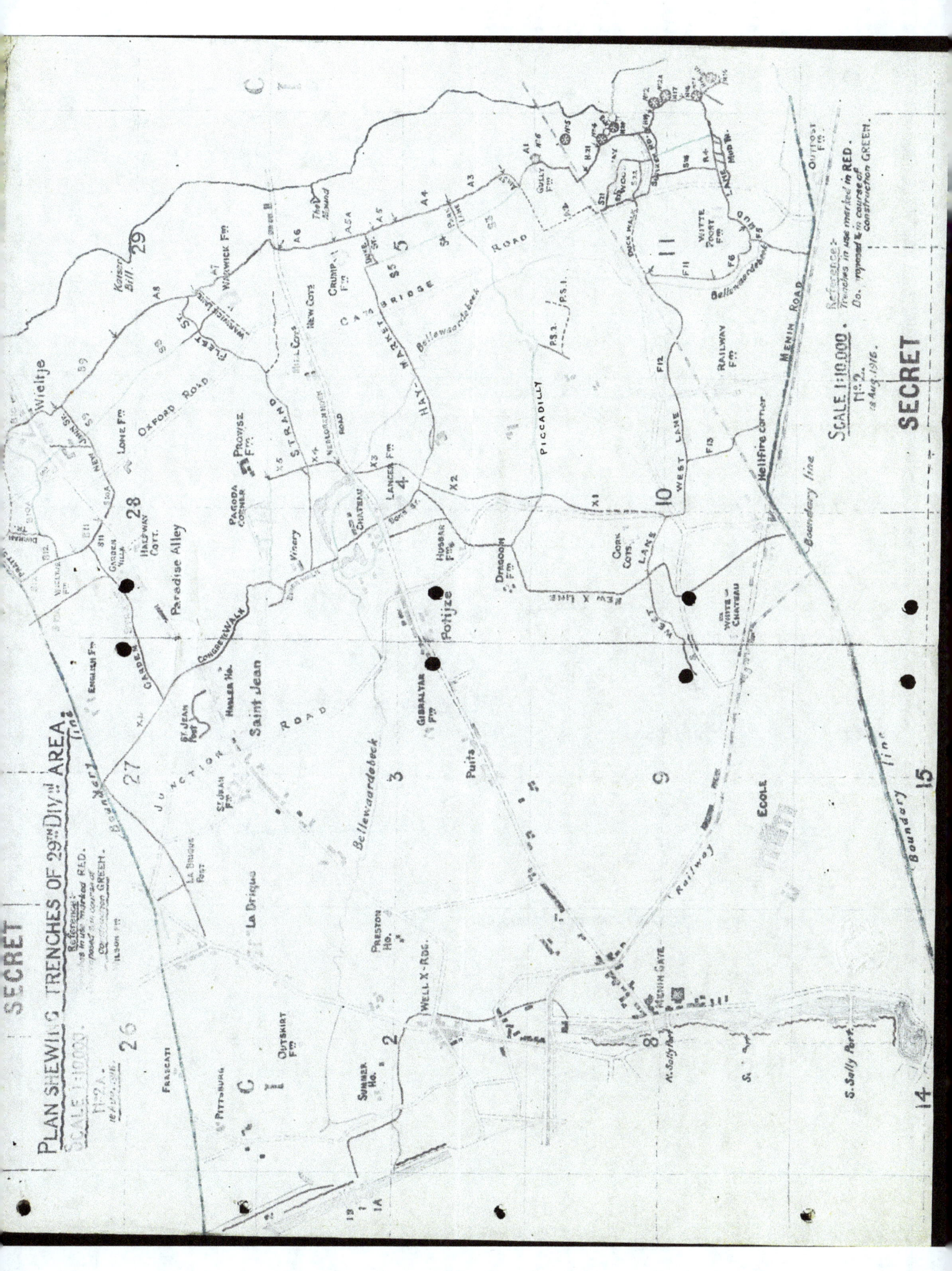

29th Division.
87th Infantry Brigade.

1st BATTALION

KING'S OWN SCOTTISH BORDERERS

SEPTEMBER 1 9 1 6

Trench Map attached.

16 .T.
8 sheets

Vol 9

CONFIDENTIAL.

WAR DIARY.

1st Bn. The King's Own Scottish Borderers.

From 1st September 1916. To 30th September 1916.

Volume No. 7.

Army Form C. 2118.
N° 132

September 1916

WAR DIARY
INTELLIGENCE SUMMARY
(Erase heading not required.)

Instructions regarding War Diaries and Intelligence Summaries are contained in F. S. Regs., Part II. and the Staff Manual respectively. Title Pages will be prepared in manuscript.

Place	Date	Hour	Summary of Events and Information	Remarks and references to Appendices
YPRES	1st Sept		Working parties on work revetting STRAND also opening up new drains to drain STRAND and FLEET ST. Casualties nil. Sick to Hospital 1 man to base under age.	
"	2nd Sept		Drainage on STRAND empty continued. Also revetting party on the STRAND.	
		2330	GAS ALARM which turned out to be the Working party disturbed by machine gun fire. Casualties 2 men wounded sick to hospital nil	
"	3rd Sept		Drainage on STRAND revetting continued. 275 men employed gas appeared. Casualties nil. Sick to hospital nil	
"	4th Sept		Drainage STRAND Revetting party continued. Casualties 9111 Thos (previously reported sick) has reported wounded (gun powder) Sick to Hospital nil.	
"	5th Sept		Working parties on MONMOUTH TRENCH and NEW TRENCH in WIELTJE AREA. supp of 29 O.R. arrived. Casualties nil. Sick to Hospital nil.	

Army Form C. 2118.
No 133

WAR DIARY
—or—
INTELLIGENCE SUMMARY
(Erase heading not required.)

Instructions regarding War Diaries and Intelligence Summaries are contained in F.S. Regs., Part II. and the Staff Manual respectively. Title Pages will be prepared in manuscript.

Place	Date	Hour	Summary of Events and Information	Remarks and references to Appendices
YPRES	6th Sept		Work continued on MONMOUTH TRENCH and NEW TRENCH. Work interfered with by machine gun fire. Casualties 1 man killed 1 wounded. Sick to Hospital nil.	
"	7th Sept		Work continued on MONMOUTH and NEW TRENCH. Casualties nil. Sick to Hospital nil.	
"B" Camp BRANDHOEK	8th Sept		Working party by day on MONMOUTH and NEW TRENCH. Work nearly completed. Coys relieved by 2nd Bn Royal Fusiliers. Coy entrained at YPRES for BRANDHOEK 23/15. On arrival at BRANDHOEK Coys occupied huts in "B" Camp. Lieut F.E. Broadway, Lieut N. Macleod, Lieut D.L. Ker, Lieut T. Gill reported their arrival. Casualties nil. Sick to hospital nil.	
"	9th Sept		Bathing parade for each Company. Conference at the disposal of O.C. Companies. Casualties nil. Sick to Hospital nil.	
"	10th Sept		Church Parade. Services. Casualties nil. Sick to Hospital nil.	
"	11th Sept	0910	Physical Drill for all Companies 0930 Adjutants Parade 11-1230 & 14.15-1530. Parades under Company arrangements of Sheldick. Camp shelled at 12.30 and again at 15.00. The Casualties. Casualties nil. Sick to Hospital nil.	

Army Form C. 2118.

WAR DIARY
INTELLIGENCE SUMMARY

(Erase heading not required.)

September 1916

Instructions regarding War Diaries and Intelligence
Summaries are contained in F. S. Regs., Part II.
and the Staff Manual respectively. Title Pages
will be prepared in manuscript.

Place	Date	Hour	Summary of Events and Information	Remarks and references to Appendices
"B" CAMP BRANDHOEK	12th Sept		Captain A.N. Lewis, R.S. Major and 190 O.R. went to Battleut to by-pass at daybreak & reports to Bilges werkplaats. Army Training programme continued throughout the day. Inspection on the range in the afternoon. 2/Lieut A.L. AITCHISON reported his arrival and taken on the strength of the Bn. Casualties nil. Shew sick to Hospital.	
"	13 Sept		Conf. wound off 2.30 pm by casualties. Route March by Companies in the morning. 4.O.C. 87th Bde. inspected Camp. Training carried on in the afternoon. Draft of 99 O.R. from 2/9 Royal Scots to arrival and taken on the strength of Bn. Casualties nil. Sick to Hospital 2.	
"	14 Sept		C.O's parade in the morning and Bn. inspected on parade by G.O.C. 87th Bde. Training continued in the afternoon. Raiding Party training commenced. Casualties nil. Sick to Hospital nil.	
"	15 Sept	11.30	Gas lecture to Officers at Dermoul Yard School in the morning. Entire Aeroplane scheme successfully carried out by 78th Squadron officer. Training continued. Raiding Party on night operations. Draft of 4 O.R. arrived. 2 O.R. from Hospital arrived. Casualties nil. Sick to Hospital 1.	
"	16 Sept	7.00	Inspection of Camp by C.O. in the morning. Company inspected in the use of new Box respirator and put through practice test in the afternoon. Regimental exercise for Officers under Brigade arrangements. Casualties nil. Sick to Hospital 2. 2/Lt Oettley sick invalided to No 10 C.C.S.	
"	17 Sept		Divine Service in the morning. 1 Sergeant transferred from 9/32 I.W.B. Casualties nil. Sick to Hospital nil.	

WAR DIARY
INTELLIGENCE SUMMARY

(Erase heading not required.)

Army Form C. 2118.

September 1916

Instructions regarding War Diaries and Intelligence Summaries are contained in F.S. Regs., Part II. and the Staff Manual respectively. Title pages will be prepared in manuscript.

Place	Date	Hour	Summary of Events and Information	Remarks and references to Appendices
"B" CAMP — BRANDHOEK	18 Sept		Rained heavily all day.	
— YPRES		2000	Bn. entrained for YPRES and relieved 2nd Bn. Royal Fusiliers in the PRISON. Companies in their former billets. Casualties nil. Sick to Hospital 1.	
FIRING LINE	19 Sept		Bn. relieved 12th Bn. [illegible] Lancashire Fusiliers in the night interval. "C" and "B" Companies in the firing line. "B" Company in support in the "X" line and "A" Company in Reserve in CONGREVE WALK. Casualties nil. Sick to Hospital 1.	
"	20 Sept	0200	Raid by 2nd Bn. Royal Fusiliers from Bn. front. Raid unsuccessful. Work carried on on front line, STRAND. Casualties 1 wounded. Sick to Hospital 2. Patrol from "H"Coy to MOUND.	
"	21 Sept		Work continued on front line, STRAND, "X" line, S.8 and new WARWICK FARM defences in WARWICK LANE. Wiring in front of "A.6." Patrol from "D" Company to KAISER BILL. Casualties 1 man slightly wounded (artillery). Evacuated from F.A. Sick 7.	
"	22 Sept		Work continued on front line. STRAND, "X" line, S.8 and new WARWICK FARM defences in WARWICK LANE. Also drain near 1.5 opened out. Wiring party in front of A.6. Patrol from "B" Company endeavour to cut wire in front of the MOUND but found string every covering party and forced to retire. Fighting Patrol from "D" Company did not encounter any enemy. Casualties nil. Sick to Hospital 3. Draft of 50 O.R. arrived.	

Army Form C. 2118.

September 1915

No 13/6

WAR DIARY

INTELLIGENCE SUMMARY.

(Erase heading not required.)

Instructions regarding War Diaries and Intelligence Summaries are contained in F. S. Regs., Part II. and the Staff Manual respectively. Title pages will be prepared in manuscript.

Place	Date	Hour	Summary of Events and Information	Remarks and references to Appendices
FIRING LINE	Sept 23rd		Work continued as before. Strong fighting patrol out from C Company for identification purposes but no enemy encountered. Our artillery active throughout the night. Casualties 1 man wounded (slightly) Sick to Hospital nil.	
FIRING LINE – YPRES	Sept 24th		Work continued during the day. Bn relieved at night by 1st Bn Royal Inniskilling Fusiliers. Relief complete 11.35. Bn in Divisional Reserve in YPRES. Companies in the former billets. Casualties 1 killed 1 wounded. Sick to Hospital 2.	
YPRES	Sept 25th		Working party WIRING on POTIZE SE Defences by day. Working parties by night to MONMOUTH TRENCH. Casualties 2 wounded for detail Wd1 Wd2 included in 73rd Bn Commanded by Major J.B. McPherson. Working parties as before. Casualties nil. Sick to Hospital nil	
"	Sept 26th			
"	Sept 27th		Working parties continued. Casualties 1 killed 2 sick to Hospital	
"	Sept 28th		Inspection of HQ & Gds by Corps Commander & Staff the following awards are now entered: MILITARY CROSS 24.8.16 Captain G.E. Malcolm	
			MILITARY MEDAL 14.8.16	
			No 7795 Pte. A. Humphrey No 7986 A/L/M.T. Prentice	
			No 18644 " J.F. Cope No 9341 C.S.M. J.J. Grusie.	
			Draft of 162 O.R. arrived. Casualties nil. Sick to Hospital nil.	

WAR DIARY

INTELLIGENCE SUMMARY

(Erase heading not required.)

Army Form C. 2118.

September 1916

Place	Date	Hour	Summary of Events and Information	Remarks and references to Appendices
YPRES FIRING LINE	29th Sept		Working parties by day on POTIJZE Defences and CRUMP FARM under R.E. Bn relieved 1st Bn Royal Inniskilling Fusiliers in the right sector at night. Relief complete 2200. Dispositions as follows "C" Company (less 1 Platoon) on right of firing line. "B" Company (less 1 Platoon) on the left. 1 Platoon "B" Company in the "GARDEN OF EDEN". 1 Platoon "C" Company in support in "X" line. "D" Company in Reserve in CONGREVE WALK with 1 Platoon "C" Company.	
		2300-2330	Raid by Division on our left. No retaliation on our front. Casualties nil. Sick to Hospital 1.	
	30th Sept		Work on general repair and upkeep of trenches throughout the line	
		2000 -	Bombardment of enemy trenches by our artillery in connection with	
		2230	two raids one from left Subsect: 87th Bde line and one from 86th Bde area. Enemy retaliation slight. Casualties 1 wounded. Sick to Hospital nil.	

Written at
by
M.B. Campbell Capt
30/9/16 A/Adjutant 1/KOSB

29th Division.
87th Infantry Brigade.

1st BATTALION

KING'S OWN SCOTTISH BORDERERS

OCTOBER 1916

Vol 10 27/29

17.T
attack

CONFIDENTIAL

WAR DIARY

1st Battn. The King's Own Scottish Borderers

From 1st October 1916.   To 31st October 1916.

VOLUME 27

Army Form C. 2118.
No 134

WAR DIARY
INTELLIGENCE SUMMARY
(Erase heading not required.)

February 1916

Place	Date	Hour	Summary of Events and Information	Remarks and references to Appendices
FIRING LINE YPRES	15/2/16		Quiet day. Work continued. Total out at night repaired enemy trenches. Quiet. Casualties nil. Sent to hospital 5.	
	16/2/16		Quiet day with the exception that enemy shot over in the vicinity of H.15.a.b.d. 8.0 rounds 77mm's H.E. and damaged dug out. Company suffered however still remained quiet at night. Very wet all day. Draft of men attached to various party of Battalion returned from 3rd/4th Brig. Leinster Regiment arrived at night. Casualties 1 wounded sent to Hospital nil.	
FIRING LINE YPRES	17/2/16		Work continued on trenches getting ready to hand over to relieving unit. Quiet night. Casualties nil. Sent to hospital nil.	
	18/2/16	2 pm	Relieved by 3rd/4th Bn. Leinster Regiment	
		9 pm	Battn. Hqtrs.	
			(B) arrived at ASYLUM to M. Govt. Casualties nil. Sent to Hospital nil.	
M.Govt. ASYLUM	19/2/16		Inspection of Bn. by Capt. Crawford Canadian army med. Corps.	
			Reported at Field Hospital of A.L. Company Casualties nil Sent to Hospital	

October 1916

Army Form C. 2118.
No 134

WAR DIARY
INTELLIGENCE SUMMARY
(Erase heading not required.)

Instructions regarding War Diaries and Intelligence Summaries are contained in F.S. Regs., Part II. and the Staff Manual respectively. Title Pages will be prepared in manuscript.

Place	Date	Hour	Summary of Events and Information	Remarks and references to Appendices
"M" CAMP POPERINGHE to CARDONETTE	7th Oct	0815 0445 0700 1815 2200	Transport and "A" Company left "M" Camp. Bn paraded and left "M" Camp for HOPOUTRE SIDING. Bn entrained. 24 Officers and 772 O.R. of left HOPOUTRE SIDING. Bn arrived and detrained at LONGEAU. Bn marched to CARDONETTE. Bn arrived CARDONETTE and went into billets. CARDONETTE is 6½ miles from LONGEAU. Casualties nil. Sick to Hospital nil.	
CARDONETTE	8th Oct	16.20	Bn resting. Divine Service held. Lt-Col A.T. Welch relinquished off leave and took over command of the Bn from Major J.B.W. Pennyman. Casualties nil. Sick to Hospital nil.	
CARDONETTE	9th Oct		Bn remained CARDONETTE awaiting orders. Casualties nil. Sick to Hospital nil.	
CARDONETTE to BUIRE-SUR-ANCRE.	10th Oct	1425 1900	Bn marched from CARDONETTE to BUIRE-SUR-ANCRE distance about 12 miles. Bn arrived BUIRE-SUR-ANCRE and camped there. Draft of 4 O.R. arrived. Casualties nil. Sick to Hospital nil.	
BUIRE-SUR-ANCRE.	11th Oct	0730	Physical Training. Remainder of day Companies at the disposal of their Company Commanders. Casualties nil. Sick to Hospital nil.	

Army Form C. 2118.
No. 140

WAR DIARY
INTELLIGENCE SUMMARY
(Erase heading not required.)

October 1916

Instructions regarding War Diaries and Intelligence Summaries are contained in F. S. Regs., Part II, and the Staff Manual respectively. Title Pages will be prepared in manuscript.

Place	Date	Hour	Summary of Events and Information	Remarks and references to Appendices
BUIRE-SUR-ANCRE	12th Oct	07:30	Companies at Physical Training	
		09:30	Companies practising attack formation.	
		14:15	Practice attack by all officers and N.C.O's in the Brigade under G.O.C. Casualties nil. Sick to Hospital nil.	
BUIRE-SUR-ANCRE	13th Oct	09:00	Bn. practised attack.	
		18:25	Bn. marched to FRICOURT (distance about 6 miles) and arrived 16:00 and went into camp. Casualties nil. Sick to Hospital nil.	
FRICOURT	14th Oct	14:00	Bn. practised attack.	
		17:30	Working parties digging drains in camp. Casualties nil. Sick to Hospital nil.	
FRICOURT	15th Oct	11:30	Bn. practised attack with 1st Border Regiment. Casualties nil. Sick to Hospital 17.	
FRICOURT	16th Oct		Companies making "Strong Points" in the morning. Church Party from Bn. out in the afternoon. Casualties nil. Sick to Hospital nil. Draft of 27 O.R. arrived.	

Army Form C. 2118.

WAR DIARY
INTELLIGENCE SUMMARY
(Erase heading not required.)

October 1916

Instructions regarding War Diaries and Intelligence Summaries are contained in F.S. Regs., Part II. and the Staff Manual respectively. Title Pages will be prepared in manuscript.

Place	Date	Hour	Summary of Events and Information	Remarks and references to Appendices
FRICOURT	17th Oct.		Working party on new road between FRICOURT and MONTAUBAN. Casualties nil. Sick to Hospital 2.	
"	18th Oct		Bn received orders to be ready to move in 2 hours. Working party on New Road continued. Casualties nil. Sick to Hospital 1.	
BERNAFAY WOOD	19th Oct	0600	Bn left FRICOURT Camp to march to BERNAFAY WOOD. Road very congested with traffic. Bn arrived 1230. Transport very late. Weather very wet. Casualties nil. Sick to Hospital nil.	
BULL'S ROAD TRENCH	20th Oct	1400	Bn left BERNAFAY WOOD and marched via DELVILLE WOOD and COCOA ALLEY to relieve 1st Bn Essex Regiment in support in BULL'S ROAD and Companies in PIONEER TRENCH. "B" & "C" Companies and H.Q. in BULL'S ROAD. Ration party of 50 supplied to carry rations from BULL'S ROAD DUMP to firing line. Casualties 1 killed 8 wounded 1 missing. 1 Sick to Hospital.	
FIRING LINE	21st Oct		Bn relieved 2nd Bn J.W. Borderers in the firing line. Relief commenced at 1900 and completed 0200. Disposition: ½ A Coy, C Coy, B Coy and D Coy in front line GREASE TRENCH. ½ A Coy, Bn Bombers and Reserve Lewis Guns with Bn HQ in PILGRIMS WAY. Casualties 1 killed. Capt. W.M. Clark and 14 O.R. wounded.	

WAR DIARY / INTELLIGENCE SUMMARY

Army Form C. 2118.

October 1916

Place	Date	Hour	Summary of Events and Information	Remarks and references to Appendices
ARMENTIERES	Oct 1/16		Quiet day and much bursts throughout the day. Patrols out at night reported no wire in front of enemy's position and enemy in very reduced condition. Patrols who had apparently lost his way thought no casualties but killed Lieut D. L. Kerr & Lieut A. L. Mitchener wounded and for Patrol missing. Weather conditions very bad. Entrances rain and very cold. 1 wounded prisoner brought in.	
"	Oct 2/16		New assembly trench in front of GRENAE TRENCH being dug as a jumping off place. Heavy bombardment by our artillery commencing at 5pm in conjunction with an attack by the Division on our right. Attack apparently successful as far as 1st Objective. Enemy's artillery cut very silent on our front line and few casualties sustained. Enemy shell fairly heavy barrage on PILGRIMS WAY. Patrols out at night had nothing further to report. Casualties 2 killed Captain F. E. Brodwig slightly wounded at duty Lieut C. B. Anderson & 17 OR wounded. Capt Grainie expired from —	
"	Oct 3/16		I Coming brought in at 2AM having given himself up in an exhausted condition. Enemy moderately artillery bombardment Enemy during the afternoon. Our artillery very active on the left throughout the night.	

Army Form C. 2118.
No 143

WAR DIARY
or
INTELLIGENCE SUMMARY

(Erase heading not required.)

Instructions regarding War Diaries and Intelligence Summaries are contained in F.S. Regs., Part II. and the Staff Manual respectively. Title Pages will be prepared in manuscript.

October 1916

Place	Date	Hour	Summary of Events and Information	Remarks and references to Appendices
FIRING LINE	24/25 (cont)		Casualties 1 killed 9 wounded 1 Lieut T.D.R. Higgins evacuated sick to hospital.	
"	25/26		Re-organisation of the line at dawn. "A" Coy from the right of GREASE TRENCH moved to M.H.Q in PILGRIMS WAY "B" and "D" Coys remained in the right of GREASE TRENCH D'. Coy having handed over their part of GREASE TRENCH to 18th Border Regt and moved to support in PIONEER TRENCH. Continued progress made with the "jumping off bus" and trench cut through to connect with Graham at Hours night. Casualties 1 killed 16 wounded 2 sick to Hospital	
MILL'S ROAD TRENCH	26/27th		Relieved by 9/HLI's a night of 25th/26th Oct'm. Relief complete 02.00. Weather conditions still very bad: and the troops found the way back to the Support very difficult. H.Q Coys in Pioneer French "B"+"C" + M.H.Q. in BULL'S ROAD TRENCH During relief enemy started sudden barrage which lasted about ½ an hour. Enemy unusually active all day Casualties nil killed 5 wounded 1 sick to Hospital.	

2449 Wt. W14957/M90 750,000 1/16 H.B.C. & A. Forms/C 2118/14.

Army Form C. 2118.

WAR DIARY
or
INTELLIGENCE SUMMARY
(Erase heading not required.)

October 1916

Place	Date	Hour	Summary of Events and Information	Remarks and references to Appendices
BERNAFAY WOOD (DUMP)			2 Coys employed as carrying party to carry stores from BULL'S ROAD DUMP to front DUMP. B⁴ relieved by Newfoundland Regiment and proceeded to BERNAFAY WOOD and placed under orders of 88 Bde.	
		19.30	B⁴ all in BERNAFAY WOOD. Casualties 1 killed (2/Lt R.T. McT Elliot and 2 OR wounded)	
BERNAFAY WOOD	27.10.16		B⁴ resting in BERNAFAY WOOD preparatory to proceeding to front line to the attack on 29th. Casualties nil. 1 killed 2 wounded sick	
MAMETZ VILLAGE CAMP	28.10.16		Orders for the attack cancelled on account of the weather. B⁴ moved to MAMETZ VILLAGE CAMP. Casualties nil Sick to Hospital nil	
PRICOURT	30.10.16		B⁴ moved to PRICOURT. Casualties nil Sick to Hospital nil	
"	31.10.16		B⁴ awaiting orders at PRICOURT. Casualties nil Sick to Hospital nil. 2/Lieut A. Douglas 2/5th British Rifles attached as Washing nil.	

Lieut A. Douglas

31.10.16

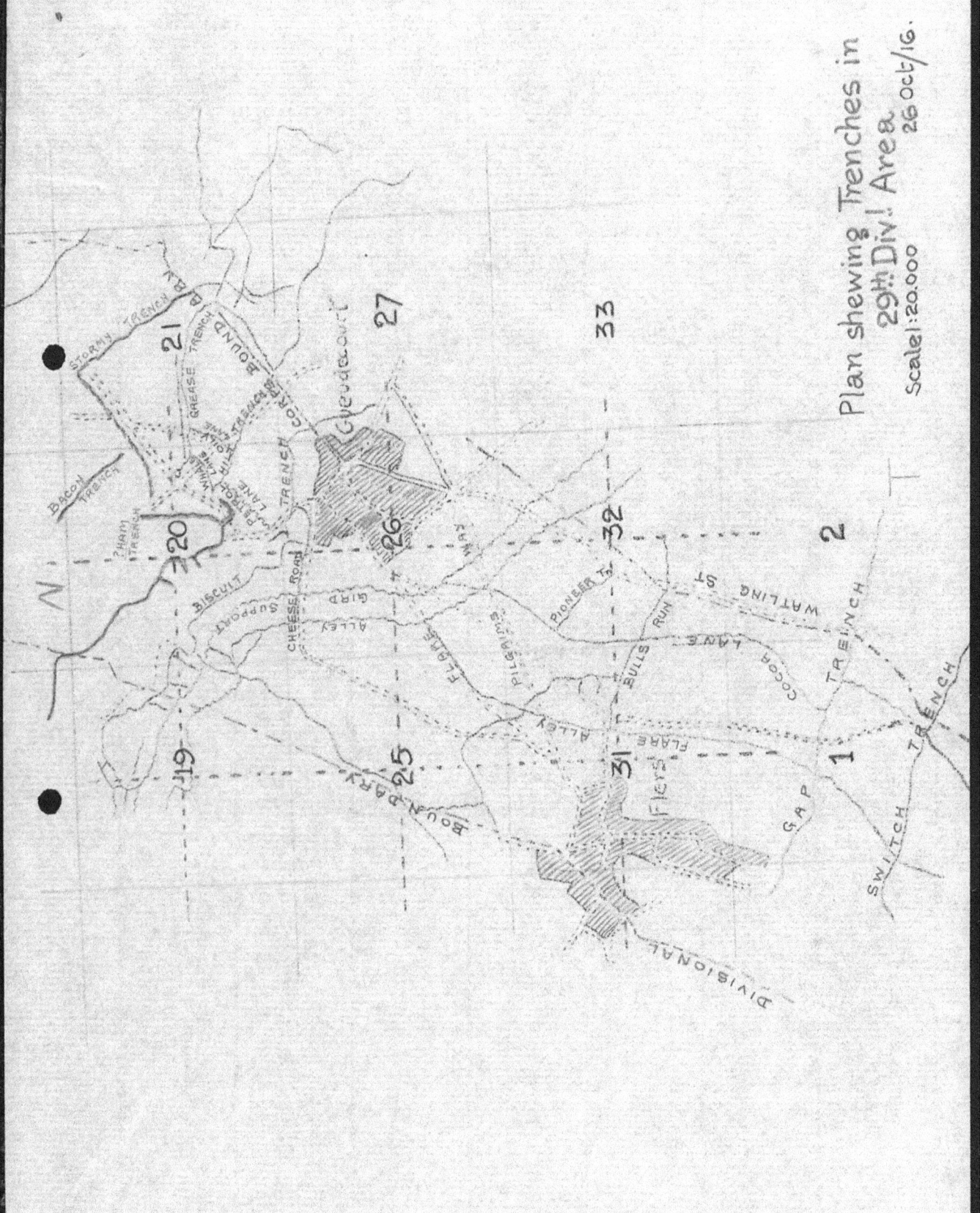

29th Division.

87th Infantry Brigade.

1st BATTALION

KINGS OWN SCOTTISH BORDERERS

NOVEMBER 1 9 1 6

CONFIDENTIAL

WAR DIARY.

1ST KING'S OWN SCOTTISH BORDERERS

FROM 1st NOVEMBER 1916

TO 30th NOVEMBER 1916

VOLUME 28.

Army Form C.2118.

WAR DIARY
INTELLIGENCE SUMMARY
(Erase heading not required.)

November 1916

Instructions regarding War Diaries and Intelligence Summaries are contained in F.S. Regs., Part II. and the Staff Manual respectively. Title Pages will be prepared in manuscript.

Place	Date	Hour	Summary of Events and Information	Remarks and references to Appendices
FRICOURT CAMP	Nov 1st	0900	B'n marched to ALBERT to go into billets. On arrival at ALBERT it was found there was no room in the town. B'n had dinner in town and returned to FRICOURT camp arriving 1700. 2/Lt G.J. McNay, 2/Lt C.W. Coyle, and 2/Lt J.Y. Thomson all from 9th B'n K.O.S.B. reported their arrival and are taken on the strength of the B'n. a draft of 78 O.R. arrived. Casualties nil. Sick to hospital 1.	
"	Nov 2nd		B'n remained in FRICOURT CAMP. Casualties nil sick to Hospital nil. Transport marched to CORBIE, where it remained.	
ARAINES	Nov 3rd		B'n marched to ALBERT and entrained in two parties for ARAINES. 1st Party consisting of Headquarters B+C Coys and 1 Platoon "A" Coy left ALBERT 15.15 and arrived ARAINES 18.00. 2nd Party consisting of 3 Platoons "A" Coy, D Coy & Lewis Gunners left ALBERT 18.00 and arrived ARAINES 01.30 4th Nov. B'n billeted in ARAINES Casualties nil sick to hospital nil. 4/Lt A.L Aitchison died of wounds received on October 22nd.	
"	Nov 4th	1600	B'n cleaning up and settling into billets. Inspection of Companies by Company Commander. Casualties nil sick to Hospital nil. Sick to Hospital 9.	
"	Nov 5th		Physical training before breakfast. Divine Services for Presbyterians and Church of England. Casualties nil Sick to Hospital nil. Walked by English C of E. J.C.B. Campbell Capt

WAR DIARY or INTELLIGENCE SUMMARY

Army Form C. 2118.

(Erase heading not required.)

From 1st Nov 1916

Instructions regarding War Diaries and Intelligence Summaries are contained in F.S. Regs., Part II. and the Staff Manual respectively. Title Pages will be prepared in manuscript.

Place	Date	Hour	Summary of Events and Information	Remarks and references to Appendices
ARAINES	Nov 6th	0900	Physical Training, Platoon Drill & Handling of Arms. 1200 Marching order inspection as far as possible, afternoon Bomb & Lewis Bomber practical. Casualties Nil – Sick to Hosp. 1. Regained from Hospital 1.	
	Nov 7th	0900	Company Drill, M.S. Trench discipline practical, afternoon Bomber practical, Casualties Nil – Sick to Hosp. 3. Regained from Hosp. 1.	
	Nov 8th	0900	Physical Training. B Coy in extended order and Coy in Attack practical. B Coy instructed in use of Rifle Bombs. Major B. Campbell Johnston 3rd K.O.S.B. reported his arrival, taken on the strength and assumed duties of 2nd in command. 2/Lts R.J. Smith & J. Routledge 2/K.O.S.B. reported their arrival from R.D. and taken on strength, a draft of 34 O.R. arrived. 2Lt J.C. Cameron 2/K.O.S.B. reported his arrival & taken on the strength. 2/Lt J.S.R. Shaggers 2/K.O.S.B. re-taken on strength, he was previously reported wounded (shell shock) now reported sick. Casualties Nil. Sick to Hospital 1. Nil regained from Hospital.	
	Nov 9th	0915	Batt. Route March. 1400 A Coy Musketry D Coy instruction in Bombs. Casualties Nil. Sick to Hosp. Coy	5.
	Nov 10th	0900	A & B Coy musketry. C & D Coy Company drill etc. 1430 Batt practical attack. Casualties Nil. Sick to strength. Captain A.E. Bennett 9/K.O.S.B. reported his arrival and taken on the strength.	
	Nov 11th	1130	The Batt. was inspected by G.O.C. 9th Division after thorough an attack was carried out in conjunction with the 9/S.A.I. (Brigade Reserve). Casualties Nil. Sick to Hosp. Nil, 1 man cut to England Available for Commission.	
	Nov 12th		The Bn Rt attended Divine Service. Casualties Nil. Sick to Hosp. 1.	

WAR DIARY or INTELLIGENCE SUMMARY

Army Form C.2118.

November 1916

Instructions regarding War Diaries and Intelligence Summaries are contained in F.S. Regs., Part II. and the Staff Manual respectively. Title Pages will be prepared in manuscript.

(Erase heading not required.)

Place	Date	Hour	Summary of Events and Information	Remarks and references to Appendices
ARAINES	13th Nov	9.00	The Batt. was entrained en Route Marching. Stranger 21 off. Provisional Bombing & 204 Bombing Brussilles Nil. Sick to Hosp'l Nil. Sgt W.E. Aitchison struck off the strength, granted a Permanent Commission in 2nd Hants Regt.	
Citadel Camp Ti: Javenuit	14th Nov & 30th		The Batt. marched to Citadel Camp. non trained by Bus to Buine, thence by march route to camp, arrived 17.00, Casualties Nil. Sick to Hosp'l Nil.	
	15th Nov	9.15	Batt. marched to BRIQUETERIE Camp. 7= 7 Officers arrived 12.15. 2/Lt PATON G. 3/R.S.F. & 2nd Lieut MAC BRYAN Northumbd. their arrival. Taken on the strength of the Battalion. Rupft of 240 O.R. arrived and taken on the strength. 2/Lt W. BARNARD 3/R.F. & 2/Lt Rupft his arrival and is taken on the strength. Casualties Nil. Sick to Hosp'l Nil.	
Hoeve time The TRENCHES	16th Nov & 17th		Batt. moved up and took over front line trenches from STINNARD Regt on left of the FRENCH near L.E. BOEFFS. Casualties 5 wounded including one attached 6 T.M.B -	
In the Field The TRENCHES	17th & 18th & 19th Nov		Quiet day except for usual spasmodic shelling. Trench digging. deepening & Rev. strafed communication trenches started. Casualties 1 men wounded by own transferred to 183 Travelling RM sick to Hosp'l Nil.	
	18th Nov		Joint Gaint Enemy Artillery more active during day. Turned to look after with trench by our drafts of 7 O.R. arrived & taken on the strength. Casualties 1 killed 5 wounded. Sick to Hosp'l 1.	

WAR DIARY or INTELLIGENCE SUMMARY

Army Form C. 2118.

November 1916

Place	Date	Hour	Summary of Events and Information	Remarks and references to Appendices
Leuzenem	19th Nov		Usual Artillery activity. Work carried on trenches. Casualties 2 killed 6 wounded. Sick to Hospital nil. Patrol sent out and estimated enemy line at 300x distance.	
-"-	20th Nov		Artillery more active during day. The Batt: was relieved by the 1/R. Innis. Fusiliers and marched to CARNOY Camp NORTH, distance about 6 miles, but Coy arrived about 4 P.M. Casualties 4 killed, 3 wounded. 2nd Lieut Barrett 2/K.O.R.L.25 reported his arrival wounded (Shell Shock) Sick to Hospital 6, 2nd Lieut R.D. Peet 3/K.O.R.L.25 reported his arrival and taken on the strength, Dept of A.O.C. arrived & taken on the strength, 1 man transferred to A.O.C.	
CARNOY Camp NORTH	21st Nov		Battalion resting. Casualties 2 wounded, Sick to Hospital 36.	
-"-	22nd Nov		Battalion 350 men for various fatigues under the R.E. Casualties 1 Wounded (bruised) Sick to Hospital 20, Rejoined from Hospital wounded 3.	
-"-	23rd Nov 14.30		Battalion moved to GUILLEMONT Camp. Distance about 3½ miles, arrived 16.00, Casualties nil Sick to Hospital nil.	

Written up by
[signature]
Capt 1/K.O. Sco. B.

WAR DIARY or INTELLIGENCE SUMMARY

Army Form C. 2118.

November 1916

Place	Date	Hour	Summary of Events and Information	Remarks and references to Appendices
GUILLEMONT CAMP.	24/Nov		Weather very wet. B: on working parties. Casualties nil. Sick to Hospital 11.	
"	25/Nov		Weather continued very wet. B: on daily working parties. Casualties nil. Sick to Hospital 1.	
FIRING LINE near LESBŒUFS	26 Nov		Working parties in the morning. B: moved up to the line at 1600 and relieved 16th Bn Middlesex Regt. Disposition as follows: Front-line 2 Platoons D Coy on the right, B Coy in the Centre and C Coy on the left. 2 Platoons of D Coy in Support in ANTELOPE Trench and A Coy in Support in FROSTY TRENCH. Night Quiet. Casualties nil. Sick to Hospital nil.	
"	27/Nov.		Companies engaged in cleaning and clearing trenches which were very bad. Some shelling in the afternoon but on the whole front very quiet. Quiet night. Casualties 1 wounded. Sick to Hospital nil.	
" and CARNOY CAMP	28th/Nov		Patrol from "B" Company out in the early morning. Nothing to report. Two of the Patrol missing. Quiet day very murky. Relieved at night	

Army Form C.2118.

November 1916

WAR DIARY
INTELLIGENCE SUMMARY
(Erase heading not required.)

Remarks and references to Appendices
150

Place	Date	Hour	Summary of Events and Information
CARNOY CAMP	28 Nov (Tuesday)		by 1st Bn. Border Regt. Relief complete 20.30. Bn. marched to CARNOY CAMP. Casualties 2 killed, 1 wounded & 1 missing. Sick to Hospital nil. Draft of 10 O.R. arrived.
"	29 Nov		Bn. resting & cleaning up. 3 O.R. transferred to Labour Bn. Casualties nil. Sick to Hospital 9.
"	30 Nov		Working party of 1 Officer & 50 O.R. on transport lines. Companies at the disposal of the Companies. Casualties nil. Sick to Hospital 3.

Written up by
J.H.B. Campbell Captain
? / ? COB
1/ / COB

29th Division
87th Infantry Brigade.

1st BATTALION

KING'S OWN SCOTTISH BORDERERS

DECEMBER 1 9 1 6

Vol 12

CONFIDENTIAL

WAR DIARY

1ST KING'S OWN SCOTTISH BORDERERS

FROM 1ST DECEMBER 1916 TO 31ST DECEMBER 1916

VOLUME 29

WAR DIARY or INTELLIGENCE SUMMARY

Army Form C. 2118.

December 1916

Place	Date	Hour	Summary of Events and Information	Remarks and references to Appendices
CARNOY CAMP	Dec 1st		Running drill 0730. Working parties furnished by Bn. Casualties nil. Sick to Hospital 1	
"	Dec 2nd		Running drill 0730. Working parties furnished by Bn. Casualties nil. Sick to Hospital 23	
GUILLEMONT	Dec 3rd		Bn. left CARNOY CAMP at 1400 and took over GUILLEMONT CAMP from 2nd Bn S.W.B. Captain J.B.W. Pennyman left the Bn to be attached to the Worcesters. 2/Lt D Armstrong 3rd Staffs arrived and is taken on the strength of the Bn. 2nd Lt Toft admitted sick to Hospital nil. Casualties nil.	
FIRING LINE MAMORAC	Dec 4th		Bn. relieved performing Trenches in right sub-sector of the area. Area lately taken over from the French. "B" Company in front line "B" Company in support in MARLBURG TRENCH "C" Company in Reserve in LEBOEUFS TRENCH Bn.HQ at T.6 a.73. Advanced Bn.HQ under Major S. Campbell. Johnston at T.6.c central. Quiet night. Casualties unwounded sick to hospital nil.	
"	Dec 5th		Work continued on trenches. Patrol out from "B" Coy at night reported enemy's line continuous unwired. Bombs and ammunition carried up to front line. Casualties 3 OR wounded. Sick to hospital nil	

WAR DIARY

December 1916

Intelligence Summaries are contained in F.S. Book 7/12/ and the Staff Manual requires title Page and headings given in the margin.

ARMY FORM C. 2118

INTELLIGENCE SUMMARY

Summary of Events & Information

PLACE	DATE	HOUR	Summary of Events & Information	Remarks & references to Appendices
FIRING LINE N. MORVAL	Dec 6th		Telephone communication with front line broken. Work in front line continued. Company patrols emerging at Combles. "Communication" Ration guard went up at night. Casualties 1 man killed. Ret. to England Lieut Gibb 24.XII.1916. Lieut J. Watt arrived on scene. Bn. strength of the Bn. achieved in the line by 12th Bn. Lancashire Fusiliers. Relief complete 20.30. Bn. marched to camp at CARNOY.	
CARNOY CAMP	Dec 7th			
"	Dec 8th		Whist Palm, & 3 other Offrs left to form Company of Divisional later Bn. Bn. resting and cleaning up. Casualties from attached 63rd Machine Gun Coy. Back to Hospital nil.	
MERICOURT	Dec 9th		Bn. entrained at the PLATEAU STATION at 12.00. Arrived MERICOURT 10.45. Bn. in billets. Drafts of 100 arrived. Casualties nil. Sick to Hospital nil.	
"	Dec 10th		Bn. resting at MERICOURT. Casualties nil. Sick to Hospital 25 O.R. evacuated from Field Ambulance.	

Written by
J.K.B. Campbell Capt
Adjutant

Army Form C. 2118.

153

WAR DIARY
or
INTELLIGENCE SUMMARY.
(Erase heading not required.)

Place	Date	Hour	Summary of Events and Information	Remarks and references to Appendices
MERICOURT l'ABBÉ	Dec 12		Draft of 309 O.R. arrived at 0100. 2 O/r & 1 O.R. Expert Graduates to England to report to War Office for duty with Colonial Branch. War Office. Team arrived the air of Captain misspelling in Training rest. at 0900 Bat. marches to CORBIE arriving at 1030. — and went to billets. Casualties nil. Sick evacuated 1.	
CORBIE	Dec 13		1300 Bn. arrived at CORBIE station for LE MESGE arriving at HANGEST & marched from the place to LE MESGE, arriving at 1740. Went to billets. Casualties nil. Sick evacuated nil.	
LE MESGE	Dec 14		Bn. cleaning up resting into billets. 1000 Inspection of billets by Transport Officer. Draft of 5 O.R. arrived. Casualties nil, sick evacuated 1 O.L. boys.	
"	Dec 15		Running and walks before breakfast. Bordow or disposal of O.C. coys. Casualties NIL. Sick evacuated 1.	
"	Dec 16		Running and walks before breakfast. Troops fighting new O.C. Coy. Changing equipment etc. In the afternoon Casualties NIL. Sick evacuated I. 1 O.R. struck off on enquire as Instructor at T.M. school. Handing of arms. Vickery and musketry. Captain's bath of N.C.Os. Inspection of billets by Commanding Officer. 2/Lt. D.M. Robertson 3rd K.O.S.B. and Lt. Colonel 3rd K.O.S.B. reported thro' and taken on strength. Troops 1, 15 O.R. arrived. Casualties NIL. Sick evacuated 1. A and B Companies bathes at PIENCOURT. Class ending was issued	

A.3834. Wt.W4973/M687. 750,000. 8/16 D.D.& L.Ltd. Forms/C2118/13.

WAR DIARY or INTELLIGENCE SUMMARY

Army Form C. 2118.

Place	Date	Hour	Summary of Events and Information	Remarks and references to Appendices
LE MESGE	Dec 17th		Physical training before breakfast. Divine service for Roman Catholics. Casualties NIL. Sick to hospital NIL. Sick to hospital NIL. Lieut. D. Bonfanti taken ill RIENCOURT.	
	Dec 18th	0945	Company at Physical training 0900 Company parade. At 1000 Lee 11-45 Company practised march discipline. Bayonet fighting. Melee and advanced arm drill	
		1200	Marching saluting for all companies. 1400 "A" Company moved to range B, C, & D Companies practised Bombing under Coy Bombing Officers	
		1430	Lecture by Officers Mess for all Officers on the attack delivered by the Commanding Officer. Casualties Sick to hospital NIL.	
	Dec 19th	0945	Running drill. 0900 Company practised Bayonet fighting march discipline Extended order drill. Gas blast drill. 1115 Gas drumhead & aeroplane control. 1400 'B' Company on the range. A, C, & D Company Bombing	
		2nd Lt. J Stanton 9th R.O.I.B reported sick to England, relieved off strength of the Batn. Casualties NIL. Sick to hospital NIL.	
	Dec 20th	0900	Batn. practised in Route Marching. Casualties & Sick to hospital NIL	
	Dec 21st		Running drill at 0745. Company parade at 0900 as strong as possible. 1000 March discipline. Company went inspection, cleansing. 1115 Execution & recognition of targets. Casualties NIL. Sick to hospital 20.	

WAR DIARY
INTELLIGENCE SUMMARY

Place	Date	Hour	Summary of Events and Information	Remarks and references to Appendices
LE MESGE	Dec 22nd		0745. Running drill under C.O.'s. 0900. Battn practices to attack under the Commanding Officer. 1430. The Battn was inspected in the attack by the Brigadier Commanding. Having overtaking of Battle stores. Pingle XC England staff appointment. 30/7/16. 2 O.R. joined from with Casualties and sick to hospital Nil. 15:30 Divisional Band played at 09:04	2nd W. R.H.
"	Dec 23rd		Running and at 07:45. Company paraded in storm to practise and practise Bayonet fighting, extended, section attacks, drill and march discipline. 1400. "A" Company on the range. B.T.A.D. bayonet bombing. Officers and NCOs. Tr. dept and leature of HANGEST culnnus of Brdg. Officer 2 officers and 193 O.R. PONT REMY for a military show. NCOs & glass for temporary commission. Casualties & Sick to Hosp. Nil.	
"	Dec 24th		Recon gun company. By Mayor. To Rayau Regt in the afternoon or probs running by 4 train C.3. Casualties Nil. Sick to hospital 2.	
"	Dec 25th		0745. Running drill. The morning was devoted to steady drill. Hovering of arms Cleo and Enlined party arm harness and Lavaruo of Target. The afternoon was observed as a half holiday. Casualties & sick Hospital Nil.	
"	Dec 26th		Running and at 07:45. At 09:00. Company practise the attack 11:45 and 14:00 Captain of Bombing and Lewis gun training. Instruction of tug and lewis with the Battn for four days. I am reported Army Service towards Casualties Nil. Sick Hospital 1.	

Army Form C. 2118.

WAR DIARY
or
INTELLIGENCE SUMMARY.
(Erase heading not required.)

Instructions regarding War Diaries and Intelligence Summaries are contained in F. S. Regs., Part II. and the Staff Manual respectively. Title pages will be prepared in manuscript.

Place	Date	Hour	Summary of Events and Information	Remarks and references to Appendices
LE MESGE	Dec 27th	0900	Route march for the Bath, accompanied by the 1st line transport. 1030 Coy Commanders met taken in a Battalion scheme by the Brigadier General 2/Lt Calloway returned on Knuckles dept for a Lewis gun course at LE TOUQUET. 2nd Lieut S Robertson dept for a staff gun course at MEAULTE and 2/Lt D.M. Robertson for a Lewis gun course at DAOURS. 1400 all companies training in Bombing and Lewis gun. Sick to hospital 1. A & B companies bathing at RIENCOURT.	
"	Dec 28th		Running drill at 0845. Company parade as strong as possible at 0900 Heading of arms, anti-gas, musketry drill. Bombing, Lewis gun training and at 1000. Bombing + Lewis gun training at 1400 octobers drill and at 1000. Bombing + Lewis gun training at 1400 1000 Brigade Bombers received instruction in Trench Mortar. Casualties NIL. Sick to Hospital. NIL	
"	Dec 29th	0945	Foot training drill. 0900 Commanding Officers Parade as strong as possible. Bombing and Lewis gun training. 1400 Bombing and Lewis gun training.	
		11.15	2/Lt McLennan & Watt and 193 O.R. returned from musketry course at PONT REMY. Casualties NIL Sick to hospital NIL 2. + D companies bathing at RIENCOURT.	
"	Dec 30th	0945	Running drill. 0900. Bombing & Lewis gun training for all companies	
		11.30	C.O. his inspection. Casualties NIL Sick to hospital 1	
"	Dec 31st	10.9 E.	headed under Capt. Broaday for Burns course at 10.9 45. R.16s at 11.00 under 2/Lt McLennan. Casualties NIL dick & hospital 2 1 man written up by Ran.Lewis Lewis. Adjt 1st K.O.S.B.	

A. 58/B.A.W973/M687 750,000 8/16 D. D. & L., Ltd. Forms/C.2118/18.

CONFIDENTIAL

Vol 13

WAR DIARY

1ST KING'S OWN SCOTTISH BORDERERS.

From 1st January 1917. to 31st January 1917.

VOLUME 30.

WAR DIARY
INTELLIGENCE SUMMARY

January 1917

Place	Date	Hour	Summary of Events and Information	Remarks and references to Appendices
LE MESGE	Jan 1st 15/1/7		Holiday for the Batt.	
	Jan 2nd		2½ Per mile march accompanied by 1st line transport, leaving at 9 am & returning at 1.15 pm. 2 pm all N.C.Os paraded for instruction under the Bombing Officer. 2 O.R. reported from hospital. 3 O.R. sick to hospital. draft of 6 O.R arrived.	
	Jan 3rd		Company tactics. Artillery formation from 0900 to 1100. 20 warrants of the day was supplies & trenching. Bayonet fighting. The hostile discipline 5 O.R. reported to hospital & 3 reported from hospital. 2 men rejoined from wounds. 1 O.R. to Base under age. 9/691 Broadway & 2 O.R. on course to FLIXECOURT.	
	Jan 4th		1000. Inspection of the Batt. by the Divisional Commander, after which Bn. was seen in an attack. 5 pm G.O.C. wining. 2 N.C.Os to England for Company Commanders. 2/Lt Wales & 2/Lt Mackinnon to England on leave. Casualties & sick to hospital NIL.	
	Jan 5th		0745. Tact training drill from 9 to 12 Noon company practices Fire Control. Bayonet fighting, trenching & bombing. 1400 all Officers on 9 Prelim. Scheme. 1400 to 1 pm wiring. draft of 9 O.R. arrived sick & hospital NIL.	

Army Form C. 2118.

WAR DIARY
INTELLIGENCE SUMMARY.
(Erase heading not required.)

Place	Date	Hour	Summary of Events and Information	Remarks and references to Appendices
LE MESCE	Jan 6		4001 warning arm byset trades 0900 Company Parad "Protection" (a. strong as possible) 1/35 officers of platoon by T.O. 1 to Bow/ford i. At E. Parade for Divis arms at 10. R.C.O. at 9.30 a Powcette NIL and b leaders 2/H. G. Pallor	
	Jan 7		4601 warning arm 900. Programme: lectures enemy and comi on made Brigaden Guard. Hawalis NIL did throttes ?	
	Jan 8			
	Jan 9		0900. Botany Route march in Strong as possible Avanue, + R. A. Guard practice also Ateung formation 1400 at intend N.C.O. was Bombing Duty N.C.O. is an by R.S.M. Livesting M S Land my Bombing Duty N.C.O. is an by R.S.M. Livesting M S Land + 3 OR. accidentally wounded. Draft of 7 OR armed. 1.O.R. joins from Kephria. Sickness 1.	
	Jan 10		Raining arm at 0945: Outside ainw anew O.C. Coys at 0900: Parands of warning awrates to Sabling, Musketing Bayonet Asting. Lectures + Gas helme drill was very G a N C Os at 1400. Lewiseettie NIL Disk to loss the NIL	
	Jan 11		0945 4001 warning drill Be Outpo arm at 9 a. Lecture of Grainerats at 9.45- by Commanding Officer. Renewal The day awl to Musketry, Bayort fighting march discipline. Map reading for all Officers at 5.30pm wends 3rd command Arrowthis NIL Sick to hospital NIL	

WAR DIARY / INTELLIGENCE SUMMARY

Army Form C. 2118.

Place	Date	Hour	Summary of Events and Information	Remarks and references to Appendices
LE MESGE	Jan 12		The Bn moved to BRESLE moving by Ervillers to AIRAINES, detrained at MERICOURT and marched from AIRAINES to BRESLE. Bn HQ and LE MESGE at 10.15 am & arrived at BRESLE at 6.15 p.m. Casualties NIL. Sick to hospital NIL.	
BRESLE	Jan 13		The Bn entrained at BRESLE at 10 am for GUILLEMONT arriving at 2.30 p.m. Relieved the 6th Yorkshire Regt who went into No. 2 Reserve — reported from hospital.	
GUILLEMONT CAMP	Jan 14		The Bn "lived" in the 10th and 9th Yorkshire Regt in the line (Left Section) A & B Companies to the line. Lieut Douglas & 3 Section D Coy in Reserve. 1 O.R. wounded. 1 O.R. reports from 12 A.C.C.S. Reflex (transport officer) to hospital sick.	
Ferry day Jan 15			Enemy artillery fairly active during very quiet day. 2 O.R. killed 4 O.R. wounded. 4 officers & 10 O.R. arrived + attended. Lt Lewis & Lt Ellis joined 3rd K.O.Y.L.I. Lewis attended 3rd K.O.Y.L.I. Brown 3rd K.O.L. Ros. the two ambulance 1st K.O.Y.L.I. Brown & Lewis & Brown took over the "C" Coy from Lieut N.G. Wilcock & Lieut Ellis took over the "D" Coy from Lieut Brown & report reports in No. two. Lieut Wilcock & Lieut Calais left Scott morning & returned to CARNOY.	

WAR DIARY
or
INTELLIGENCE SUMMARY
(Erase heading not required.)

Army Form C. 2118.

Place	Date	Hour	Summary of Events and Information	Remarks and references to Appendices
FIRING LINE	Jan 16th		Enemy very quiet. Our own very active. At 5.30 p.m. the Bn. got relieved by the 7th Buffs & marching from Citadel Camp returns to CARNOY CAMP. Arriving in Camp at 7.30 p.m. the Bn. are formed up and dismissed (on arrival in Camp). Casualties Nil. Sent to hospital Nil.	
CARNOY CAMP	Jan 17th		Breakfast at 9.30 in the day in changing into Drill order & cleaning up. From 9 M.L. dress & adjustment kept. M.O.L. Bn. y P.A. wounded aid. Error in Muster. Permission granted to Offr & NCO.	
CARNOY CAMP	Jan 18th		The Bn. training in CARNOY. Gas mask regiment inspection among the morning. Lectures turned as relieval of the greatest of low movement & CARNOY MAIN DRESSING STATION. The finale relation for the honourn of trench feet. Draft of 4 Other ranks posted to A. & B. Companies arrived 10 A. to England to take up temporary Commissions. Casualties Nil. Sent to hospital Nil.	
CARNOY CAMP	Jan 19th		At 3 p.m. the Bn. paraded & moved forward to GUILLEMONT CAMP. B Bn. moving at CARNEY at 3 hofner we along range to take due to the lengthening accommodation at GUILLEMONT CAMP. & its not Casualties were more available to battalion Nil. Sent to hospital Nil.	

Army Form C. 2118.

WAR DIARY
INTELLIGENCE SUMMARY
(Erase heading not required.)

Instructions regarding War Diaries and Intelligence Summaries are contained in F. S. Regs., Part II. and the Staff Manual respectively. Title pages will be prepared in manuscript.

Place	Date	Hour	Summary of Events and Information	Remarks and references to Appendices
GUILLEMONT CAMP	Jan 20		In the morning Gen. [?] and went from the Brigade Head qrs. Very satisfied with what I had. In the By. Standard etc. to B.H. returned the 7 Eveng. Regt to the firing line. D & C Coys in a front line. A Coy in support (in a more fairly advanced & open attack on front line) & I had each available. I had. Some uneasiness.	
FIRING LINE	Jan 21		From here told by forts. moving to the state of the trenches concerned in cleaning up moving up these fronts. Enemy artillery fairly quiet. Units safe. We were [?] from. Our of Coy. [?] enemy sniping. I saw wounded. Died & taken by 1st Border Regt. returned to GUILLEMONT CAMP NIL.	
GUILLEMONT CAMP	Jan 22nd		In the morning our ranks developed extra trench were drawn to the opinion on the Bn. relieved to the line returned to the firing line. Wrote to B.B. going into the front line. A & D Coys into outpost. C Coy into support. Bn. relieved & looked NIL Coy relieved to GUILLEMONT CAMP.	
FIRING LINE	Jan 23rd		Very hard frost. School enlarged to dug. Every artillery action somewhat as artillery replied. 2 on killed 1 on wounded Strength of 13 off around trenches. Res. & tropical NIL	

A 5834 Wt. W 4973/M 687 750,000 8/16 D. D. & L. Ltd. Forms/C.2118/13.

WAR DIARY
INTELLIGENCE SUMMARY

Army Form C. 2118.

Place	Date	Hour	Summary of Events and Information	Remarks and references to Appendices
FIRING LINE	Jan 24"		Enemy guns & DEVIL'S Wood caught a party of the enemy in the open. Many casualties. Enemy guns & Bray & S9 O.P. caused heavy shelling. Our artillery very active. Men were much exhausted, many wounded to send out to hospital. 3 men reported for hospital. The Bn. was relieved by 1" Essex Regt. & returned to CARNOY CAMP not far from tramways. The Bn. arrived down at CAMP and felt it was what was never seen before down as this.	
CARNOY CAMP	Jan 25"		Rifles, kit, equipment, uniforms in the morning & materials in the afternoon. Men sent to hospital.	
"	Jan 26"		Got warning order cancelled. The Bn now to GUILLEMONT CAMP a/c 3 p.m. arrived ab. 4.30 p.m. Relieved Anzac nr. 2 week & hospital.	
GUILLEMONT CAMP	Jan 27"		2 Baths for men, & distributing of new & old extra rounds of S.A.A. were drawn for the purpose of taking into the line. At 4.30 pm the Bn. moved off to the line & relieved the 1st Essex Regt. & 1st R. Berks there, taking over the position there the Bn. had relieved from the enemy two 3 days before. 4 men wounded going up to the line. 2 M.G. Bns of Portland to take up Lewis Guns (wounded from hostile missiles unknown).	

A.5834. Wt. W4973/M687. 750,000. 8/16. D. D. & L. Ltd. Forms/C.2118/13.

WAR DIARY
INTELLIGENCE SUMMARY

Place	Date	Hour	Summary of Events and Information	Remarks and references to Appendices
FIRING LINE	Jan 28th	—	Very heavy [enemy] reinforcements being [brought?] [up?] Enemy continually shelling the captured position. Did no [damage?]. Lights not [manned?] of our men. 9 O.R. killed. Lt. W.H. Atkins & one Officer having gone out [could not?] to locate the [enemy?]. They are [taking?] what [shelter?] they can. Capt. Hackett & Lt. Harris [both?] wounded. Sent to [Hospital?] N/L.	
	Jan 29th	—	Enemy shelling very heavy. Infantry fire to the front & [by day?] & [shrapnel?] as [cut off?] from our [centre?]. 3 men killed & 19 wounded. Sick & Hospital N/L.	
	Jan 30th	—	1 Officer + 21 O.R. of the enemy was captured by B Coy in the morning. They [had?] [...] come up to take one of [...]. [...] by the 9 R.[...]. Yrs in the days previous. They lost their way & [is?] the morning were seen to [...] an not advanced. Told [...] to the old front line. Did no voluntaries to get out & attack them after getting round they [remain?] throwing a few bombs. The enemy [surrenders?] [The enemy were seen [...] from trenches at work in artillery.] 12 [...] killed, 16 [...] wounded [...] 27 men [...] Hospital 1 also reporting from trenches.	

Army Form C. 2118.

WAR DIARY
INTELLIGENCE SUMMARY
(Erase heading not required).

Instructions regarding War Diaries and Intelligence Summaries are contained in F. S. Regs., Part II and the Staff Manual respectively. Title pages will be prepared in manuscript.

Place	Date	Hour	Summary of Events and Information	Remarks and references to Appendices
Firing LINE	Jan 30.		(Continued) the Bn. were relieved by the 1st R Innis. Fus (?) & marched back to CARNOY CAMP. not having had time as Bn. at GUILLEMONT CAMP and has since however on coming to CARNOY.	
CARNOY CAMP	Jan 31.		Rifles &c. equipment entertainer in the morning the Bn. rests for the remainder of the day. (no working &c. wanted) 9 men left to hospital.	

Written up by Lt Lewis ?
a/ adjt
1st K.D.L. Bn.

87/39
Vol 14

21 J.
9 sheet

CONFIDENTIAL.

WAR DIARY

of

1st BATT. THE KING'S OWN SCOTTISH BORDERERS.

from 1st FEBRUARY, 1917 to 28th FEBRUARY, 1917

VOLUME NO. 31

WAR DIARY or INTELLIGENCE SUMMARY

Army Form C. 2118.

165

Place	Date	Hour	Summary of Events and Information	Remarks and references to Appendices
CARNOY CAMP	Feb 1st		Wet morning and at 7.45 am Battalion paraded at an inlying (?) quarter of an hour to march to trenches if required at the enemy attack CARNOY. Bn. Released at 3 pm & marched to GUILLEMONT CAMP relieving the 1st BORDER Regt. thereabouts. Dick & trenches NIL.	
GUILLEMONT CAMP	Feb 2nd		The morning was devoted by all ranks to keeping in touch to the Bn. paraded at 4.30 pm and moved forward & relieved the Newfoundland Regt. in the left sector. Enemy's artillery very active. Enemy patrols were now & anxious to all patrol activity. They were advised by our teams giving rifle fire. Casualties NIL. Our trench casualties 1 OR.	
	Feb 3rd		(A quiet day with little activity by either side. At night the enemy carried on front line trenches shot out and inflicted any casualties. Enemy artillery retaliated. Casualties NIL. Dick & Trenches NIL.	
Young Line	Feb 4th		An enemy aeroplane came over lines in the morning. Our artillery was fairly active throughout the day. The Bn. was relieved by 1st R Sussex Fusiliers in the evening & marched back to GUILLEMONT CAMP where they settled in for the night. Casualties rank & file NIL. 1 OR (Regl Pte) killed in action at the 5th Aust. Div school.	

WAR DIARY or INTELLIGENCE SUMMARY

Army Form C. 2118.
106

Place	Date	Hour	Summary of Events and Information	Remarks and references to Appendices
CARNOY CAMP	Feb 5th		The morning was devoted to clearing up & preparing [for] a move to CARNOY CAMP. Col. S. from the Bn. was always by the 1st R Irish Fus. have J.B.W. moved back to CARNIY. heavily down for so mgs. Det to trophies NIL. Anzres reported from livine Beaulieu NIL	
—	Feb 6th		Rest, equipment, &c. examined and were told away. The Bn. rested for the reminder of the day. The last 4 weeks sent from them...Lewisville NIL Det to trophies NIL. Reports from there draft of 71 OR arrived Beaulieu. OR reported from trophies. 1 OR Reinhardt reported missing reported.	
—	Feb 7th		The Bn. paraded at 12.30 am marched by transport to MEAULTE arriving at 2.15 p.m. and settled into billets & had dinner 2.45 p.m. Early Z S W. Division moving from Carn. 1 OR previously reported missing reported. Casualties NIL Reg. to trophies NIL	
MEAULTE	Feb 8th		Rifles, equipment cleaning inspected & brown etc abbrevis continued the remainder of the day. The Bn. moved. 5 NC. O.s + 95 m. we to the CITADEL at 4 pm in Company fatigues. Casualties NIL Det trophies 1 OR to. 1 OR out f the Bn. to infly	
—	Feb 9th		7.30 Running and trade early, the remainder inspection in the morning Bomb throwing practices in the afternoon A B + D Coys Parade + march of the Beaux Casualties NIL Det trophies NIL	

WAR DIARY
INTELLIGENCE SUMMARY

Army Form C. 2118.

167

Place	Date	Hour	Summary of Events and Information	Remarks and references to Appendices
MEALTF	Feb 10		Running with water [illegible]. To remainder of the morning at disposal of O.C. Rept. Dark throwing practice in the afternoon. 1 W.N.C.O. + 30 Oth ranks in fatigue at TOWN MAJOR'S office. Casualties NIL. Sick to hospital 4 O.R. Roll of 19th Armed.	
	Feb 11		Yl. Bn. Wet rec for Duties. dump left C.E.I. Push war from component Officer by returning to Camp by A.P.L. station. Sick to hospital 9. Casualties NIL.	
	Feb 12		7.30 am. Running drill. The remainder of the morning was devoted to handling of arm. Saluting drill + musketry. 1400 Bombing was O.C. Repl. Casualties 1. Sick to hospital NIL. 2 O.R. transferred to A.O.C. 1 O.R. returned from hospital	
	Feb 13		07.30. Running drill. 2 O's Parade as during the remainder of the morning. Lecture of O.B. by the remaining officers. 5 hrs study A.R.U. The remainder of the morning at the disposal of O.C. Bomps. Bombing war O.C. Repr at 1400. The fatigue party of 5 N.R.O.S. + 95 other ranks were relieved by a party of the same strength. Casualties NIL. Sick to hospital 2. 2 Lt. W. R. Evans 4th Batn 4 Rep K.O.S. Bn turned 9. 4 K.O.S. Bn ex alt. 4th F.M. the acorn. 7th O.S. Bn arrived	
	Feb 14		Dispensed with the disposal of O.C. Rept. Angr. Baynes fighting Repr Mgr for fracting to O.O.Y. fracting the attack. Casualties NIL. Sick to hospital 1 O.R.	

Army Form C. 2118.
168

WAR DIARY
INTELLIGENCE SUMMARY
(Erase heading not required)

Place	Date	Hour	Summary of Events and Information	Remarks and references to Appendices
MEAULTE	Feb. 15"		Throughout day we fighting bombing attacks among the sunken road under O.C. Coys. Enclosed. Nil sent to hospital. N.9.	
—	Feb. 16	At 0530	arrival enemy aeroplanes flew over the sunken road. A large number of Coy bombs were used by O.C. Coys. 2/Lt at Welch took over command of the Brigade H.Q. & B.W. Perryman took over command of the Batn: Casualties: Nil. Sick to hospital: Nil.	
—	Feb. 17"		Raining, and at 0730. Lt W. Parker a/0915 a/s strong reported Company at arrival of O.C. Corps named as day Casualties. Nil sick to hospital: 2 OR. 1 Officer & 25 OR ordered to report 6 to 6 RESTRONQ=WOOD wood. 153rd Trenching Bay. R.E. 1 O.R. & 25 O.R. ordered to report to RESTRONQ=WOOD working as ordered.	
BRONFAY CAMP	Feb. 18"		The Batn. formed at 11.30 & marched to BRONFAY CAMP No 107 arriving by Companies with a distance of 300 yds between Companies. The Batn. arrived at 14.25 and about 1 mile of ditches the hills returning the 9th Bn. Balce at Accrington with Perkh. & 3rd S.M.L. Lnrel & O.R. to storecarrier in a guards room at DAOURS. Lawrence 2/4 O.C. Banner. " 4 O.R. to Guards room as DAOURS Lawrence Nil dies to hospital Nil.	
SUPPORT LINE	Feb. 19"		The morning was available to cleaning up & preparing to move. At 2.30 pm the Bn. headed moved into the SUPPORT LINE, relieving the	

WAR DIARY or INTELLIGENCE SUMMARY

Army Form C. 2118.

Place	Date	Hour	Summary of Events and Information	Remarks and references to Appendices
SUPPORT LINE	Sep 19th		The 9th West Ridings & Coy was battalion to the INTERMEDIATE LINE. A Coy under Capt. Broadway, "B" Coy under Shuttleworth in MORVAL ROAD and "D" Coy in MUTTON TRENCH under Lieut. F. Cole. Bn HQ in overflow dug out in COMBLES. 90 officers rank & file taken to the line, the attack being left as BROWFAY on arrival OC. Coys were instructed to send an officer to locate Bn. HQ Dr. casualties NIL. Lieut. F. Robertson reconnoitred the position of French Bn. on our Rt. No further preparation for reaction in afternoon. Our Sta. Sheriff et their Dressing Station COMBLES in the afternoon.	
FIRING LINE	Sep 20th		Relieved the 9th West Ridings in the Firing Line B & C Coys in the front line, A & D in close support. A guide & up. Enemy fairly active with trench mortars & rifle grenades during the night. Night casualties of each rank & file out of the trenches. 2/Lieut. T. O'Neill & Battle awarded the Military Medal and No's 9246, 12725, 20241 T.S.R. Battle awarded the Distinguished Conduct Medal for gallantry in the field. Sing returned to captaincy. 2/Lieut. Offord was ill when went to Hospital NIL. the casualties 1 killed 4 wounded died in Hospital NIL.	
FIRING LINE	Sep 21st		A fairly quiet day. Shelling on both sides and hostile machine gun active. Casualties 2 OR died in Hospital NIL. 13 OR wounded remain in duty	

Place	Date	Hour	Summary of Events and Information	Remarks and references to Appendices
FIRING LINE	Feb 23rd		On front line and CHARLES STRONG POINT the latter occupied by "A" Coy. Fairly quiet day. No enemy attack. Enemy shelled Support trench and HARDECOURT was shelled by the 1st Gloster Yuela morning. Kew T.B. arriving at 6.20 am. A fatigue party was in the new Coy. carrying our dead to Maricourt. 11 O.R. casualties coming out. NIL. Major Beythew proceeded to ENGLAND for duty. 14 Lieut. D.H.C. Jeacock Revd. C.F. transferred to 55th Bde to take up the appointment of D.A.P.C.	
BRONFAY CAMP	Feb 23rd		The Bn moved from HARDECOURT to BRONFAY at 12.30 pm. arriving at 2.30 pm. Dinners served on arrival in Camp. New OTC.G Army being formed (sic.) of the A.Coy. 2nd Hertfs, 21st Bns. moved into BOIS DORE CAMP, and others to stay for review of the attack. The attack marched to BOIS DORE CAMP, and others marched a carrying party which returned arms in the line. 2nd Hertfs. carrying attached to the West Riding R.E.'s. Casualties NIL. Men to Maricourt 16 O.R.	
SUPPORT LINE	Feb 24th		The Bn paraded at 9.30 am moved into support relieving the 1st Staffs. Men in Camp marched independently "B" Coy found 1 Officer and 50 O.R. to "A" Coy. 1 Officer and 50 O.R. for carrying to Max "B" Coy. / Officer and 50 O.R. for carrying to the West dict. Casualties NIL.	

Army Form C. 2118.

170

WAR DIARY
or
INTELLIGENCE SUMMARY.

(Erase heading not required.)

Place	Date	Hour	Summary of Events and Information	Remarks and references to Appendices
FIRING LINE	Sept. 25th		Company paraded & marched to COMBLES to take the Australia [position?] at the junction of French line & trench of the NEWFOUNDLAND Regt. in the firing line. 5 bn. the Batt. moved forward & relieved B Coy. the CHARLES STRONG POINT and C Coy. to COPSE RESERVE and CHEESE SUPPORT. A heavy barrage was put on the line by the Batt. and moving into the line two patrols out from 'A' Coy & 'D' Coy, under 2/Lt Routledge and 2/Lt D.H. Robertson attempted to enter the enemy's front line but were unsuccessful owing to rifle fire. One man of 'A' Coy killed & Enemy trench mortar very active during the night. Casualties 1 O.R.	
FIRING LINE	Sept. 26th		Enemy very active with artillery & trench mortars. Work was carried out to heavy shelling of our trenches. 6 patrols from 'A' Coy under 2/Lt Routledge succeeded in cutting through to enemy's wire and exchanging rifle bombs with a group of the enemy. One N.C.O. of this patrol missing & one wounded. Casualties 1 O.R. killed & 5 wounded.	
HARDE-COURT	Sept. 27th		The Bn was relieved in the firing line by the 1st Lanc. Fusilrs & marched to HARDECOURT. The first Co. arriving at 9 P.M. and the last 2.0 A.M. 12 M.N. Coys. were issued to the Bn at HAIE WOOD, on arriving at HARDECOURT [?] fell in [?] the hutts. 2/Lt McKay & 2/Lt Bond & 10 O [?] outside [?]	

Army Form C. 2118.
171

WAR DIARY
or
INTELLIGENCE SUMMARY.
(Erase heading not required.)

Place	Date	Hour	Summary of Events and Information	Remarks and references to Appendices
HARDE-COURT	Feb 24th		100 men from "A" details at BRONFAY march to BOIS DORE to bring in Stretcher Bearers. 2 O.R. killed + 11 O.R. wounded. 1 O.R. missing.	
BRONFAY	Feb 25th		At 10.30 a.m. 7th Bn. parades to BRONFAY arriving at 2 p.m. relieving the 16th Manchester Regt. Yer. were inspected various means after which the Bn. rested. 3 other ranks wounded + 6 O.R. sick to hospital.	Written up by C.M. Lewis R. at rear. 7th K.O.S.R.

No. 15

CONFIDENTIAL

WAR DIARY

OF

1st Battn. The King's Own Scottish Borderers

From March 1st 1917 to March 31st 1917

VOLUME 32.

WAR DIARY or INTELLIGENCE SUMMARY

March, 1917. Army Form C. 2118.

Place	Date	Hour	Summary of Events and Information	Remarks and references to Appendices
BRONFAY	March 1st		350 O.R. attacked the Batts. O.C. Coys held inspection of Rifles, Bayonets & webbing. 2 Officers & 100 O.R. and to BOIS DORÉ to leave party of the number already there. 1 O.R. of Long transferred to R.F.C. Kit inspection. 4 O.R. killed & 4 O.R. wounded. 5 O.R. sick admission. 1 O.R. to England for y/d munition. Major Townshend Junction to England for duty. 22.2.17.	
VILLE	March 2nd		The Bn. paraded at 10.30 a.m. and marched to VILLE being relieved at BRONFAY by the Welsh Guards. Bn. arrived at 2.10 p.m. Dinner was served & settled into billets. Bn. advance party left on previous day 7 a.m. to take over billets, which consisted of 1 Officer & 5 N.C.Os. Casualties NIL. Sick to hospital NIL. 5 ORs arrived hospital. Par transferred to Y/F K.O.S.Bs. at signallers	
LA NEUVILLE	March 3rd		Y/o left VILLE at 10 a.m. and marched to LA NEUVILLE arriving at 2 p.m. Bn. arriving there was relieved for the Bath by the day. 2 Officers & 100 men from BOIS DORÉ reported. Casualties 1 O.R. sick to hospital. 4 O.Rs	
LA NEUVILLE	4th		Lootham attended the Baths at CORBIE at an interval of an hour and a half. Kit, Rifle, Equipment & clothing inspected by O.C. Coys. Bath at 6.30 a.m.	

WAR DIARY

INTELLIGENCE SUMMARY

Army Form C. 2118.

Place	Date	Hour	Summary of Events and Information	Remarks and references to Appendices
LA NEU-VILLE	March 5th		Companies at the disposal of the Commanders for the purpose of having a general overhauling of kits, equipment, clothing etc. Kits inspected. From today's return, consist of 'B' Coy. Casualties NIL. Stick to hospital 2 O.Rs. 2 Ors. joined from hospital. Rev. D. Farnon arrived today.	
	March 6th		Steady and drenching rainwater continued all day. Casualties 1 O.R. 2 O.Rs. joined from hospital. Casualties NIL. Sick to hospital 1.	
	March 7th		Commanding Officers' tour of observation by the T.O. Rounds at 9.15 am of the Bn. inspected by Bn. Rounds of Arm. Reserves of day devoted to looking over. Lt. Armstrong returned O.C. Coys. Lt. Armstrong NIL Sick to hospital 1. with Recce R.E.'s Casualties NIL	
	March 8th		Running drill at 9.20 am. dry anti Bayonet fighting. Rapid loading, running, Bowing & Trench Gun instruction during remainder of the day. Coy. Commanders returned to attend a Lecture. The Control Reports on the use of the Bombard 2/Lt. Galloway proceeded to CAMIERS. for Machine Instructor Course. Armourer S/Sgt Hayward to arrived today. 10 ORs to hospital sick	
	March 9th		Corps at disposal of O.C. Coys, in the morning. Lecture by C. O. Hygiene, in the afternoon. 2 Officers and 140 other ranks attached to Bombing Brigade Hdqtrs as at 2.30 pm Casualties NIL. Sick to hospital 1. 6.R. 4 O.Rs rejoined from hospital	

WAR DIARY or INTELLIGENCE SUMMARY

Army Form C. 2118.

Place	Date	Hour	Summary of Events and Information	Remarks and references to Appendices
AT NEU-VILLE	March 10		Sunday. Band gave recital on Lady Ann under O.C. Bays in the morning. The afternoon was attended by a Lady Hickey at 2nd Lunch & 2nd from R.E.R. Henverton to come at the Divisional School. Staff of 5 A.R. officers attached to the Division sick and 1 O.R. moved from hospital.	
—	March 11		Lieut. E's attend church at 11.00 t. L.S under H/ C. Brown. Fatigue at 10 am. Presbyterian at 10 am and R.E.s may 12 am East morning at 11.30 am. Lecture for all officers by t.C. at 9 am.	
—	March 12		Training carried out under O.C. Bays. All Officers assembled at the Gallows guardroom by t.O. on the review action of outpost. 1 O.R. sick to hospital.	
—	March 13		O.C. Parade at 9.15 am. Numbers on parade 5.56 not including Officers. Remainder of day devoted to training Lewis gunners & Rifle Grenadiers and throwing out advanced guards. 2 O.Rs sick to hospital. 1 O.R. returned to R.E. & 1 O.R. returned from hospital.	
—	March 14		Sunday. R.C.'s parade. (Caviarea Guard & Caviarea Guard action taken on route test) by R.C. Officer by L.O. at 6 pm. Brunetti. 1 O.R. sick to hospital. 1 O.R. reported from hospital & 1 O.R. moved from hospital.	

WAR DIARY or INTELLIGENCE SUMMARY

Army Form C. 2118.

Place	Date	Hour	Summary of Events and Information	Remarks and references to Appendices
LA NEU-VILLE	15th March		Coys were at the disposal of O.C. Coys. Trench guard practised. Night outpost for all Companies at 6 p.m. Casualties NIL. Divs. to trenches. 1 other rank 3 O.R. rejoined from hospital	
"	16th March		Training in Bayonet fighting, Bombing & musketry carried out under O.C. Coys. 14 O.R. des. to trenches. 2/Lt G.d. Ross to England 3"/L 2/Lt. T. K.G. Roberton 3rd K.O.S.B. reported for T.M. Batty. 6 O.R. to Base reinft.	
"	17th March		Bn. continued training. Draft of 5/11 other ranks arrived trenches. 1 O.R. des. to hospital. Casualties NIL.	
"	18th March		Divine Service were attended by the L.A. Coys. Prestyknow Reinforcements. 1 O.R. to Base reinft. and 1 O.R. and R. des. y O.R. des. to hospital. Coys kept up a temporary tramway.	
"	19th March		The Bn. turned out at 9 a.m. and marched to EDGEHILL Platform cleaning at 2 p.m. The Bn. arrived at HANGEST at 4.20 p.m. and marched to billets at LE MESGE arriving at 5.25 p.m. All ranks proceeded to their billets. 4 O.R's to hospital sick	
LE MESGE	20th March		The Bn. parade as strong as possible at 9.15 a.m. after which toys practised Artillery formation. The afternoon was another to chamy up Kilt etc also lecture by L.O. to an officer & Men. Draft of 4 ORs arrived & OR to an Outpost at 5.15 pm	

Army Form C. 2118.

WAR DIARY
or
INTELLIGENCE SUMMARY.
(Erase heading not required.)

Instructions regarding War Diaries and Intelligence Summaries are contained in F.S. Regs., Part II. and the Staff Manual respectively. Title pages will be prepared in manuscript.

Place	Date	Hour	Summary of Events and Information	Remarks and references to Appendices
LE MESGE	21st March		Enemies renewed at 6.15 am the attack followed by intense digging, but no continuation of a strong point. All ranks were warned against being taken by surprise or any acceptation from any of the fill in the village to evening. NIL dies to trenches 2 O.R. Relief by 7. O. & an officer at 6.15 pm. Death of 4 ORs arriva trenches.	2 O.R.
	22nd March		Movement in attack was carried out by all companies in the morning. In afternoon was issued to the further training of Lewis Gunners. Bombers and rifle grenadiers helped by L.O. & officers in the officers was at 5.15 pm. Subject "Bombers". All officers and orders to all officers to be on the lookout of enemy aircrafts and in transporting baggage to meeting NIL to beyond the supplying to transporting baggage to meeting NIL to beyond the 4 Rl. & B.R. to Base was not so. 2 O.R. 2 O.R. 4 wounded during the day.	
	23rd March		Bn paraded at 9.15 am for Brig of attack. The reviews of the day who inspected the training of Lewis gunners bombers & rifle grenadiers translation NIL dies to trenches NIL 24. O.R. Lewis 5th K.O. I.B. hotes	
	24th March		The Bn practiced the Manoeuvre in attack. In afternoon on return to Unit lining. All ranks for our return to Hosps. a Rugby Ballers ???? into match. Trenches NIL dies trenches NIL ??? 3rd K.O.Y.L.Bs arrived trenches	

A.D. Foulis
Bn ???
3rd K.O.Y.L.I.

Army Form C. 2118.

WAR DIARY
or
INTELLIGENCE SUMMARY.
(Erase heading not required.)

Instructions regarding War Diaries and Intelligence Summaries are contained in F. S. Regs., Part II. and the Staff Manual respectively. Title pages will be prepared in manuscript.

Place	Date	Hour	Summary of Events and Information	Remarks and references to Appendices
LE MESSL	25th March		Divine service was held. C of E service was conducted mainly by E.E. Brockway, the RCs & L Solomon & Q sections were R/s by Maj TK Dept honorary Murdoch & Lt Murray and R/s was baptised. Divt honorary Lewallie. Nil. Sick to hospital 1 OR, B.M.H. S OR arriv. Deft. 1 OR rejoined from hospital 1 to Base refs 1 to Transportation deft. BOULOGNE	
""	26th ""		The Bn paraded at 7.15am & marched to the training area taking part in a Divisional Field day, returning to billet at 4pm when all were served.	
""	27th March		Reveille was at 7.30am Bn paraded at 11.15am and took part in a Brigade scheme returning to billet at 4pm. 3 OR sick to hospital 1 OR to Base refs.	
""	28th March		The Bnth at RIENCOURT was ordered to the Bn from 9am to 5pm. Coys worked to RIENCOURT at intervals of 25 hours & all men had their clothing washed. During the rifle Examination fires off all rifles greased & experimented with the Norton-Pryer Grease No 22. Offs rtning from the Baths detaining - one made for army 13 OHs rotr evacuated sick. 3 to Base refs + 9 to Transportation Deft. BOULOGNE	

WAR DIARY or INTELLIGENCE SUMMARY

Army Form C. 2118.

Place	Date	Hour	Summary of Events and Information	Remarks and references to Appendices
FLESSELLES	29th March		The Bn. paraded at 9.15 a.m. full marching order & marched to FLESSELLES via PICQUIGNY, LA CHAUSSÉE ST. VAST & PICQUIGNY. The Bn in process of being fitted out as 1st Rein for RE. Distance of march 11 mile. On arriving at FLESSELLES, dinners were served & all ranks billeted. 10 m.n failed to keep up with the Bn on the march. Staff of 9 O.R. arrived. Total 2 O.R. evacuation sick.	
BONNEVILLE	30th March		The Bn. left FLESSELLES at 10.10 a.m. en marche to BONNEVILLE via HAVERNAS, CANAPLES and FIEFFS. Arriving at 1 p.m. Dinners were served after which men billeted. Weather showery all day. 4 men failed to come in with the Bn, but arrived later. 2 O.R. evacuated sick.	
	31st March		Running order for all troops at 7.30 a.m. From 9 a.m. troops were at the disposal of O.C. Coys. Lads Tilmats and inspected. Lect to Lowrie	

Written up by C.S.M. Lewis L.
& Capt
17 K.O.Y.L.I.

Vol 16

Confidential

1st Bn. King's Own Scottish Borderers

War Diary

Month of April 1917

Volume No 33

REGISTRY
No. 2 DISTRICT and
INFANTRY RECORD OFFICE
25 OCT 1917
HAMILTON

18887/8.

Officer i/c
    Historical Section,
        Committee of Imperial Defence,
            (Military Branch),
            Public Record Office,
            Chancery Lane,
              LONDON. W.C.2.

      I beg to return with thanks the War Diary of 1st Bn. King's Own Scottish Borderers for April 1917. A duplicate has been prepared for custody in this office.

                                              Colonel.
                            i/c No. 1. Record Office,
Hamilton.   No. 2. District.
25-10-17.

Army Form C. 2118.

WAR DIARY
or
INTELLIGENCE SUMMARY.
(Erase heading not required.)

April, 1917.

Place	Date	Hour	Summary of Events and Information	Remarks and references to Appendices
HEM	1st April		The Bn. paraded at 9 a.m. & marched to HEM a distance of about 7 mls. via MONTRELET, FIENVILLERS and HARDINVAL. Bn. arriving at HEM at 12.30 p.m. Billets were good but no stables available. Billets party of 35 O.Rs arrived prior to Bn. 2 ORs. rejoined from hospital.	
LUCHEUX	2nd April		The Bn. paraded at 12.5 & marched to LUCHEUX via DOULLENS. MILLY (distance about 6 mls). Bn. arrived at 3.30 p.m. & "A" & "B" coys. were accommodated in huts & "B" coy in billets. Draft of 2 other Ranks and intelligen[ce] men with nothing known & 1 other rank rejoined from hospital.	
	3rd April		The Bn. meeting at LUCHEUX. Physical training at 7.30 a.m. under O.C. Coys. The Bn. paraded at 9.30 a.m. for training and again at 2 p.m. Training took a little of Platoon minus the village. A gallows erected with their respective contango. Orders were issued for all ranks to have their hair cut close to the head. A latrines in the charge of superior mounds in the village during the evening. 4 O.Rs evacuated sick.	
	4th April		The Bn. still resting at LUCHEUX and the Bn. continued training as of April [illegible]. 2 O.R. wounded at PAS to return to duty [illegible]	

Army Form C. 2118.

WAR DIARY
or
INTELLIGENCE SUMMARY.

(Erase heading not required.)

Instructions regarding War Diaries and Intelligence Summaries are contained in F.S. Regs., Part II and the Staff Manual respectively. Title pages will be prepared in manuscript.

Place	Date	Hour	Summary of Events and Information	Remarks and references to Appendices
LUCHEUX	4th April		Course of cycling & Lewis gun attached & 1 OR transferred to cadres. Horse transport detail. ABBEVILLE. 2 ORs transferred to Pnrs. of war draft.	
LIENVILLERS	5th April		The Bn left LUCHEUX at 1.30 pm marched to LIENVILLERS via SUS-ST-LEGER and GRAND RULLECOURT arriving at 3.30 pm when billets were issued. Both Companies included the Bn during the march from ACHEUX. Billets & rations & ammunition & rifles etc. being sent. M.O. Capt. 4th K.O.S. Bn transferred to R.F.C. 1 O.R. struck off strength of Bn.	
"	6th April		The Bn rested at LIENVILLERS and continued training. Bty was running at 7.30 am Pvts grenadiers & all platoon commanders 10 am and 11.30 am 2/Lt R. Mackay lecturing to subaltern at 9.15 am and others digging. Casualties NIL	
GRAND RULLECOURT	7th April		The Bn marched at 9.15 am marched to GRAND RULLECOURT via the march en route GOC and 8 Off'k lorry arrived heartily interested arriving billetes P.15 & 12.45 bn saw were served on the boys arriving. 3 Mess sacks evacuated sick. 1 man return from hospital. 5 Officers and 40 O.R. sent to Corps Schl. at ST POL. 3 (Hp) ranks invalided sick. 1 Offr. and report from hospital.	

Army Form C. 2118.
182

WAR DIARY
or
INTELLIGENCE SUMMARY.
(Erase heading not required.)

Place	Date	Hour	Summary of Events and Information	Remarks and references to Appendices
MONCHIET	9th April		The Bn. paraded at 9.30 a.m. & marched to MONCHIET via BARLY – FOSSEUX – GOUY-EN-ARTOIS. Distance about 7 miles. Arrived at 12.30 p.m. Dinners were served soon after for the remainder of the day. Billets taken over were very dirty. Casualties NIL	
"	9th April		Resting at MONCHIET until orders to move at 6 hours notice. W. & allowed to have the vicinity of the village. During the rest of the day was devoted to Physical training. The remainder of the day was devoted to cleaning up & cutting down — and Officers' kits. A suitable ground for inspection were used by O.C. Coys. A suitable ground for training was found about 1 mile from the village. Casualties NIL.	
"	10th April		Bn. paraded at 9.30 a.m. for P.T. & for Gymnastics. The Bn. paraded at 10.15 a.m. & proceeded to the training area to carry out such training as they thought necessary. A return was given by the C.O. to all Officers at 6.70.p.m. A future party of 1 N.C.O., 20 O.Rs. under were orders orderly to TOWN MAJOR at 9.30, who 2 Limbers & no heavy draught horses. Casualties NIL.	

A 5834 Wt.W4973/M687 750,000 8/16 D.D.& L. Ltd. Forms/C.2118/13.

Army Form C. 2118.

WAR DIARY
or
INTELLIGENCE SUMMARY.
(Erase heading not required)

Instructions regarding War Diaries and Intelligence Summaries are contained in F.S. Regs., Part II and the Staff Manual respectively. Title pages will be prepared in manuscript.

183

Place	Date	Hour	Summary of Events and Information	Remarks and references to Appendices
MONCHIET	11th April		7.30 a.m. Running order. The morning of the day kept at the disposal of 10th Corps for training & infantry tank. (Other rank sent to hospital)	
ARRAS	12th April		Bn. paraded at 11 a.m. marched to ARRAS arriving at 4 p.m. Shelters about 1 mile distant were served out, & the Bn. rested whilst awaiting for return to move at 7.30 p.m. the Bn. moved up to the support (BROWN) line. Arriving # at 12 M.N. Casualties NIL.	
Wb BROWN LINE	13th April		Work during the day was devoted to cleaning and a walk from the trenches. Bn. moved forward at 12 M.N. to reach the 1st northumberland Fus. in the fighting line. Relief complete was reported at 4.45 a.m. Whilst waiting for the guides to conduct the Bn. to the line a large number of Eno artillery fell close to the Bn. which necessitated the wearing of Box Respirators. During the move 3 other ranks killed. 2/Lt R.D. Peat + 5 O.R. wounded. slightly gassed.	

A.8834. Wt. W4973/M687 750,000 8/16 D.D. & L. Ltd. Forms/C.2118/13.

WAR DIARY or INTELLIGENCE SUMMARY

Army Form C. 2118.

18A.

Place	Date	Hour	Summary of Events and Information	Remarks and references to Appendices
FIRING LINE	14 April		village of MARLIERE. The Bn held the line from LABERGERE X ROADS to the hedge and worked to aid in the line at the SUNKEN RD in N18.c. The patrol under Lt Ling was sent forward to patrol the road from which trouble was being given. A line was then dug about 200x E of the Sunken Rd. A & B Coys furnishing one platoon each as a covering party to the working party. C Coy available by 150 other ranks from the 1st Bord. Regt. dug the line. Work ceased just before daybreak. The new line dug was 24. 2/Lt D.H. Robertson and 2/Lt P.S. Mackay killed. 10 Oers [other ranks] killed + 5 Oers ORs wounded.	
	15th April		During the day work consisted of improving the line + revetting. Report received GUEMAPPE had been evacuated by the enemy. An officers patrol was made reconnoitre the village. It was knowing it was ascertained that the enemy was still held the place. At 4.20 p.m. orders were received for a moor operation, occupying + consolidating a road along N18.c.16. Three platoons of D Coy taking part in this operation. At 9 p.m. orders from the Bn cancelled this. 1 D Coy trooper wounded. 1 B Coy trooper 1 to aug + 2Lt Ling to line dug the Sunken road. 4. OR wounded.	

Army Form C. 2118.

WAR DIARY
or
INTELLIGENCE SUMMARY.
(Erase heading not required.)

Place	Date	Hour	Summary of Events and Information	Remarks and references to Appendices
FIRING LINE	16th April		At dawn "A" & "D" Coys moved forward from the new line. On with during the day was arduous & wearisome, involving retirement the screen. At night one Coy of the R. Berks. was placed at the disposal of the C.O. & aug the Coys between "A" & "D" Coys. thereby making a continuous line. The hefty moved forward as fm when the orders of Capt Scott Moncrieff. 1 Officer (2/Lt S. Rowbotham) + 4 O.R. killed. 4 O.R. wounded.	
"	17th April		At 3.30 a.m. "B" Coy moved forward from the support line & reinforced the newly dug line of trees. All Coys now being in the firing line, every aug by the 1/Bn. was now of advice. Coys are all in length. The line had been pushed forward about 600 yards in Bradway) + 5 O.R. wounded. 2nd Lt Eller + 2 O.R. struck off strength of Bn.	
"	18th April		At 1 a.m. the Bn. was relieved from the firing line by the 1st Bn. Essex Regt. All ranks having been in the line with without refreshment or practical food having been the Bn (less C Coy now) were looking forward being returned to the support line. of the ranks wounded. into the BROWN LINE "C" Coy	

A 5834. Wt. W.4973/M687 750,000 8/16 D.D. & L., Ltd. Forms/C/2118/13.

WAR DIARY
INTELLIGENCE SUMMARY

Place	Date	Hour	Summary of Events and Information	Remarks and references to Appendices
BROWN LINE	19th April		Men were allowed to rest in the morning & in the afternoon men were sent for Coys to clear impact to him so far as possible. At night "B" Coy were ordered to work on the C.7 turning and MARLIERE. 1 O.R. killed & 4 O.R. wounded.	
ARRAS.	20th April		Through the day inspections were held in the line & a general cleaning up ordered. At night the Bn was relieved by the 11th 9th Black Watch & came back to ARRAS. M.C.O. men going to the Cams & Officers into billets. Strength of Bn 33 O.R. arriving at the 13th Corps Depot. 2 O.R. transferred to Transportation Depot. BOULOGNE.	
	21st April		The new rebus & platoons were reorganised. The Baths at the Seay & Dumb Institute having been allotted to the Bn. Coys proceeded there as follows:- "B" Co. from 6 a.m to 8 a.m. "B" Coy from 8 to 10 a.m. "A" Coy from 10 a.m to 12 Noon & "D" Co from 12 Noon to 2 p.m. Orders received from the Brigade, stating the Bn taking part in a Big offensive commencing on MONDAY the 23rd inst. Casualties NIL.	

April 1917   XXX   87th Bde   1/25"

Army Form C. 2118.
187

WAR DIARY
or
INTELLIGENCE SUMMARY.
(Erase heading not required.)

Place	Date	Hour	Summary of Events and Information	Remarks and references to Appendices
FIRING LINE MONCHY LE PREUX	22nd April		During the day infantry were being used for the Bn. going into the line. At 7.30 p.m. the Bn. did an advance to the new meeting the line on the right through the old front line from 0.4.b.16¼.7½ to 0.1.d.4.4. Very heavy shelling during the night, the enemy shelling MONCHY LE PREUX very effectively. 2 other ranks wounded.	
FIRING LINE MONCHY LE PREUX	23rd April		At 4.45 a.m. heavy volume of our artillery barrage on the Bn. left the front of attack extended a long way from 0.2.d.0.0 to 0.2 central. Report of forward message from the front line at 4.46 a.m. Everything nice + quiet, no will. H.48 a.m. line of our shells dropping just H.59 a.m. Our troops 400" from jumping off line 4.57 a.m. bridges go have crossed our old front line 5.1 a.m. Our troops on the front German trench 5.7 a.m. Have got German front trench and left are moving forward. As read us 5.19 a.m. Our troops on not have reached German front line, South of MONCHY 5.26 bridges go nothing or German trench and our troops nothing towards Windmill the Hayfield are reported as taken. 5.30 Our artillery on our firing short, one of our shells dropping just in front of our old front line. 5.36 a.m. This is a very heavy mist and we cannot see anything at present. 5.50 German machine guns are opening fire from FRITS... across the road. 5.53 We have	

WAR DIARY
or
INTELLIGENCE SUMMARY.
(Erase heading not required.)

Army Form C. 2118.

Place	Date	Hour	Summary of Events and Information	Remarks and references to Appendices
			Got the whole of the BLUE LINE and consolidating. 6 a.m. Consolidating our attack O2 a 0.4 to O2 a 6.4. The Barrage has opened out by the time we are about from O.L. A Co. 6.10 a.m. has taken up position holding up artillery fire along the whole of our front. 6.13 a.m. The Wounders report they have suffered no casualties and there is evidence of reaction by our own artillery. Infantry at still in advance of the Company trench. 6.15 a.m. The Bn is digging in on a line running from N.S 700.10 at BOIS DU SART. L lines that 9 in Bn on our right and the S.W. Bn on our left. Barrage at heavy. Further reports tell us by our own Runner. Enemy sniping from BOIS DU SART from O.C. B. Co. 6.17 Enemy firing Machine Gun from a true bearing of 93 degree from our position. 6.20. Report white flares going up on our RH. 6.35 Enemy shelling us on our right. 6.36. Our artillery still firing short. 6.43 Enemy sending up light flares in front of our original front line. 6.45 Enemy shelling with heavy on the right. 6.50 Shelling in between the Consolidation and the BLUE LINE. At this stage we are heavy aug shelling with heavy on the right. 7.5 a.m. German seen running in areas about O2 a a. are now under cover. 9 am. Enemy shelling our rear from the very heavy. 10.10 a.m. Shells exploding with terrific heavy in our cut right. 10.15 a.m. Enemy coming over cut in the artil.	188

A3584 Wt.W4973/M687. 750,000. 8/16. D.D. & L. Ltd. Forms C.2118/13

WAR DIARY or INTELLIGENCE SUMMARY

Army Form C. 2118.

189

Place	Date	Hour	Summary of Events and Information	Remarks and references to Appendices

BOIS DU VERT. Artillery necessary to shift them. An airman early manoeuvring to take up a position O.9.a.38 to O.9.a.36. The message sent in by O.C. 'A' Co. (Lt. WEST M.C.) and an artillery informed of the thought fit to this on this report, causing many casualties to the enemy who fired in the direction. While many took to the open rifles & Lewis gun fire was opened causing more casualties to the enemy.

3 p.m. Enemy preparing for a counter attack on our right flank. One of our troops on our right flank seen to be falling back. At 3 p.m. our troops to our original from this 4 p.m. Counter attack [illegible] seen back to our original from this 4 p.m. Counter attack [illegible] There are the [illegible] as [illegible] a line in continuation with our line. Position of the Bn at 10 p.m. The rgt of the line was at 0.5.6.2.9. (approx) just N of the road, the left of the line with a at 0.2.a.3.1. The trench was continuous the 50× which had not been dug through across 0.2.a.5.2. Orders were given for this to be dug through during the night. The trench was from 5 to 6 ft. deep throughout. There was a gap of about 100× between the right of the line & the left of the PP to Lt. BELL. The O.C. 'A' Co. taking the left of the line was in touch with a [unit] of the Borax Regt situated aligning to our left flank & front of 0.2.a.3.F. Three patrols had been pushed out in front of our line by all along were led by O.C. 'A' Co. in the

WAR DIARY
or
INTELLIGENCE SUMMARY

Army Form C. 2118.

Place	Date	Hour	Summary of Events and Information	Remarks and references to Appendices
SUPPORT LINE.	24th April		SUNKEN ROAD on at O.2.d.45 and the other at O.2.a.55. A good deal of fire came the piraser from all parts of the line. The west of the troops are good. Owing to the Bn being so [near?] the enemy the Company trenches are very shallow and cover dug during the night by the men as they could use the trench during the morning for use temp- HQ Bn HQ Bn three uses and trued to FEUCHY CHAPEL X ROADS and Reserve nr. At 11 p.m others were moved from the Bde to new Cry Stn say moved to reserve at the Tenedosne trench & Royal trench (B & D Coys were relieved by the trench tend in at 2 p.m. and they show signs out of the night daytime. These two Companies harassed is Reserve had by to STRING TRENCH. The Royal Irish not being able to PICK and STRING TRENCH. The Royal Irish not being able to get into the line B & C Coys were not relieved. Bn HQ was moved to the dugout at LA PERGERE X ROAD. B & D Coys were move down to the dugout at LA PERGERE X ROAD. B & D Coys were move relieved from the trench line at 9.30 p.m. and to the Bn moved back to ARRAS. Lewallan during this town Amounted to 3 Officers and 16 other ranks killed & 4 Officers and 116 other ranks wounded, and 20 other ranks missing of whom about 10 were shortly after being wounded & 20 other ranks were found afterwards slightly killed. Arrived at ARRAS.	2 Officers and 16 other ranks killed 2/Lt [?] at H.M. Routs 4 Officers and 116 other ranks wounded 20 other ranks missing

Army Form C. 2118.

WAR DIARY
or
INTELLIGENCE SUMMARY.
(Erase heading not required.)

Instructions regarding War Diaries and Intelligence Summaries are contained in F.S. Regs., Part II. and the Staff Manual respectively. Title pages will be prepared in manuscript.

Place	Date	Hour	Summary of Events and Information	Remarks and references to Appendices
DUISSANS	25th April		The Bn paraded at 1.30pm & marched to the railway station ARRAS entraining at 2pm and was borne on to DUISSANS. We route marched to the nameless of the day. Throughout the event necessary for the landing of the N 29th Reinforcements were sent to the H.M.S.s against the Sapphire and Granat. Les Hants Winston war spa also named from the H.M.Ss AMETHYST, the SAPPHIRE and Granat. Thanks Weston Casualties NIL.	
LATTRE ST. QUENTIN	26th April		O.C. Coys were ordered to hold full inspections and a general cleaning up of everything. Battle Scouts were organised & stores were issued. 11.30 am orders were received from the Bde for the Bn to move at 1pm. This was confirmed at 12 noon. The Bn marched at 1pm and arrived at LATTRE ST. QUENTIN (distance about 8 mls.) arriving at the Casualties NIL	
ST. AMAND	27th April		The Bn paraded at 10.30 am and marched to ST AMAND (distance about 12 mls.) order of march B.L.D.A. Coys. The first Coy arrived at 3.30 pm followed by the other Coys at 20' intervals. We made use allowed of 5 pt. for 20 rounds of the day. Men killed	

A 5834 Wt.W4973/M687 750,000 8/16 D.D.&L. Ltd. Forms/C.2113/13.

Army Form C. 2118.

WAR DIARY
or
INTELLIGENCE SUMMARY.
(Erase heading not required.)

Instructions regarding War Diaries and Intelligence Summaries are contained in F. S. Regs., Part II. and the Staff Manual respectively. Title pages will be prepared in manuscript.

Place	Date	Hour	Summary of Events and Information	Remarks and references to Appendices
ST AMAND	27th April (contd)		in huts, men in huts, and are comfortable. 6 other ranks evacuated sick.	
	28th April		Boys were at the disposal of O.C. Coys for the purpose of inspections, cleaning up, & c. There was arrival of NCOs & warrant officers during the day. Bn Battle Stores were not available. Platoons reorganised. Draft of 49 other ranks arrived from D. POL & posted.	
	29th April		The Bn paraded in lorries in lorries at 9.45 am & was marched by the C.O. for this good walk on the 23" + 24" inst. The draft was inspected after the Bn was assembled. Pretty firm. The draft was inspected at 10.30 am for private arms. No conformity paraded at 11.30 am. A tray form from the Bn reports & A.P.C. paraded. Issues & Awards of Gong & DOUBLETS. 6. A.d. Orr to take officers classes of 2 ROS Br. 4 "A.d. Orr to take officers classes & Bn B A Crnode & 2 ROS Bn transferred to 2nd ROS Bn. 2 other ranks evacuated sick.	
	30th April		7.30 am Physical training. 9 am Company drill. The remainder of the day was devoted to Rifle training, fire control and training Lewis Gunners, Rifle Grenadiers & Bombers. At 1.45 pm all Officers & men were	

Army Form C. 2118.

WAR DIARY
or
INTELLIGENCE SUMMARY.
(Erase heading not required.)

Instructions regarding War Diaries and Intelligence Summaries are contained in F. S. Regs., Part II. and the Staff Manual respectively. Title pages will be prepared in manuscript.

Place	Date	Hour	Summary of Events and Information	Remarks and references to Appendices
ST AMAND	3rd April		For the Bn to be prepared to move on the 1st proximo. An advance party on and forward at 3 pm to take over billets at WANQUETIN from the units evacuated such	

Written up to by Att. Lieut. Lewis
A/Adjutant
1st K.O.S. Borderers

Army Form C. 2118.

180

WAR DIARY
or
INTELLIGENCE SUMMARY.
(Erase heading not required.)

Instructions regarding War Diaries and Intelligence Summaries are contained in F.S. Regs., Part II and the Staff Manual respectively. Title pages will be prepared in manuscript.

Place	Date	Hour	Summary of Events and Information	Remarks and references to Appendices
HEM	1st April		The Bn. paraded at 9 am. marched to HEM, a distance of about 8 miles via MONTRELET FIENVILLERS and HARDINVAL. On arriving at HEM at 12.50 p.m. lunch was served and men settled into billets. Strength 35 O/Rs. Nurses reported a O/R rejoined from Isolation sick.	
LUCHEUX	2nd April		The Bn. paraded at 12.5 p.m. marched to LUCHEUX via DOULLENS-MILLY. A distance about 6 miles. Bn. arrived at 2.30 p.m. "A" "B" "C" "D" "Coys" here accommodated in huts. "E" Coy in billets. Dinners served on arrival and anaesterious tea after settling down. 2 other ranks rejoined from hospital.	
"	3rd April		The Bn. resting at LUCHEUX. Physical training at 9.30 am. under O.B. Boys. The Bn. paraded at 9.30 am for training and again at 2 p.m. training and athletics 1 kilometre outside the village. Signalling paraded with their respective Companies. Orders were issued for all ranks to have their hair cut close to the head to minimise the danger of infectious wounds in the head. A performance in the Cinema was given in the village during the evening. 1 O.R. evacuated sick.	
"	4th April		The Bn. still resting at LUCHEUX and the Bn. continued training on 3/4/18. Lieut .... was forwarded to PAS to attend a	

Army Form C. 2118.

WAR DIARY
or
INTELLIGENCE SUMMARY.

(Erase heading not required.)

Place	Date	Hour	Summary of Events and Information	Remarks and references to Appendices
LUCHEUX	4th April		Course on erecting Wireless apparatus. I.O.R transferred to Ammn Horse Transport depot ABBEVILLE 2 O.R transferred to Div. of W. Coys.	
LIENVILLERS	5th April		The Bn. left LUCHEUX at 1.3 pm. marched to SUS-ST. LEGER and GRAND RULLECOURT arriving at 3.30 pm when dinners were served. Coys. commanders inspected the Bn. during the halt, then settled into billets & rested. 2 o/Rs. Amtn. week. knocked 4th KO S. Bns. transferred to R.F.C. 1 O/R trans. officers 5 eng 8th A.B.	
"	6th April		The Bn. moved at LIENVILLERS and continued training. Physical training at 7.30 am. Rifle grenadiers + all platoon commanders paraded at 9.15 hrs. under 2/Lts L.G. KeRoy. Coy. companies carried out Intensive digging. 4 O/R O/R N16	
GRAND RULLECOURT	7th April		The Bn. paraded at 9.15 am. marched to GRAND RULLECOURT knees using the attack in route. After boys marched to billets independently arriving between 12.15 & 12.45 pm. Dinners were served on the boys arriving. 3 other ranks evacuated sick. 1 man injured from hospital. 5 officers & 110 O/R sent to Tanks OKs at ST. POL. 3 o/Rs rejoined from hospital.	

A 5834 Wt.W.4973/M687 750,000 8/16 D.D.&L. Ltd. Forms/C.2118/13.

WAR DIARY or INTELLIGENCE SUMMARY

Army Form C. 2118.

Place	Date	Hour	Summary of Events and Information	Remarks and references to Appendices
MONCHIET	8th April		The Bn formed at 9.30 am & marched to MONCHIET via BARLY–FOSSEUX–GOUY-EN-ARTOIS distance about 8 miles. Arrived at 12.30 pm. Dinners were served then rested for the remainder of the day. Billets taken over. Run very dirty. Casualties NIL.	
"	9th April		Resting at MONCHIET with orders to move at 6 hours notice. As men were allowed to leave the vicinity of the village Bn had one 9.30 a.m. Physical training. The remainder of the day was devoted to cleaning billets, cleaning up & setting down. Kit inspections were held by O.C. Coys. A suitable ground for training was found about 1 mile from the village. Casualties NIL.	
"	10th April		Reveille sounded at 4.30 am for P.T. & few gymnastics. The Bn paraded at 10.15 am & marched to the training area to carry out such training as they thought necessary. A lecture given by the C.O. to all Officers at 5 p.m. A fatigue party of 2 N.C.O. & 30 other ranks was ordered to report to TOWN MAJOR at 9.30 with 2 limbers one heavy draught horse. Casualties Nil.	

Army Form C. 2118.

WAR DIARY
or
INTELLIGENCE SUMMARY.
(Erase heading not required.)

183

Place	Date	Hour	Summary of Events and Information	Remarks and references to Appendices
MONCHIET	11th 6/4/17		Given training area. The remainder of the day kept at the disposal of Coy Commanders for training & preparing kits + equipment.	nil
ARRAS	12th 6/4/17		Bn paraded at 11 a.m. marched to ARRAS arriving at 4 p.m. advance parties were round & the Bn & LEWIS GUNS billets awaiting about 7 mile. Dinner were round & the Bn & LEWIS GUNS billets awaiting for return to them at 7.30 p.m. Bn moved into the support line (BROWN) arriving at 12 M.N. Laen attacks NIL.	
The BROWN LINE	13th 6/4/17		Work during the day was done in strengthening wire & wells from the trench. Bn. ordered to attack at 12 M.N. to assume the 1 northwesterly face to the firing line. Relief complete was reported at 4.45 a.m. Whilst awaiting for the Zero hr to commence the Bn. to the line. a large number of Bn one shells fell above to the Bn lines which necessitated the moving of Bn. Headquarters twice and caused slightly fewer d. 3 other ranks killed. Offrs R.H Peate + 5 O.R. wounded.	

A5834. Wt. W4973/M687 750,000 8/16 D. D. & L. Ltd. Forms/C.2118/13.

Place	Date	Hour	Summary of Events and Information	Remarks and references to Appendices
FIRING LINE	14th April		The Bn held the line from LA BERGERE X ROADS to the SUNKEN Rd. in N17c. Orders were received at aug. 6 a.m. at the SUNKEN Rd. in N17c. Patrols were sent forward to the high ground which was found to be strongly held by the enemy. While in front of this line during day, C Coy were dug in about 200y E of the Sunken Rd. A & B Coys were dug in echelon on a covering party to the working party of Bry A. Coy available by 150 other ranks from the 17. Border Regt. dug the held work close to just before daybreak. C. Coy employed 150 ready dug in position — one 2/Lt & P.S. Mackay killed, 10 other ranks killed & 5 other ranks wounded.	
	15th April		During the day work consisted of improving all trenches recently taken round GUEUDECOURT & A new succeeded by the enemy in efforts but it was arranged to reconnoitre the village of the evening. It was ascertained that the village was vacated by the enemy. At 4.30 p.m. account was made of carrying out a minor operation, occupying & consolidating a forward trench N17c.14. Three patrols of D Coy, being of the Battalion not in the situation at 9 p.m. men from the Bn entered the village to D Coy moved to a position in the line during the hour was vyd. Y. O.R. wounded.	

WAR DIARY or INTELLIGENCE SUMMARY

Army Form C. 2118.

Place	Date	Hour	Summary of Events and Information	Remarks and references to Appendices
FIRING LINE	16th April		At Dawn A & D Coys moved forward into the new line. Our work during the day was chiefly to make possible moving the trench. At night one Coy of the R. Bers, two new Plats of A & D Coys the whole of the C.O.'s and the Sap Reliever A & D Coys thereby making a continuous line. Casualty moved forward as follows :— the whole of Capt Scott movements. 10 Others (Lt E Routledge?) the 1st & R. killed. 4 O.R. wounded.	
	17th April		(1) 7.30 a.m. B Coy moved forward from the support line to occupy the newly dug line of trench. As Coys now being in the firing line, supply by the Bn. was now of a more closer nature, almost one mile in length. The line had been pushed forward about 600x. Though the day was with some artillery & infantry fire (Capt E Broadway) & 5 O.R. wounded. Lieut Gillon 1 O.R. smith off strength of Bn.	
	18th April		(1) night the Bn. was relieved from the firing line by the 1st Bde. Irish Fus. in all ranks having being in the line six nights, without blankets or great coat, & having had no sleep on two reasons were looking very ragged. On being relieved the Bn (A & C Coy) moved into the BROWNLINE in the support line. 4 Other ranks wounded	

185

Place	Date	Hour	Summary of Events and Information	Remarks and references to Appendices
BROWN LINE	19th April		Now quite secure to & is in the morning by the afternoon trench was used for Coys to clear repair. The trenches as far as possible. At night B. Coy were moved to work on the C.T. running into MARLIERE. 1 O.R. killed & 7 O.R. wounded	
ARRAS	20th April		Through the day work. Items were had been in the line & a general clearing up ordered. At night the Bn. was relieved by the 11th/9th Black Watch & moved back to ARRAS. N.C.O's were sent to the camps & others into billets. Draft of 33 O.R. arrived at 18th Corps Depot. 2 O.R. transferred to transportation Dept. BOULOGNE.	
	21st April		The men rested & Platoons were reorganised. The Batln. is the Post & Dump Insilite having been allotted to the Bn. Coys found as did there as follows:- "C" Co. from 6 a.m. to 10 a.m. "A" Coy from 10 a.m. to 12 noon & "D" Coy from 8 to 10 a.m. "A" Coy from 10 a.m. to 12 noon & "A" Coy from 12 noon to 2 p.m. Orders received from the Brigade relative to the Bn. taking part in a big offensive commencing on MONDAY the 23rd inst.	

WAR DIARY or INTELLIGENCE SUMMARY

Army Form C. 2118.

Place	Date	Hour	Summary of Events and Information	Remarks and references to Appendices
FIRING LINE	22/4/ April		During the day typhostigers were being made for the Bn going into the line. At 4.30 p.m. Bn HQrs. paraded and marched to the line relieving the Middlesex Regt. Front line from O.7.b.1½.8½. to O.1.d.7.9. Very heavy shelling during night. Enemy shelling MONCHY-LE-PREUX very frequently.	
FIRING LINE MONCHY LE PREUX	23rd April		At 4.45 am under cover of an artillery barrage the Bn left thy trench to capture & consolidate a line running from O.2.d.2.0. 0.2 ...... Khartis as follows received from the front line. 4.46 am Everybody over + doing well. 4.48 am Some of our shells dropping short. 4.517 am Our troops 400' from jumping off trench. 4.58 am Inhabitants have reached our old front line. 5.1 am Our troops in the first German trench. 5.8 am Have got German front trench and many are moving towards the 2nd trench. 5.19 am Our troops on heights are nearing the German 2nd line, South of Wancourt. 5.20 Inhabitants passing on German trench and our troops making towards Wancourt. 5.30 Our artillery are still shelling our trench. 5.30 Our artillery knocking our own rear line. 5.26 am There is a very heavy mist and we cannot see anything at present. 5.50. German machine guns are opening fire in front of our own front line. 5.53 We have ...	

WAR DIARY or INTELLIGENCE SUMMARY

Army Form C. 2118.
188

Got the whole of the BLUE LINE and were consolidating 6 a.m. bombarding in our objective O.2.d.0.4 to O.2.d.0.9. The Barrage then moved on. My left and a little short from O.6.A.c. 6.10 a.m. Our troops pushing out from along the whole of our front. 6.13 a.m. The Worcesters report they have been shelled out of their most advance position by our own Artillery. However they are still in occupation of the General Trench. 6.15 a.m. Enemy digging in in a line running due N. & S. 700' W. of the BOIS DU SART. I lined up the 91st Bde on our right and the 5 W Bde on our left. Barrage not heavy. Further came up by our own Barrage. Enemy sniping from BOIS DU SART from O.E.B.60. 6.18 a.m. Enemy firing Machine Guns from a true bearing of 53° from our position. 6.20 a.m. heavy white flares going up on our left. 6.35. Enemy shelling on our right. 6.36. Our Artillery still firing short. 6.43. a.m. Enemy shelling wood ravine in front of our original from line. 6.45 a.m. Enemy helding very heavy on old right. 6.50 a.m. The shelling in between the Red Sunken Trench & the BLUE LINE. At the dugout on my left dug in were wall away cover. 7.5 a.m. Enemy own Machine Gun small wood at O.2.a. 9. a.m. Enemy shelling on our front line heavy. 10.10 a.m. Attack v Worcesters last duggg [?] [?] near Enemy looking up a position on our new tench

Place	Date	Hour	Summary of Events and Information	Remarks and references to Appendices
Bf BOIS DU VERT			Artillery necessary to shift them. O.G. disposed on faulty endeavouring to take up a position O.9.a.38 to O.9.a.36. This manage was apt. By O.C. (B/Lt Batt N.C.) an artillery informed wks brought here to bear on the trench causing heavy casualties to the enemy ris this in all directions. Whilst moving back in the three M.G. Lewis Gun fire was fired knowing our casualties to the enemy.	
		3 pm	Enemy trying to a counter attack on our right front.	
		3 pm	Our troops on our right flank seen to be falling back. Enemy have gone back to own original front line & an counter attack seems also the Worcesters and letting & his in continuation with our line. Position of the Bn at 10 h.m. the right of the line rested at O.R.t.2.9. (Alphee) just N of the road. The left of the line was not at O.2.a.36. The trench was continuous too 50° which had not been dug through about O.2.a.52. Points were given for this to be dug through during the night. The trench was from 5 to 6 ft deep throughout. Were five stepped there was a gap of about 100° between the right of the line & the left of the 8°th S.R. Bee. the O.b."A" bn holding the left of the line was in touch with a post of the Border Regt situation slightly to our left flank at O.2.a.3.F. small posts had been pushed out in front of our line by "A" bn holding by O.b.a.66. in the	

WAR DIARY or INTELLIGENCE SUMMARY

Army Form C. 2118.

Place	Date	Hour	Summary of Events and Information	Remarks and references to Appendices
SUPPORT LINE	24th	6 a.m.	SUNKEN ROAD one at O.2.a.45 and the other at O.2.a.55. A good field of fire could be obtained from all parts of the line. The state of the trench was good. Owing to the Bn having to hand over the German trench trenches, very few prisoners were taken, several killed by the men as they passed over the trench. During the morning five were brought to Bn HQ Dg these were sent back to FEUCHY CHAPEL X ROAD and nearer our. At 11 pm orders were received from the Bde to warn boys that they would be relieved by the Lancashire Fusiliers Royal Scots. "A" "B" boys were relieved by the Borders at 2 pm, this enabling them to get out of the trench before daybreak that two bombers however to overtake PICK and STRING TRENCH. The Royal Scots not being able to get up to the line "B" "D" boys were not relieved. Bn HQ Ors moved to the dugouts at LA BERGERE X ROADS. "B" "D" boys were relieved from the firing line at 8.30 pm, and the whole Bn moved back to ARRAS. Casualties during the two amounted to 3 Officers and 16 other ranks killed, 7 Officers and 116 other ranks wounded, one of whom died of wounds shortly after being wounded, 20 other ranks missing. Between 1 am. 3 am and settled into billets in the Barracks	

WAR DIARY or INTELLIGENCE SUMMARY

Army Form C. 2118.

Place	Date	Hour	Summary of Events and Information	Remarks and references to Appendices
DUISSANS	25th April		The Bn. paraded at 1.30 p.m and marched to the railway station, ARRAS entraining at 2 p.m and on to DUISSANS. The rain was allowed to rest for the remainder of the day. This being the second anniversary of the landing of the 29th Division at Gallipoli wires were sent to H.M.S. The Euryalus & Sapphire and to General de Lisle. Wires were also received from H.M.S. Amethyst & Sapphire and General de Lisle. Weston. Casualties NIL.	
LATTRE ST. QUENTIN	26th April		O.C. Coys were ordered to hold foot inspections and a general cleaning up, & overhaul Battle Stores, respirers, platoons &c. 11.30 a.m orders were received from Bde. for the Bn. to proceed & move off 1 p.m this also applies at 12 noon the Bn. B. received orders 1 p.m and marched to LATTRE ST QUENTIN billets arriving at 4 p.m. Casualties NIL.	
ST. AMAND	27th April		The Bn. paraded at 10.30 a.m and marched to ST. AMAND (Billets about 12 m.) en route (on march) R.L.A. Coys 26 hrs (by a mile about) & 30 Lu Oplions(?) by the 14th Coys at 200y distance All ranks were allowed to fall out for 10 minutes at end of the day, [so that] blister[?]	

Army Form C. 2118.

WAR DIARY
or
INTELLIGENCE SUMMARY.
(Erase heading not required.)

192

Place	Date	Hour	Summary of Events and Information	Remarks and references to Appendices
ST AMAND	27th April (contd)		in billets. men in huts and all comfortable. 6 men sent evacuated sick.	
"	28th April		Boys were at the disposal of O.C. Coys to the purpose of interior cleaning up. 1 hr was devoted to leg exercises & Physical training during the day. Bath time was arranged & platoon organized drills & rifle & Lewis gun drill carried on.	
"	29th April		Bn paraded as strong as possible at 9.45 am & went through by the C.O. for their good work on the 23rd & 24th inst. The draft was inspected c/s the Bn was aniversed. Divdg Gerns. Non-conform paraded at 10.30 am for burial service the draft at 11.30 am. A tea party from the Bn went to H.Q. Reserve at 11.30 am. A tea party of 5 offs & 6 O.R.s to DOULLENS. At 11.40 On it's late officers for G.O.C G.A. invited & R.C.S. Bn. Lieutenants & 5th F.O.C. 150. 2 other ranks were attached.	
"	30th April		7.30 am Physical training. 9 am attack or the rahis of the day. was available to Rafia towards the training the Lehrt and training Lewis gunners Rifle Grenadier Bomber at 3 pm. the L.O. delivered a lecture to all officers & 11.45 pm firders/hessares	

Army Form. C. 2118.

WAR DIARY
or
INTELLIGENCE SUMMARY.
(Erase heading not required.)

193

Place	Date	Hour	Summary of Events and Information	Remarks and references to Appendices
ST AMAND	30th April		For the first time in the war the Bn. 210 1st proceeded into the trenches and furnished 3 pm. to take over billets at WANQUETIN it others were enabled to the	
			instructions sent by A.U. Lewis, Lieut A/Adjutant 1st K.O.1 Borders	

INSTRUCTIONS FOR OFFICERS GOING INTO THE FRONT LINE TO-NIGHT.

One Officer per Company and 1 N.C.O. per Platoon will report this evening at the 88th. Brigade Headquarters, situated in H.34.Central, namely in the BROWN LINE 1000 yards North of where the BROWN LINE crosses the ARRAS-CAMBRAI main road. Guides will then take them up to the Front Line trench East of MONCHY from where the Battalion will jump off. They will take with them the boards showing the Flanks of Companies and will mark off the trench as follows:-

The RIGHT of "D" Company at the corner and junction of trench at O.7.b.6½.8½. and the Left of "D" Company at O.1.d.7.3½. (Total length of trench about 225yds.)

"A" Company will have its Right resting on the Left of "D" Coy. at the above mentioned point, namely, O.1.d.7.3½. and its Left at the junction of the Front Line Trench and the Communication Trench at O.1.d.7.7. (total length of trench about, 225yds.)

The Two right Platoons of "C" Company will be extended along the trench behind "D" Company's front, and the two left platoons of "C" Company extended behind "A" Company's front, similarly the two right platoons of "B" Company will be extended behind "D" Company's front, and the two left platoons of "B" Company extended along "A" Company's front.

The Senior Officer will select a site for Battalion Headquarters in "D" Company's Sector, taking the best dug-out available.

All Officers and N.C.O's during the day must carefully study the Country over which the attack is to be made and must note, ready to point out to the Companies on arriving in position where wire has to be cut, to enable the Battalion to debouch to the attack. They will leave the front line the next afternoon if possible or just after dark if they cannot leave by day to meet the Battalion at the 88th. Brigade Headquarters at H.34.Central, to help guide their Platoons up.

21/4/17.

Lieutenant,
A/Adjutant, 1st. Battn. K.O.S.Borderers.

XXIX 87.

BATTALION WILL MOVE INTO THE FRONT LINE TO-NIGHT.

One Officer per Company and 1 N.C.O. per Platoon will report this evening at the 86th Brigade Headquarters, situated in H.34.Central, namely in the BROWN LINE 400 yards North of where the BROWN LINE crosses the ARRAS-CAMBRAI main road. Guides will then take them up to the Front Line trench East of MONCHY from where the Battalion will jump off. They will take with them the boards shewing the flanks of Companies and will mark off the trench as follows:-

    The RIGHT of "D" Company at the corner and junction of trench at O.7.b.61.9½. and the Left of "D" Company at O.1.d.7.3½.
    (Total length of trench about 220yds.)
    "A" Company will have its Right resting on the Left of "D" Coy. at the above mentioned point, namely, O.1.d.7.3½. and its Left at the junction of the Front Line Trench and the Communication Trench at O.1.d.7.9. (Total length of trench about 200yds.)

The Two right Platoons of "C" Company will be extended along the trench behind "D" Company's front, and the two left platoons of "C" Company extended behind "A" Company's front, similarly the two right platoons of "B" Company will be extended behind "D" Company's front, and the two left platoons of "B" Company extended along "A" Company's front.

The Senior Officer will select a site for Battalion Headquarters in "D" Company's Sector, taking the best dug-out available.

All Officers and N.C.O's during the day must carefully study the Country over which the attack is to be made and must note, ready to point out to the Companies on arriving in position where wire has to be cut, to enable the Battalion to deploy to the attack. They will leave the front line the next afternoon if possible or just after dark if they cannot leave by day to meet the Battalion at the 86th.Brigade Headquarters at H.34.Central, to help guide their Platoons up.

24/4/17.

Lieutenant,
A/Adjutant, 1st.Battn. K.O.S.Borderers.

OPERATION ORDER NO: 5
BY LIEUT.COLONEL A.J.WELCH,
COMMDG. 1st.BATT.THE KING'S OWN SCOTTISH BORDERERS.
In the Field. 22nd.APRIL, 1917.

1. The general advance will be continued at a date, and at a ZERO hour to be notified later.

2. The 87th.Infy.Bde.will take part. The 1st.Batt.K.O.S.Borderers will take and consolidate the First Objective, having the S.W.Brs. on their LEFT, and the 88th.Infy.Bde. on their RIGHT.

3. JUMPING OFF PLACE-The Battalion will take over and jump off from the First Line trench EAST of MONCHY, as per "Instructions for Officers going into the line to-night", a copy of which is attached.

4. OBJECTIVE-B L U E L I N E. This will be occupied and consolidated by a continuous line of trench running due North and South, approximately along the GRID LINE, running North and South from O.2.d.0.0. to O.2.Central. In addition to the consolidation of this line, Strong Points to hold one Platoon will be consolidated as under:-

    "B" Company about O.2.c.6.1. facing South-East.

    "D" Company near road about O.2.d.3.3.

    "C" Company in the vicinity of the Road junction at O.2.d.3.5. (this Post must be so sited as to sweep the Sunken Road in front of it).

    "A" Company about O.2.d.4.7. facing North-East.

    It will not be possible to construct the three last named Posts until our Barrage has jumped forward for the Second phase of the Operation.

5. FORMATION FOR THE ATTACK-"A" & "D" Companies will take the final objective as indicated above, passing over the German trench which runs North and South across the front from O.2.c.2½.0., to the junction with the S.W.Brs at O.2.c.2½.8. These Companies will go forward in two waves, each of two lines, the Right of "D" Company leading on a bearing due East from the Right of its jumping-off place to the Northern corner of the BOIS DU VERT, and the Left of "A" Company on a true bearing of 80 degrees from the Left of its jumping-off place.

    "C" Company will follow in close support at 50 yards distance from the rear line of the two front Companies, moving in one wave of two lines, its flank front line sections consisting of Bombers ready to block the German trench, which it will drop into as the mopping-up party to "A" & "D" Companies. When it has mopped up this trench and the leading Companies have attained, and are established in their objective line, it will go forward and join them. At this stage it must be prepared to assist the attack on its Right or Left if either is held up.

"B" Company will go forward behind "C" Company at 100 yards distance, and in the same formation. Its outer flank sections will consist of Lewis Gunners instead of Bombers. It will pass through "C" Company on the line of the German trench and will follow the leading Companies into the final objective as a support. Prior to passing through the German trench this Company must be prepared to assist the units on its flanks if necessary, but it must not cross over our Right boundary until the Barrage of the Brigade on our Right has got level with it.

6. Diagram of the Attack Formation, Barrage Table, and Map are attached.

7. ADMINISTRATIVE- Companies will go over the top about 125 strong.
DRESS- Fighting Order. Packs will be carried.
Three days' Iron Rations will be carried in the pack on leaving ARRAS, Rifle Grenades will not be carried but will be handed in to the Qr.Mr. All Rifle Grenadiers will be made up to 120 rounds of S.A.A. per man. Every man must start with his water bottle full which must be used most sparingly.
Bombers will carry their full complement of bombs and every man will carry one bomb in his pocket.
Two sandbags per man will be carried, also one ground flare per man, which will be lit by the most advanced troops only, and then only when called for by our aeroplanes which will probably be between 7 a.m.& 2 p.m.
Every man except Lewis Gunners will carry one tool and an extra bandolier of S.A.A. The extra bandolier will be collected in the final objective when Companies re-organise, and will be sent forward as opportunity offers to the 1/Rl.Innis.Fusiliers.
24 Lewis Gun magazines per gun will be carried.

7. (cont). Stretcher-bearers will accompany their Companies.

Officers will carry Very Pistols and Red & White flares, the former being for the S.O.S.

Battalion Headquarters will be in the right of the jumping-off trench, to which all Runners should be directed.

The Signalling Sergeant will detail a party of 6 men to run out a wire following the advance, and will establish telephonic communication between Battalion H.Q. and the German trench with in the final objective.

The Medical Officer will arrange for his Aid Post to be in the most convenient place.

There will be an Advanced Dressing Station at N.3.Central.

A. Lewis
Lieutenant,
A/Adjutant, 1st. K.O.S.Borderers.

OPERATION ORDER NO. 5.
BY LIEUT. COLONEL A.J. WELCH.
COMDG. 1st. BATT. THE KING'S OWN SCOTTISH BORDERERS.
In the Field-22nd. APRIL, 1917.

1. The general advance will be continued at a date, and at a ZERO hour to be notified later.

2. The 87th. Infy. Bde. will take part. The 1st. Batt. K.O.S. Borderers will take and consolidate the First Objective, having the S.W. Brs. on their LEFT, and the 88th. Infy. Bde. on their RIGHT.

3. JUMPING OFF PLACE.- The Battalion will take over and jump off from the First Line trench EAST of MONCHY, as per "Instructions for Officers going into the line to-night", a copy of which is attached.

4. OBJECTIVE- B L U E L I N E. This will be occupied and consolidated by a continuous line of trench running due North and South, approximately along the GRID LINE, running North and South from O.3.d.O.O. to O.2.Central. In addition to the consolidation of this line, Strong Points to hold one Platoon will be consolidated as under:-

   "B" Company about O.2.c.8.1. facing South-East.

   "D" Company near road about O.3.d.3.3.

   "C" Company in the vicinity of the Road junction at O.3.d.3.5. (this Post must be so sited as to sweep the Sunken Road in front of it).

   "A" Company about O.3.d.4.7. facing North-East.

It will not be possible to construct the three last named Posts until our Barrage has jumped forward for the Second phase of the Operation.

5. FORMATION FOR THE ATTACK- "A" & "D" Companies will take the final objective as indicated above, passing over the German trench which runs North and South across the front from O.3.c.0.0., to the junction with the S.W. Brs. at O.3.c.5.8. These Companies will go forward in two waves, each of two lines, the Right of "D" Company leading on a bearing due East from the Right of its jumping-off place to the Northern corner of the BOIS DU VERT, and the Left of "A" Company on a true bearing of 80 degrees from the Left of its jumping-off place.

   "C" Company will follow in close support at 50 yards distance from the rear line of the two front Companies, moving in one wave of two lines, its flank front line sections consisting of Bombers ready to block the German trench, which it will drop into as the mopping-up party to "A" & "D" Companies. When it has mopped up this trench and the leading Companies have attained, and are established in their objective line, it will go forward and join them. At this stage it must be prepared to assist the attack on its Right or Left if either is held up.

"B" Company will go forward behind "C" Company at 100 yards distance, and in the same formation. Its outer flank sections will consist of Lewis Gunners instead of Bombers. It will pass through "C" Company on the line of the German trench and will follow the leading Companies into the final objective as a support. Prior to passing through the German trench this Company must be prepared to assist the units on its flanks if necessary, but it must not cross over our Right boundary until the Barrage of the Brigade on our Right has got level with it.

6. Diagram of the Attack Formation, Barrage Table, and Map are attached.

7. ADMINISTRATIVE - Companies will go over the top about 125 strong.
DRESS - Fighting Order. Packs will be carried.
Three days' Iron Rations will be carried in the pack on leaving ARRAS. Rifle Grenades will not be carried but will be handed in to the Qr.Mr. All Rifle Grenadiers will be made up to 120 rounds of S.A.A. per man. Every man must start with his water bottle full which must be used most sparingly.
Bombers will carry their full complement of bombs and every man will carry one bomb in his pocket.
Two sandbags per man will be carried, also one ground flare per man, which will be lit by the most advanced troops only, and then only when called for by our aeroplanes which will probably be between 7 a.m & 2 p.m.
Every man except Lewis Gunners will carry one tool and an extra bandolier of S.A.A. The extra bandolier will be collected in the final objective when Companies re-organise, and will be sent forward as opportunity offers to the 1/Rl.Innis.Fusiliers.
24 Lewis Gun magazines per gun will be carried.

7.
(cont). Stretcher-bearers will accompany their Companies.

Officers will carry Very Pistols and Red and White flares, the former being for the S.O.S.

Battalion Headquarters will be in the Right of the jumping-off trench to which all Runners should be directed.

The Signalling Sergeant will detail a party of 6 men to run out a wire following the advance and will establish telephonic communication between Battalion H.Q. and the German trench in the final objective.

The Medical Officer will arrange for his Aid Post to be in the most convenient place.

There will be an Advanced Dressing Station at M.3.Central.

A. Lear

Lieutenant,
A/Adjutant, 1st.Batt.K.O.S.Borderers.

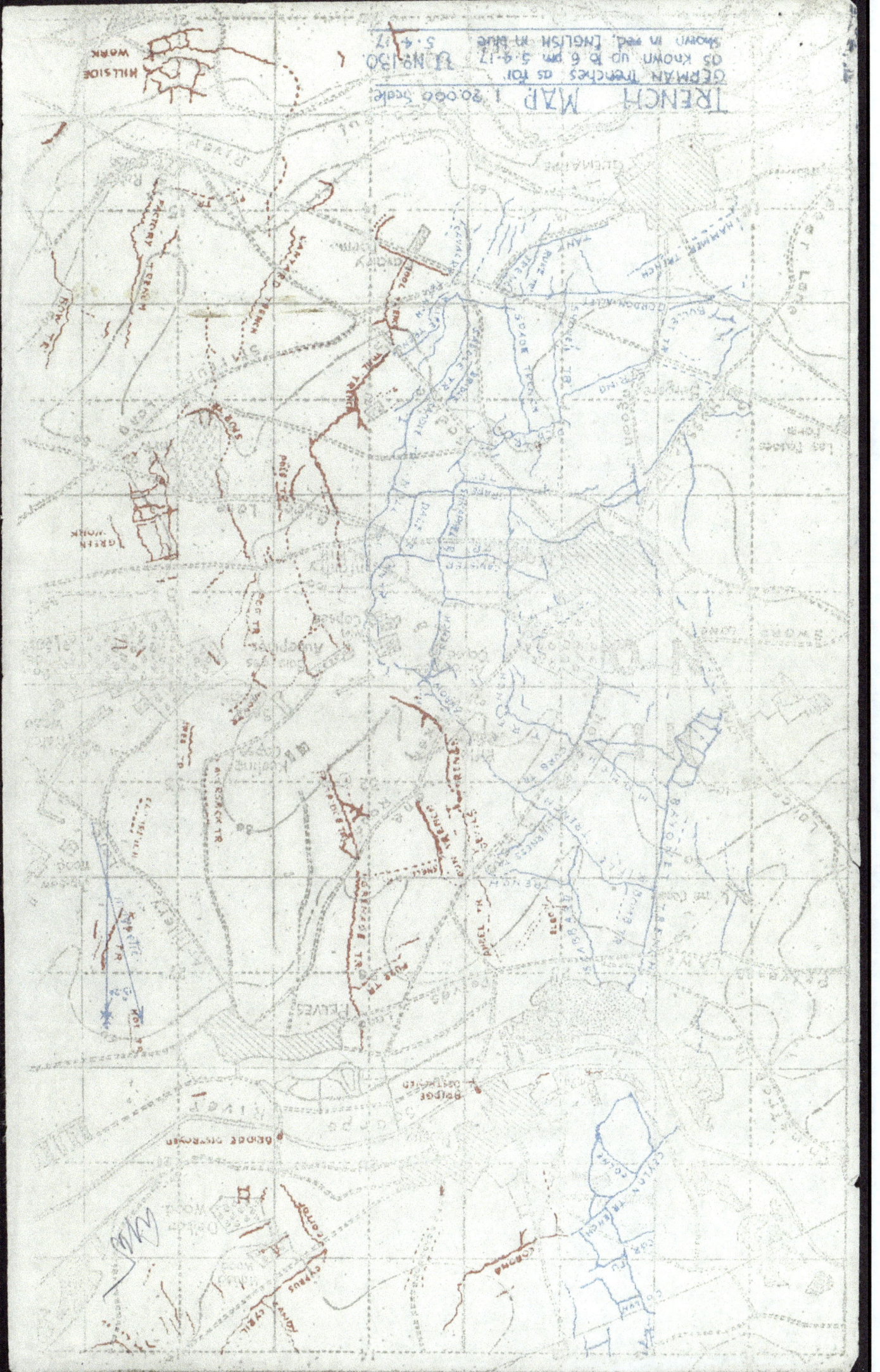

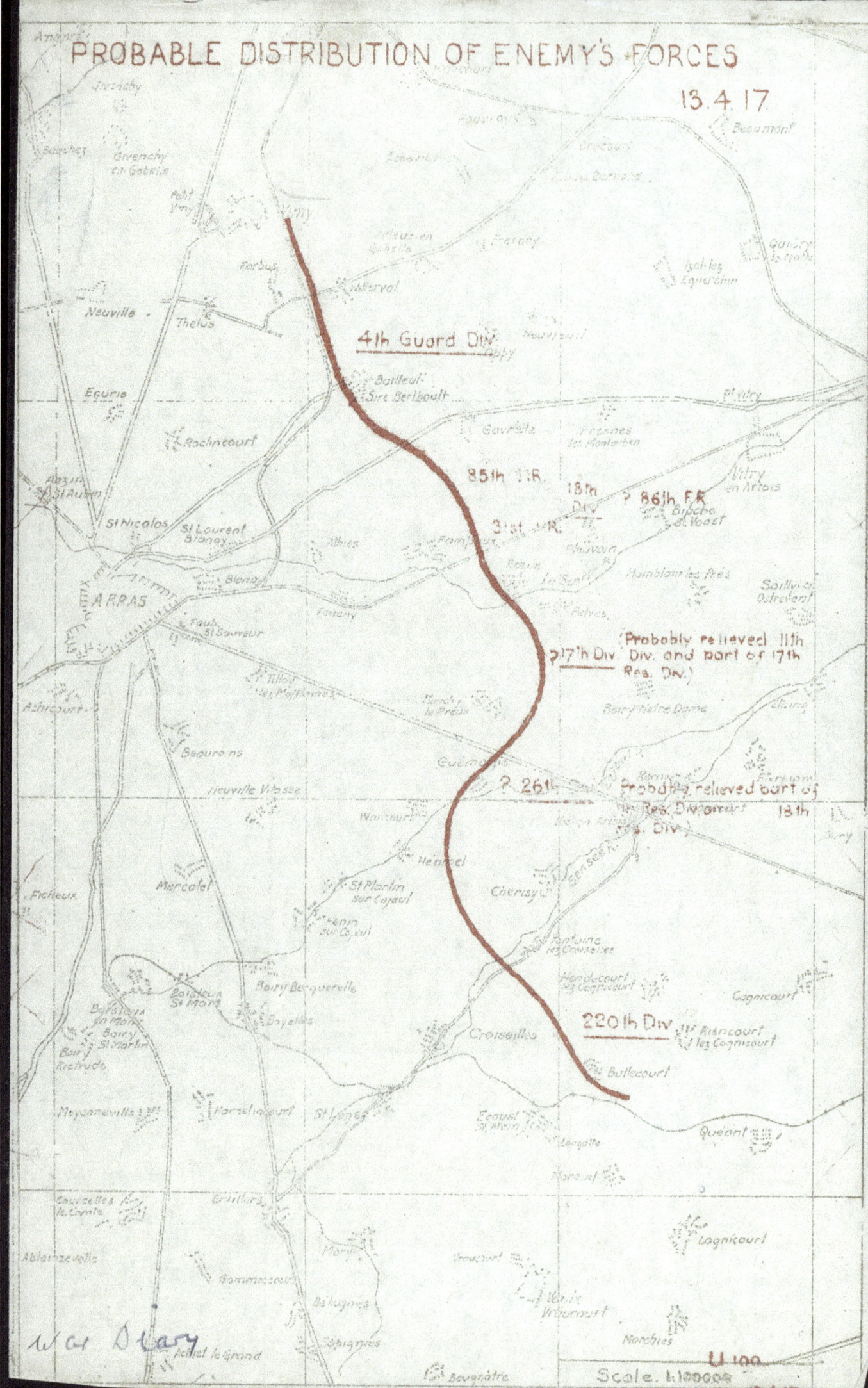

West Diary

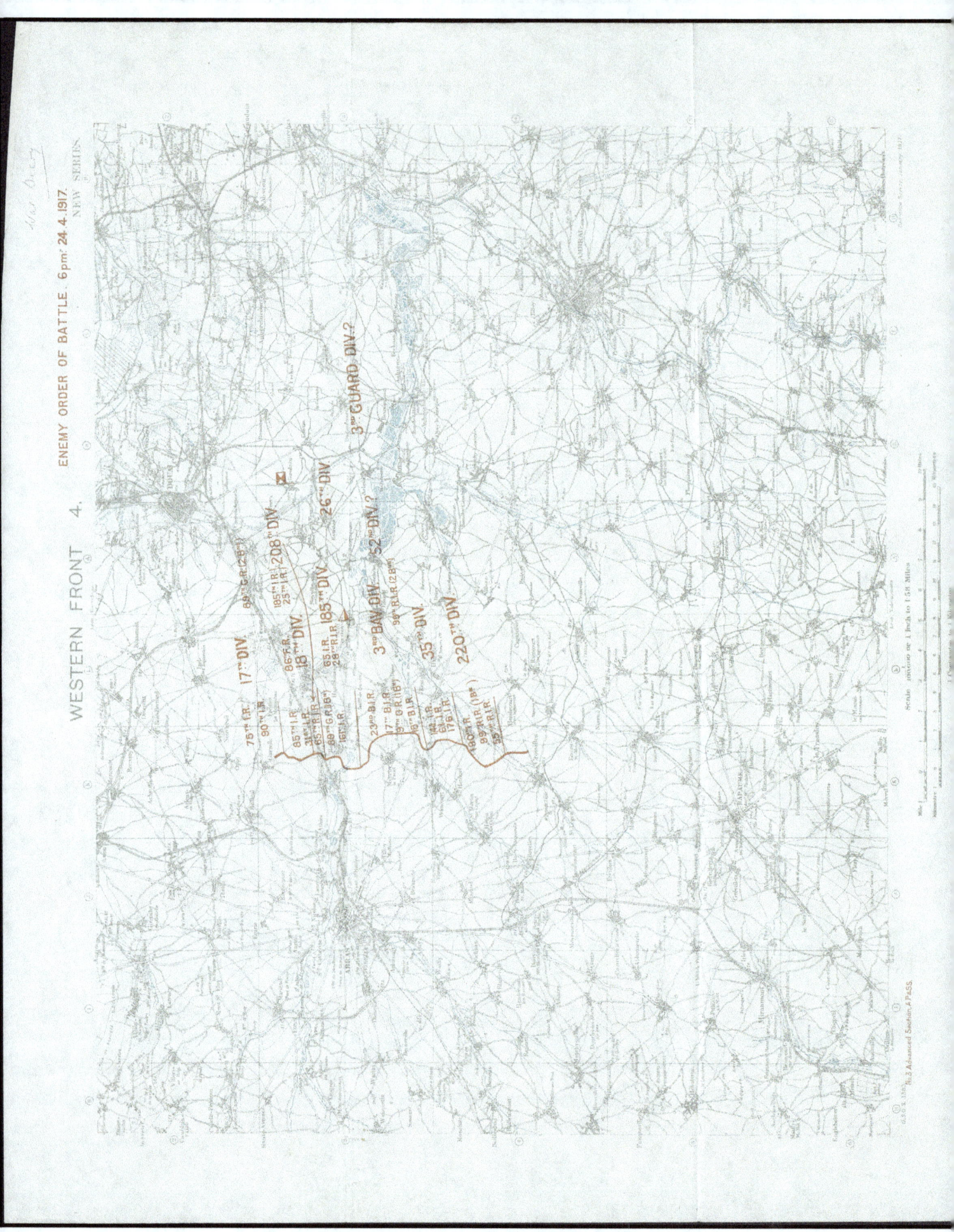

German trenches as far as known up to 4 pm
26.4.17 shown in RED
o - MOUND
British Trenches in Blue
Hostile Activity shown in Blue
SITUATION (our troops)
as far as known 6.0 pm 26.4.17 shown
by BLUE LINE (Approx)
BRIDGE DAMAGED
REGENT'S FORK
OXFORD TRENCH
PICCADILLY TRENCH
PARK WORK
BOIRY TRENCH
Sandpt
HAT TR
KIT TR
CAP TR
AXE
LANE
HAVERSACK TRENCH
TREE TR
WOOD TR
DOG TR
GREEN WORK
CARTRIDGE TR
GRENADE TRENCH
FUZE TR
SHELL TR
RIFLE TRENCH
BOMB TR
TRENCH
SPUR TR
LANYARD TRENCH
FACTORY TR
BOW TR
PIT TR
Crater reported by R.F.C.
HILLSIDE WORK
VILLAGE
ARTOIS
TRENCH
LONG LANE
Pick Tr
String Tr
Bullet Tr
Hammer Tr
Road passable for heavy traffic to this Point
SCALE 1:10,000

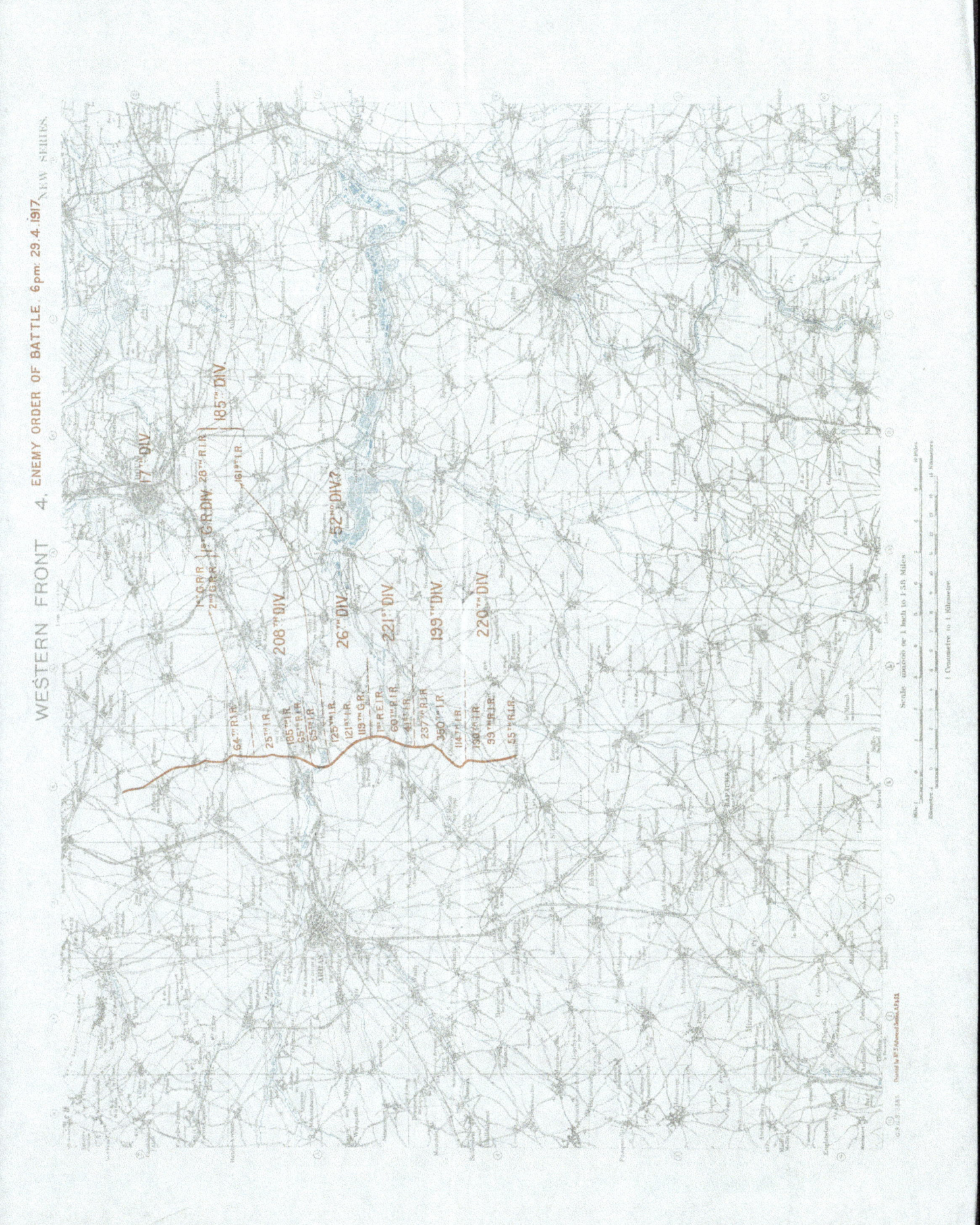

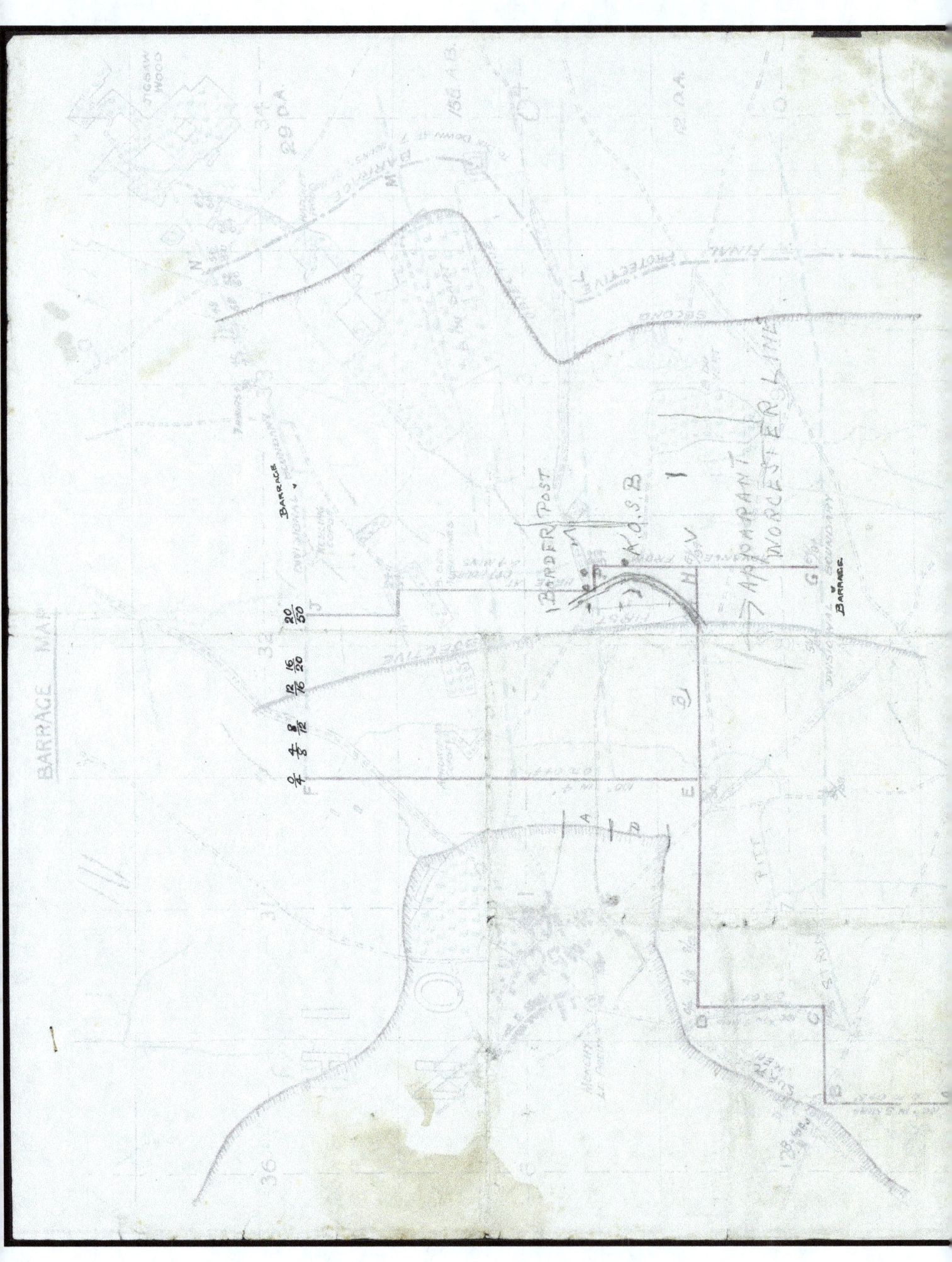

CONFIDENTIAL. Vol 17

WAR DIARY

OF

1st Battn. The Kings' Own Scottish Borderers.

From 1st May 1917. To. 31st May 1917.

(Volume 34)

Army Form C. 2118.

WAR DIARY
or
INTELLIGENCE SUMMARY.
(Erase heading not required.)

Instructions regarding War Diaries and Intelligence Summaries are contained in F.S. Regs., Part II and the Staff Manual respectively. Title pages will be prepared in manuscript.

Place	Date	Hour	Summary of Events and Information	Remarks and references to Appendices
WANQUETIN	1st May		The Bn left ST AMAND at 6am and marched to WANQUETIN via HALTE-SAULTY – BARLY – FOSSEUX arriving at 10.30 am. (Distance about 12 miles.) The 97 "B" Bn H.Q. and Royal Irish Rifles 2nd Inniskilling Brigade Staff. Both 2/Lt Rex. R.I. to England sick. Regimental Band billeted in the village.	
ARRAS	2nd May		I took 97 before breakfast. The training of Lewis Gunners, bombers & rifle Grenadiers was continued during the morning. At 6.15 pm the Bn paraded and marched to ARRAS (a distance of 20 kms) arriving at 9.20 pm. Lieutenants were billeted before hand (Lieutn. Kerr?) being at S.I.R. 10 Official sick in the Barracks. S.I.R. 10 Official sick.	
SUPPORT 3rd LINE May			At 6.15 am the Bn then the 10th who remained in billets, paraded & moved with the Support line & Bn Dunmore being in support to the Dunmore attacking beaulieu N.W. back to position N.K.	
ARRAS 4th May			The Bn left the Sullot Line at 12.15 pm and came back to ARRAS and resumed the billets in the Barracks. Piper Alayn, Private Jc Harris & 2/Lt Halcrow A.H. Goward sent to C.C.S. 2/Lt. O.R. wounded 1 O.R. and 1 O.R. intoxicated sick.	

A834 W^t W4928/M687 750,000 8/16 D.D. & L. Ltd. Forms/C2118/13

Army Form C. 2118.

195

WAR DIARY
or
INTELLIGENCE SUMMARY.
(Erase heading not required.)

Place	Date	Hour	Summary of Events and Information	Remarks and references to Appendices
ARRAS	5th May		At 2.30 am 2 Officers + 100 men were sent to the canal bank to hunt to A.P.M. for guns accessories as a fire which had broken out was in ammunition dump. 7.15 am P.T. + boxing exercises for the remainder of the day as on the arrival of O.C. Boys for the further changing up, casting. Town guard, bombers etc. 1.O.R. to Hyperdentation Depôt BOULOGNE. 3 O.R. returned Bn. whilst in ARRAS attending Divine services.	
"	6th May		Bn. held in ARRAS attending Divine services	
DUISSANS	7th May		At 10.50 am the Bn. paraded & marched to DUISSANS arriving about 1 pm. settled into huts & held a for the names of the day. Draft of 51 O.R. arrived. 1 man transferred to 2nd K.O.S.B.	
"	8th May		The training of the Bn. was continued, see claims of Lewis Gunners, Scouts, Bombers, Rifle Grenadiers, forma, Bayonets parade marched to the baths at AGNEZ. Casualties NIL. Sick to hospital NIL	

WAR DIARY or INTELLIGENCE SUMMARY

Army Form C. 2118.

196

Place	Date	Hour	Summary of Events and Information 9th K.O.S.B	Remarks and references to Appendices
DUISSANS	9th May		The Bn continued training. 2nd Cyclists off the strength of the Bn, being taken P.B.	
"	10th 11th 12th May		The training of all specialist was continued. Brigade Sports on the afternoon of the 11th. 3 O.R. reearly wounded on the 10th. 2 O.R. to hospital sick and 2 O.R. to Base ena on the 10th.	
"	13th May		Divine Service was held in the morning. At 5.30 pm the Bn paraded & marched to ARRAS. Gas was enused on arriving in ARRAS. 1 O.R. evacuated. 2 boys went to their Billets in the Schools.	
FIRING LINE (MONCHY LE PREUX)	14th May		During the day preparations were made for moving into the line. At 4.55 pm the Bn moved off and relieved the 9th K.O.Y.L.I. and the 10th R.W. Gns in the firing line (TWIN TRENCH) and SHRAPNEL TRENCH. The support line: 'A', 'C' and 2 Platoons of 'B' Coy in the front line, and 'D' Coy and 2 Platoons of 'B' Coy in the support line. 1 Coy of the Bn not the Coy of duty in the line, this boy holding the left of the line. Relief complete was reported at 5 am. Delay to the Bn HQ the Coy of duty in the line. Relief complete was reported at 5 am. Delay	

Army Form C. 2118.

WAR DIARY
or
INTELLIGENCE SUMMARY.
(Erase heading not required.)

Place	Date	Hour	Summary of Events and Information	Remarks and references to Appendices
FIRING LINE	14th May	(6.0 a.m.)	Worth relief was carried through the Guides losing the way. Casualties nil. Sick to hospital Nil.	
"	15th May		Both the enemy Artillery + men was active during the day. Bn H.Q. in MONCHY. Two horses killed. Very little shelling on front line. Enemy snipers had horrible success. Active during the night. A patrol under Lt. Howse reconnoitered the enemy front line + found it strongly held. 2 O.R. killed. 9 O.R. wounded. 2nd Lt. Malcolm killed.	
"	16th May		At 3 am our Artillery fired on enemy's trench in front of our line. On our front several shells dropped in our front line causing several casualties. Artillery active on both sides. Enemy took the opportunity of the sniper active during the night. A patrol was sent out to bring in a wounded but was observed by the enemy + forced to return. 2 O.R. killed. 4 O.R. wounded.	
-	17th May		A fairly quiet day. At 4 p.m. front of our 'plane flew low over the enemy lines. The Bn. was relieved by the 1st BORDER Regt. A.B. & C. Coys in being moved back to the BROWN LINE. D Coy to strong point behind MONCHY. 2nd Lt. Watt received a third to dug a new trench across TWIN COPSE. 2 O.R. killed. 1 O.R. wounded.	

A 5834 Wt. W4973/M687 750,000 8/16 D. D. & L. Ltd. Forms/C.2118/13.

Army Form C. 2118.

WAR DIARY
or
INTELLIGENCE SUMMARY.

(Erase heading not required.)

Place	Date	Hour	Summary of Events and Information	Remarks and references to Appendices
BROWN LINE	18th Sept 1916		The Bn rested during the day in the BROWN LINE. A Bombing attack was carried out by all Bombers + during the night the trenches were cleaned out by 3 men of D Coy. 1 wounded in one of the strong point. 4 O.R. wounded. 3 O.R. missing.	
	19th Sept 1916		The Bn. occupied the BROWN LINE during the day. At 11 pm A & C Coys. moved forward to SHRAPNEL TR. in support to the BORDER Regt. EAST and INNISKILLING Fusiliers who attacked at 9 p.m. These two Battalions were relieved by the 16th Middlesex Regt. in the BROWN LINE, at 3 am B Coy. relieved to Coy in EAST TR. and A Coy and forward to SHRAPNEL TR. Bn Hd. Qrs. and to RED HOUSE, MONCHY, and shared the dug out with the 1st BORDER Regt. 4 O.R. killed. 6 O.R. wounded.	
MONCHY LE PREUX	20th Sept 1916		Enemy shelled MONCHY very heavily during the day. Guns were silenced by the enemy on the dug out occupied by Bn. Hd. Qrs. at night. The 1st Lancashire Fus. relieved Coys in the line, and the D Coy in the Strong points.	

1: Roy. Dub. Fus. IN POST

Place	Date	Hour	Summary of Events and Information	Remarks and references to Appendices
MONCHY LE PREUX (contd)	20th (contd)		On being handed boys march back to ARRAS + sent hellalin the GRAND PLACE. Coys were again to all ranks before settling down. 1 Platoon of A, B + C Coy were left behind to man HILL TRENCH. This party arrived in ARRAS about 4 a.m. T.O.R. evacuated sick	
ARRAS	21st April		Coys were allowed to rest during the morning. Inspections of clothing + equipment etc were held in the afternoon. At 8 p.m. 3 Officers + 100 O.R. was sent forward to the front line to finish burying HILL TR. Body returned at 5 a.m. 6. O.R. wounded. 2 O.R. evacuated sick. Draft of 45 O.R. arrived.	
" "	22nd April	6.00 a.m.	Coys were at disposal of O C Coys for a general clean up. 8 O.R. evacuated sick. 1 O.R. transferred to 3rd Army H.Q. 1 O.R. trans- ferred to H. Coy H.Q.	
" "	23rd April		Bn still resting in ARRAS. Coy route marches in the morning. Training of the Bn was carried out during the day. 1 O.R. wounded. 1 O.R. evacuated sick. Draft of 4 O.R. arrived. 1 new temporary C	

R L

Army Form C. 2118.

WAR DIARY
or
INTELLIGENCE SUMMARY.
(Erase heading not required.)

Place	Date	Hour	Summary of Events and Information	Remarks and references to Appendices
ARRAS	24th May		Bn continued training & put shelters near firing line. Bn known during the morning & again during the night. 4 O.R. evacuated sick. 2 O.R. to field hospital.	
"	25th May		Training continued. During the afternoon the Bn was under the enemy batteries in ARRAS & air raids attained. 6 O.R. evacuated sick.	
"	26th May		Training continued. The Bn carried out night operation. Rifle bombs fired in the vicinity of where the Bn was operating. 4 O.R. evacuated sick. 1 O.R. wounded.	1
"	27th May		The Bn attended divine service & relief the remainder of the day. H.B.R. went to hospital sick. Barnelier N1C. Evacuated sick N1C.	
"	28th July		Boys were at the disposal of O.C. boys for training. The boys attended the evening battle during the afternoon. 1 O.R. evacuated sick. 6 O.R. to India. 3 O.R. transferred to 34 & 35 Regt Rly. Operating section. 4 Army. New draft. R.F.A. Sections 1. K.O. L.Br. North.	

Army Form C. 2118.

WAR DIARY
INTELLIGENCE SUMMARY.
(Erase heading not required.)

Place	Date	Hour	Summary of Events and Information	Remarks and references to Appendices
ARRAS LINE	25th May	4 am 9 T Sri	au days the remainder of the day was at the disposal of O.C. Coys for cleaning up & preparing to move to the BROWN LINE.	
		9.30 pm	the Bn. paraded & moved off to take over the BROWN LINE. Before reaching the BROWN LINE orders were received that the Bn. would return to the billets in ARRAS. The enemy had been ranging in our trenches from which an attack was to be made in the day. As it was known from the willing that the enemy knew that an attack was to be made the attack was cancelled and the Bn. was not moved in support. 1 O.R. wounded. 1 O.R. wounded with 2 O.R. and + 2.O.R. remained ???.
BROWN LINE (NEUX)	30th May		Owing to the hostility of the Bn. taking over the BROWN LINE in the evening all ranks were warned not to leave the vicinity of bivis. At 9.15 pm the Bn. paraded + moved by Coys to the BROWN LINE + remained in support to the 2/Lanc. Fus. + 16th M'dlesex who attacked HOOK TRENCH at 11.MO. pm. attack was unsuccessful. 2. O.R. wounded with 7.O.R. armed Mortar.	
FIRING LINE (MONCHY LE PREUX)	31st May		During the day the Bn. moved into the BROWN LINE where orders were received for the Bn. to ??? ??? relieve in the BROWN line by the 1st Roy. Luc. Fus & Gds.	

A 3834 Wt W4973/M687 750,000 8/16 D.D.&L.Ltd Forms/C.2118/13.

Army Form C. 2118.

202

WAR DIARY
or
INTELLIGENCE SUMMARY.
(Erase heading not required)

Place	Date	Hour	Summary of Events and Information	Remarks and references to Appendices
FIRING LINE	31st May		From the trenches reported at 9.45 p.m. that we were supported by 2 platoons of "B" Coy taking on the firing line and "A" Coy with 2 platoons of "B" Coy took our SHRAPNEL TR. whilst on their way to the line. Coys were where a trench nearly but got into the line without any casualties. Portion of the line by the Battalion. GRAPE TRENCH & S.E. Corner of TWIN COPSES. Taken over from 2 Coys Punjs. 1 I.O.R. wounded.	Written up by C.H. Lewis. Lieut a/Adjutant 1st K.O.S.B.

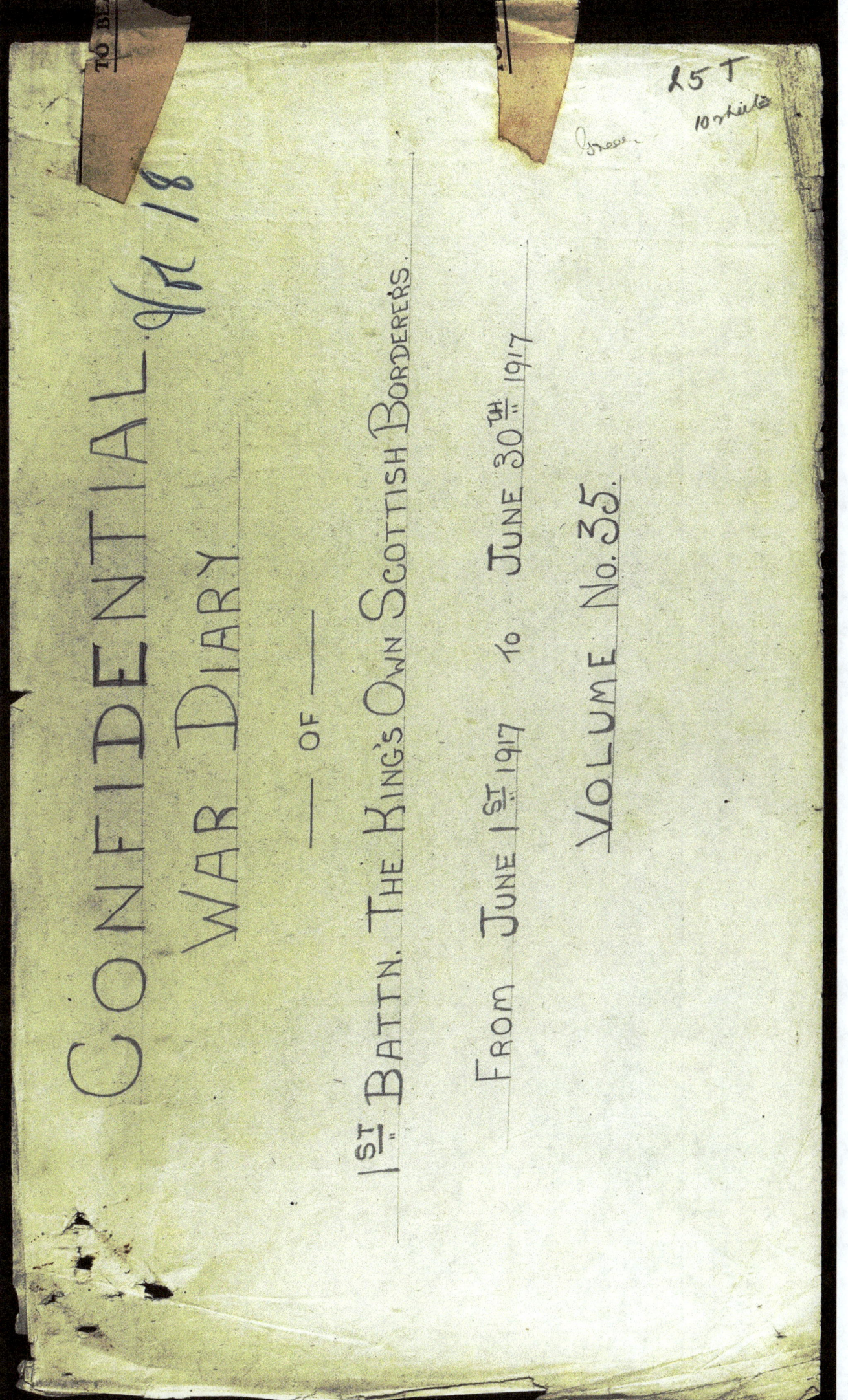

CONFIDENTIAL Vol 18

WAR DIARY

— OF —

1ST BATTN. THE KING'S OWN SCOTTISH BORDERERS.

FROM JUNE 1ST 1917 TO JUNE 30TH 1917

VOLUME No. 35.

WAR DIARY
INTELLIGENCE SUMMARY
Army Form C. 2118.

1 KOSB

Place	Date	Hour	Summary of Events and Information	Remarks and references to Appendices
FIRING LINE. MONCHY LE PREUX	1st June		Heavy shelling and reciprocal bursts of machine gun fire by the enemy during the night. The guarded down at daybreak. Our artillery fire continually during the day. 2 O.R. evacuated sick.	
"	2nd June		We boys worked hard during the night in repairing the trenches. Our support bays were shelled during the night. Three enemy aeroplanes were brought down during the morning, + one was seen to fall behind the German lines. Our support trenches shelled at 8.20 p.m. which caused several casualties. The Bn. was relieved by the 8th East Yorkshire Coys and our boys marched independently back to huts in ARRAS. 3 O.R. wounded 2 O.R. killed. 12 O.R. wounded. Coys arrived from 28th employment	
ARRAS	3rd June		Companies were allowed to rest during the morning. Exercises held during the afternoon. 1 O.R. wounded. 16 O.R. evacuated sick. S.O.R. posted. 1 O.R. transferred. 2/Lt R. McDonald 3rd K.O.S.B. arrived + posted A Coy - Lt. B W Pennyman K.O.J. B. transferred to Small Arms School. G.H.Q.	

Army Form C. 2118.

WAR DIARY
or
INTELLIGENCE SUMMARY.
(Erase heading not required.)

Place	Date	Hour	Summary of Events and Information	Remarks and references to Appendices
ARRAS	4th June		The Bn. trained in ARRAS and Companies were at the disposal of O.C. Corps. Preparations were made for moving back to rest. Advance Party left in the morning to take over billets for the Bn. at AUTHEUX. Rations N.K.	
AUTHEUX	5th June		The Bn. paraded at 9 a.m. marched to ARRAS station & entrained at 9.40 a.m. and detrained at 3.30 p.m. at CANDAS and marched from that station to AUTHEUX arriving about 4.30 p.m. Men were sent out and all ranks settled into billets which were than comfortable. I.O.R. reveilled a.s.a	
	6th June		Reorganising & the training of the Bn. commenced. During the day Coy's Commanders were shown the ground allotted to the Bn. for training purposes. 2h & O.C. bren gunners holes. I.O.R. reveilled a.s	

Place	Date	Hour	Summary of Events and Information	Remarks and references to Appendices
AUTHEUX	8th June		The training of the Bn. continues. New drafts eleven horses & covered leaving today. A.C. Baylin #70 A Bn came to take over drafts of 2 O.R. came today.	
"	9th June		Bn. training. Lieut. T.C. NOEL M.C. & A. Dooley 4th R.W.K. 2 Lt. K.O.S.Bs. and 4th Sh.T. Kings came to take over. 17 Y.O.Rs came.	
"	9th June		The morning was another of training & half holiday for all ranks in the afternoon. 6 O.R. evacuated sick. 2 O.R. rejoined from hospital.	
"	10th June		Divine service carried on. In the evening 2 O.R. evacuation sick.	
"	11th June		Bn. continues training. Divinelli Aw.	

WAR DIARY
or
INTELLIGENCE SUMMARY.
(Erase heading not required.)

Army Form C. 2118.

Place	Date	Hour	Summary of Events and Information	Remarks and references to Appendices
AUTHEUX	12th June		Training of the Bn continued. Draft of 11 O.Rs arrived, 1 O.R as England, he is invalidation together 1 O.R to Base depot.	
"	13th June		Training of the Bn continued 1 O.R rejoined 5 sick. 3 O.Rs reported to 10th & 18th Corps Sch. & Lewis Gun school	
"	14th June		Training of the Bn continued. 1 O.R rejoined 5 sick	
"	15th		Training of the Bn continued. 4 O.Rs evacuated sick	
"	16th		Bn continued training during the morning. Div Horse show held in the afternoon. the Bn being awarded 2nd prize for Jack Lot. Competition + 3rd in the "Mule turn out" for 1 gun limber. Half holiday in the afternoon. 2 O.Rs transferred to 22nd Employment Coy Labour Corps.	

Army Form C. 2118.

WAR DIARY
or
INTELLIGENCE SUMMARY.
(Erase heading not required.)

Place	Date	Hour	Summary of Events and Information	Remarks and references to Appendices
AUTHEUX	17th		R.G. trained hard. Drive of 4 a boys attacked the balls during the day. 2 O.Rs. evacuated sick.	
"	18th		Training continues. 9 O.Rs. cricket XI v the boys. I am in command & visited & boy's tournament of the Brigade. Rackets were increased. 2 O.Rs. evacuated sick.	
"	19th		Training continued. Special attention being paid to the open attack. 4 O.Rs. transferred to D.G.T.	
"	20th		Corps at the disposal of Coy. Commanders. Draws in the morning. Half holiday. Whole batt. went to baths. 2 O.Rs evacuated sick sent away.	
"	21st		Night operations under Coy. Commander. The weather being very broken all day. 4 O.Rs evacuated sick. Draft of 15 O.Rs arrived. 1 O.R. to Investigation Depot.	
"	22nd		Practice ceremonial parade for tomorrows great event. This finished training was resumed. 1 O.R. evacuated sick.	

208

Army Form C. 2118.

WAR DIARY
or
INTELLIGENCE SUMMARY.
(Erase heading not required.)

Place	Date	Hour	Summary of Events and Information	Remarks and references to Appendices
AUTHEUX	June 23rd 1917	11 a.m.	Battalion parade for ceremonial to receive the Colonel of the Regiment, Lt Gen Sir Charles Woolcombe K.C.B. Commanding 4th Army Corps. The Battalion was drawn up in two ranks and on a plot of ground near "B" Coy lines, and received the Inspecting Officer in the present. The Battn. was then inspected after which it marched past in column and quarter column. The Colonel of the Regiment then addressed the battalion congratulating them on their past success and wishing them further success in the future. He then took all officers and luncheon together in a small mosque. The afternoon was occupied by sports. In addition there were present during the whole day as guests of the Officers of the battalion Major General Sir Beauvoir de Lisle Commanding the 29th Division and Brigadier-General C.H.T. Lucas D.S.O. Commanding 12 87th Brigade. No rain from 9.30 a.m. onwards. 1 O.R. wounded acc.	
		14th	Church parades and collecting and despatch of training material. 1 O.R. from hospital. 9 O.Rs transferred to Trainier Montreuil 29th Division	

Army Form C. 2118.

WAR DIARY
or
INTELLIGENCE SUMMARY.
(Erase heading not required.)

Instructions regarding War Diaries and Intelligence Summaries are contained in F. S. Regs., Part II. and the Staff Manual respectively. Title pages will be prepared in manuscript.

Place	Date 1917	Hour	Summary of Events and Information	Remarks and references to Appendices
AUTHEUX	June 25th		Morning training continued. Afternoon Coys at disposal of Coy Commanders for cleaning up billets etc.	
	26th		Batt'n paraded for moving up line 3.25 p.m. marched to DOULLENS, entrained and started by 7.15 p.m. arrived HOPOUTRE 2.30 a.m. 27th	
HOPOUTRE	27th	2 a.m.	marched to battalion camp 3 kilo east of PROVEN and 6 kilo S.E. of KROMBEKE.	
KROMBEKE	28th		Paraded 7.15 p.m. to be moving into line. Met by guides at DAWSONS CORNER. Carried out support line YPRES SALIENT (Approx. S.P. Jatar I25°a.m 29.5). Battalion in left support.	
Line	29th		Situation Quiet, intermittent hostile shelling. Lt O'C. sent post on patrol from our line 11 p.m. until midn't. Objective ascertain condition of enemy wire opposite. Report forwarded to Bgde. H.Q. and own operate order.	

Army Form C. 2118.

WAR DIARY
or
INTELLIGENCE SUMMARY.
(Erase heading not required.)

Place	Date	Hour	Summary of Events and Information	Remarks and references to Appendices
[illegible]	June 30		Box 197 sents in expendix and R.E. entering food line again. Running party continues at training [illegible] etc.	
			Written out by Col Lewis from Napierbw. F. K.O.S. Rd.	

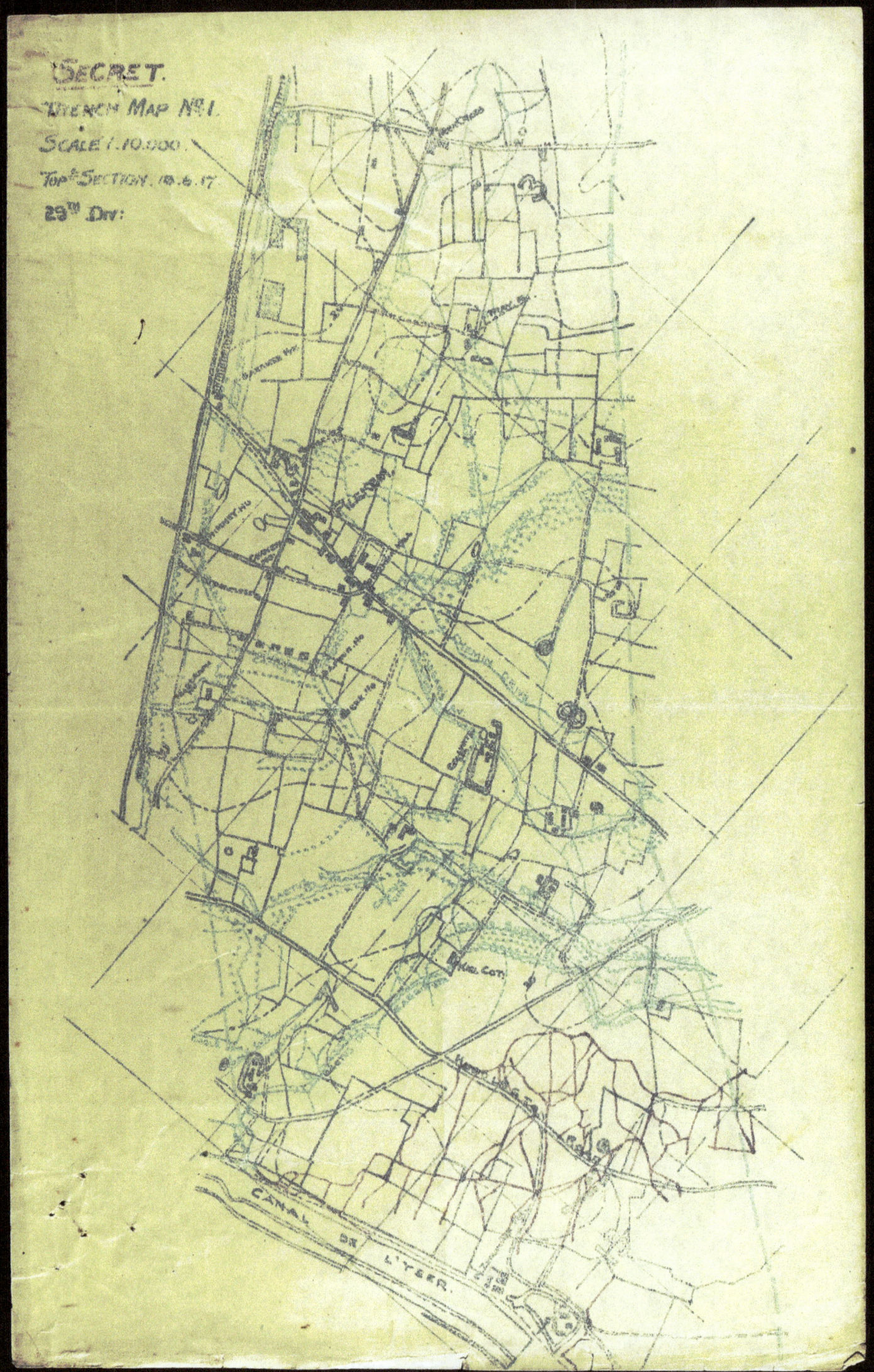

No 19

26 T
Broad 9 sheets

CONFIDENTIAL.

WAR DIARY

1st KING'S OWN SCOTTISH BORDERERS.

From 1st July 1917 to 31st July 1917

Volume 36.

WAR DIARY
or
INTELLIGENCE SUMMARY

Army Form C. 2118.

Place	Date	Hour	Summary of Events and Information	Remarks and references to Appendices
Sept. on the (CANAL BANK)	July 1st		Relieved 1/1st T.N.D.F.R. memorialised every unit before leaving for our stations & prepared to Bn. to Qr. Mrs. Quarters. Killed by hostile Guns. Evacuated to civilisation. 1 O.R. wounded. 1 O.R. wounded. Draft of 9 O.R. Guns arrived 1 B.R. Toures from hospital & O.Rs. evacuated sick.	
	July 2nd		"B" took over lift section of front line from 1/ Border Regt. in the approved A + D Coy. to firing line. C. Coy. the support line and B. Coy. the reserve line. By 11a. O.Rs. evacuated sick. 1 O.R. wounded.	
	July 3rd		1 Org. and off. "B-C" wounded and his in early morning S.G shell killing 4 + wounding 6 O.R. all of ration party later in day 10 O.R. wounded, 3 O.Rs evacuated sick.	
	July 4th		Work on R.G.B. + Left carried out made heavy hostile shelling on CANAL BANK throughout the day. Very heavy shelling over the line ran al- were laying carrying out R.E. Coy. dies hours carrying DEUTSCHE Baloon descended in "B" Coys lives Heavy incendiary DEUTSCHE FALCON Forward to Bn. H.Q. 2 O.Rs wounded draft of 11 O.Rs arrived Feta.	

WAR DIARY
INTELLIGENCE SUMMARY

Army Form C. 2118.

212

Place	Date	Hour	Summary of Events and Information	Remarks and references to Appendices
Line	July 5		CANAL BANK teams about try the enemy work on improving the trenches. Now reliever of OR evacuated sick. Lieut. T.W.J Agar, 1st K.O.S.B. posted.	
"	July 6		On back area artillery the enemy the CANAL BANK are also having shown evidence of activity (a Raid was carried out by a retained intermittents. of 20 shell each were fired on the portion of Lufty, of 20 shell each were now 4½ T.E. Non. for the purpose of reinforcing with by present nr movement from near German Runes left at 1.30 in Inner cones of Artillery & reached the enemy trench & what note very slightly him, the story for rai ant Boschs etc. Bombs were thrown & rimlists fired in the trench which will them caused many casualties. At 11.30 pm the HAMPSHIRE Regt commanced a retaking the Battn Trayment (being relieved noticed) taken to the trains at CROM PITS. De 22's w occupied by the Battn before going into the time Trench came where 4 x 6 on Laming marched 13 miles y ORs returned. 2 ORs evacuated sick. Capt. L.G. Campbell 1st K.O.S.Bos. Evacuated sick. Capt. L.G. Campbell 1st K.O.S.Bos. transferred to 6th K.O.S.Bos	

Army Form C. 2118.

WAR DIARY
or
INTELLIGENCE SUMMARY.
(Erase heading not required.)

Place	Date	Hour	Summary of Events and Information	Remarks and references to Appendices
CROMBEKE	July 8		The Bn. rested during the morning. The state of the day was recorded in reflections. Staff of 25 O.R. arrived upthis 1. O.R. wounded.	
	July 9.		Training commenced under O.C. Coys. 2 O.Rs. rejoined from hospital.	
	July 10.		Coys. continued to train under O.C. Coys. 1 O.R. evacuated sick. 1 O.R. transferred to 19 Division mtd. Coy.	
			Training continued. 39th Divnl Cinema Entertainment Company gave a performance to the Bn. in the evening. A & B Coys bathed during the day. Revielle 7 a.m.	
	July 11.		Training continued. C & D Coys bathed during the day. Revielle 7 a.m.	
	July 12.		D Co. moved into CAMP A.26.a. at 6 a.m. in PROVEN AREA. A Coy. under O.C. Coy. preparing to move. At 4 pm the Bn. paraded and moved forward to CARIBOU CAMP. All ranks were em- ployed on fatigues under R.E. on arrival in CAMP. 4 O.Rs evacuated sick.	

Army Form C. 2118.

WAR DIARY or INTELLIGENCE SUMMARY

(Erase heading not required.)

Place	Date	Hour	Summary of Events and Information	Remarks and references to Appendices
CARIBOO CAMP	July 13th		7 Officers and 336 O.R. were drawn for fatigues to R.E. Dump. The party landed at different times. Enemy shelling the area with H.V guns. 3 O.Rs Been wnded.	
"	July 14th		Fatigues found for R.E's. 1 Officer + 30 O.R sick off duty to practice training. Enemy shells fell close to the camp during the day. 3 O.Rs wounded. 1 O.R evacuated sick.	
"	July 15th		Bn. employed on work near R.E. Dump. Enemy shelling of 1 Officer 2 dogs & 14 OR suffered in the dive & katholica party. the rain raids reconnoitring the enemy's new trenches to east in front of Post 45. Draft of 51 O.Rs arrived.	
"	July 16th		Bn. working near R.E. enjoying erratic respts. Vicinity of the Dump shelled + wounded by the enemy. 2 O.Rs wounded. 2 O.Rs wounded sick.	

Army Form C. 2118.

WAR DIARY
or
INTELLIGENCE SUMMARY.

(Erase heading not required.)

Place	Date	Hour	Summary of Events and Information	Remarks and references to Appendices
KARIBOU	July 17		Bn working under the R.E. 6th night + last + 5 O.R's got cases to the front line + remained the enemy positions from of Post 45 Rang from Box H4 vicinity of the clump shelled by Hostile artillery. 1 O.R. wounded sick.	
	July 18		Bn working under the R.E. 6th night raiders left for the front line being reconnoitered in small parties on the CANAL BANK. Hostile artillery very active during the night. It's where our artillery replied. 21 O.Rs wounded sick. 2 O.Rs wounded.	
	July 19		Bn working under the R.E. At 12 MN. a portion of the raiders left the front line. About 12:30 a another party of raiders left. At 12:35 an all raiders were out in "No Man's Land" at 12:50 an wire missing that all raiders had started moving forward to enemy trench. At 1 am midrange message "all raiders in enemy trench". At 1:35 an message from O.C. "B" Coy raiders returned Russian Sap. been unsuccessful owing to our own artillery fire + Stokes guns during amongst four	

WAR DIARY or INTELLIGENCE SUMMARY

Army Form C. 2118.

Place	Date	Hour	Summary of Events and Information	Remarks and references to Appendices
CARIBOU CAMP	July 19th contd.		But men taken to the enemy front line trench. Owing to heavy casualties from this fire the rations had to be taken up the communication trench every morning in the 140' trenches by the rations parties. 1 O.R. evacuated sick. 1 O.R. rejoined from hospital. 14 O.R.	
"	July 20.		The Bn. working under R.E. repairing & making tracks leading to the front line system of trenches. All officers & men employed, the attached & not available & every day parties on convenience with parties communication. 2 ORs missing. 3 ORs evacuated sick. 2 ORs wounded.	
"	July 21st		The Bn. employed under the R.E. in repairing trenches & roads. 1 O.R. wounded. 1 O.R. evacuated sick. Draft of 25 O.R. arrived + rota.	
"	July 22nd		Bn. working under the R.Es. Prussian run confirmed attached Divs. Drive at 10 a.m. 2 ORs wounded. 2 ORs transferred to entry unit body. 1 O.R. rejoined from hospital.	
July 23rd - July 24th			Bn. working under the R.E.s. 1 O.R. wounded. Bn. working under R.E. Bn. officers rejoining from leave, 2 O.R. 1 O.R. to front line. 1 O.R. evacuated sick. 1 O.R. rejoined from hospital. 13 ORs wounded. 2/Lt. R. Kirk wounded.	

WAR DIARY or INTELLIGENCE SUMMARY

Army Form C. 2118.

Place	Date	Hour	Summary of Events and Information	Remarks and references to Appendices
CARIBOU CAMP	July 25th		Bn. working under the R.E. the weekly of the Camp Reveals eleven I.O.R. missing from tropical I.O.R. casualty over.	
Support X 27 & (Hut 19) PROVEN AREA	July 26th		The Bn. found fatigue for the R.E. till 10 hrs. The Bn. less those on fatigue moved back to the PROVEN Area, leaving at 2.30 pm and arriving at 6.30 pm. We were temporarily billeted in Huts & rested remainder day.	
—	July 27th		Boys at the disposal of O.C. Coys for cleaning up etc. Bath scores, equipment claims. 10 R reinforcements arrived.	
—	July 28th		Coys at the disposal of O.C. Coys for inspection & preparing for the forthcoming Review. Staff of T.U.R. arrived today.	
—	July 29th		Coys were clothes the Baths & attended Divine service. The remainder of the day was devoted to rest. I.O.R. casualties over.	

WAR DIARY
or
INTELLIGENCE SUMMARY.
(Erase heading not required.)

Army Form C. 2118.

Place	Date	Hour	Summary of Events and Information	Remarks and references to Appendices
CAMP 16 FOREST CAMP AREA.	July 30th		During the day the Bn were preparing for moving up for the attack. Reinforcements of the 10 % kept to join the attack on the 27th Bn. & at 10.50 pm the Bn paraded & marched by Coys to Camp 16, arriving at 1.50 am. Resting in the bivouacs the Bn then settled down in bivouac trenches in the West until at 5 am were told to join the attack on the right, and not until 5.30 am at which time in the enemy area on the Railway area & heavy bombardment. The Barrage is now in action to the 5th Division who took part in the attack, 1 O.R. wounded from shrapnel. Bn still in support to the Guards & awaiting orders. 1 O.R. evacuated sick.	
	31/7/17			written up by A.T. Lewis Lieutenant b/Adjutant 1st K.O.L. Bn.

27T
9 sheets

Vol 20

CONFIDENTIAL.

WAR DIARY

OF

1ST BATT. THE KING'S OWN SCOTTISH BORDERERS

FROM AUGUST 1st 1917   TO AUGUST 31st 1917

VOLUME NO. 37.

Army Form C. 2118.

219

WAR DIARY
or
INTELLIGENCE SUMMARY.
(Erase heading not required.)

Instructions regarding War Diaries and Intelligence Summaries are contained in F. S. Regs., Part II. and the Staff Manual respectively. Title pages will be prepared in manuscript.

Place	Date	Hour	Summary of Events and Information	Remarks and references to Appendices
CAMP 16 FOREST AREA	Aug 1st		Boys were at the address of O.A. Coys for the Chaplain. Platoon action scheme known & for the intensive Coy of men going to the rain. The camp both officers and men turned out by mess turns out in clearing the camp of grown rats.	
"	Aug 2nd		1. Off + 120 O.R's. for fatigue parade at 6.30 a.m. position was the R.E. in Entrench Post order of Fd. CANAL BANK. Remainder of Bn. continue on clearing away mud & rats.	
PUTNEY CAMP (PROVEN AREA)	Aug 3rd	ca 11 am	The Bn. Paraded and marched to the Camp left by the Bn in the 30 Division, arriving at 1.45 p.m. All ranks arrived wet through owing to the heavy rain during the march. Dinners were served at 2 p.m. Men were allowed to rest & make themselves as comfortable as possible under the circumstances.	

Army Form C. 2118.

229

WAR DIARY
or
INTELLIGENCE SUMMARY.
(Erase heading not required.)

Instructions regarding War Diaries and Intelligence Summaries are contained in F. S. Regs., Part II and the Staff Manual respectively. Title pages will be prepared in manuscript.

Place	Date	Hour	Summary of Events and Information	Remarks and references to Appendices
PUTNEY CAMP	Aug 4		Boys out at the sound of O.C. Coy for the purpose of laying cables, linking up the Brigade different places to Coy boundaries. S. Ps in preceding exercise. The Bde Bomb Relays in the lamp, at 5.16 pm.	
"	Aug 5		Damp. Armed wire Cinema during the morning. Office arrived all ranks not allowed to leave lines the day & homeless.	
"	Aug 6		Having carried out exercise O. & G. boys. The C.O. delivered to all Officers in the forthcoming operations.	
"	Aug 7		Training carried out by O.C. Coys during the morning. At S.K. the Bn. paraded & marched by Coys to the FOREST CAMP area. Taking our bivouac tents. S. Keryo arrived between 8 & 9 pm & ordered into tents.	

Army Form C. 2118.

WAR DIARY
or
INTELLIGENCE SUMMARY.
(Erase heading not required.)

22

Place	Date	Hour	Summary of Events and Information	Remarks and references to Appendices
FOREST AREA (CAMP 3)	Aug 8th		Training carried out under O.C. Coys. Vicinity of the hard shelled clearing of men and roads.	
	Aug 9th		Training of companies continued. Tracks running through the hard clear of men & roads.	
	Aug 10		At 1 pm the Brigade marked into the hand received by the 16 Royal Dublin Fus: B.Y.C. army at 2 pm. Dinner on arrival. Written up by Lieut A.N. [?]	
			Continued by Captain T. Watt M.C.	
ABINGEY CAMP (E.V.C)	Aug 11		Battalion busy preparing to go out. Line to take part in a general action. Companies marked out in miniature showing objectives & the mountains. Lectures on plan of attack, etc. were given by O.C. Companies. Examination Nil.	Companies marked good.
	Aug 12th		At 5 P.M. the Bon. paraded and marched up to the line where it took over the left subsect in the WIDJENDRIFT sector, as follows. "A" Coy — front of BOURNE FM — "B" Coy and Bn Q. in Dugouts at BOULES FM — "C" and "D" Coys front 15 — 5th Welch were left in Bugrace 13 in that area. Relief was complete without and casualties.	

Army Form C. 2118.

WAR DIARY
or
INTELLIGENCE SUMMARY.
(Erase heading not required.)

Instructions regarding War Diaries and Intelligence Summaries are contained in F. S. Regs., Part II. and the Staff Manual respectively. Title pages will be prepared in manuscript.

Place	Date	Hour	Summary of Events and Information	Remarks and references to Appendices
MIDSENDRIFT Encampment	Aug 13th		Occasional shelling throughout the day. 15 rooks 15 being shelled with Gas shell. A Cooker in front of FOURCHE Fm was hurried & received with 5.9" barrage. The trench being blown in. Casualties - killed - 9, wounded 11.	TANNENBERG 10,000
	Aug 14th		The Bn took over the front line trenches from the 7th Bn Border Regt in the MIDSENDRIFT Sector - Dispositions being as follows - Hd Qrs in FOURCHE Fm - "A" Coy in Breastwork SENTIER Fm with one platoon across the STEENBEEK at W.30.b.O.1.N. "B" Coy in Brewery near SIGNAL Fm - "C" Coy in Brewery huts near FOURCHE Fm and "D" Coy in SIGN. 9L. Fm Enemy's near PASSERELLE Fm heavily shelled all round Kitchen. 6 wounded. B.I. Snowing. 1	
	Aug 15th		were heavily shelled at intervals during the day. Enemy aeroplanes being particularly active and trained machine gun attack. Platoon on EAST bank of STEENBEEK withdrawn towards our position & dealt with MIDSENDRIFT. Our aircraft observed walks on the direction compelling the Enemy Aircraft to - Casualties were Killed - 5, Wounded - 1 Officer A.R.O.R Hewins R.E.	
	Aug 16th		Early in the morning of 16th August 1917, the Australian troops - 16pnr. ready for a great attack "D" and "B" Companies extending along a line, bearing 133°True from 75 left Square hear PASSERELLE Fm and covering 400' from W.D.n.a.3.2.5. 140 B.2.4. A & C Coys being the yards behind must connected with D Bn & W & B & to Ban in and on the right ½ a Coy 10th Bn Northumberland Regiment the B having positions to Fm	

Army Form C. 2118.

WAR DIARY
or
INTELLIGENCE SUMMARY.
(Erase heading not required.)

Place	Date	Hour	Summary of Events and Information	Remarks and references to Appendices
	1917 Aug 16th		At 4.45 P.M. the B[attalio]n attacked on a general bearing of E by N. True. The Holdfasters was taken out completely without much trouble — the coy along a line from U.21.4.10 - 46. to U.21.6.6.3. — B + C Coys were the next through the first objective and attacked the second objective - success strong positions were encountered and 6 G.M.'s Guns + 7 Chain p. Pns and G.P.W.s in P[???] of "B" Coy. displayed great gallantry in attacking this point and in[?] single handed and capturing them. At 4.50 P.M. the final line was from U.13. D.6.35. to U.22.12. 3.-9. — Enemy aeroplanes nearly hindered the work by swooping up and down the line firing with our ranks with machine guns — During the day we Captured 6 O. R. [?] Machine Gun and — 5 Officers 1 O.R. — Our Casualties: D. S. Killed 1 Officer + 25 O.R. wounded 6 Officers + 71 O.R. — Our P.J. Hick being severely injured — Early in the morning of the 17/18 Aug 1917 The B[attalio]n retired on the Blue+Green line by Sheet 28N to 1 Compy R.E. Sandridge Camp, 1 Contour 16th Bd Heavy Brigade and 1/2 Company 1st Lancashire entrenched had KETON Camp (B.4.c.) where it rested for the day (B.9.D). At [?] 6.a.m. the Bn paraded and marched to EMILE Fm where it	LINDENBERG 11,000 Sheet 28N 10,000
	Aug 17th		erected camp and settled down Casualties Killed 3 wounded 2	

Army Form C. 2118.

WAR DIARY
or
INTELLIGENCE SUMMARY.
(Erase heading not required.)

224

Instructions regarding War Diaries and Intelligence Summaries are contained in F. S. Regs., Part II. and the Staff Manual respectively. Title pages will be prepared in manuscript.

Place	Date	Hour	Summary of Events and Information	Remarks and references to Appendices
B.Q.E	August 18th		Company parade reorganisation of platoons and chosing Equipment and Battle Stores Settled accounts for expenses for Dinner at first interview came over and booked EVERIDGE Gloucester R?	
	Aug 19th		Bathing parade every man attended and got a clean change of underclothing. Church parade at 3.30 p.m. Camp Service followed by service at Dock Workshop many hours all ranks attended. Communion ??	
	Aug 20th		Companies at disposal of Coy Comdr. Worked to camp at 6.0 at 11 P.M. Orders received from army H.Y to ???? thence proceeded at Dusk by ????? Autoloren Evenite All. Company to entrain to 6 Coy. ????? ??? out ??? at Duree, names ?????? and leaving Sussex 10	
	Aug 21st		All Company ?????? ?????? ????? ???? ?? ???? ???? ???? ????? ???? ???? ???? ????? for the ???? ?????	
	Aug 22nd			

Army Form C. 2118.

225

WAR DIARY
or
INTELLIGENCE SUMMARY.
(Erase heading not required.)

Place	Date	Hour	Summary of Events and Information	Remarks and references to Appendices
B.9.c	Aug 24th		All communications with front line being cut. Breaumont Sleeping Mounders. No casualties. Enemy did no harm shortly twice awoke no fresh work. Congratulations from Corps South for good work in forward area.	
	Aug 24th		Coys & Bn organised working parties. Bn bivouacked at 1/30 pm and marched off. Received the 2nd Bn Hants in the line.	Ref. BROOMBEEK 1/10 000
LANGEMARCK Station B.9.c	Aug 25th		LANGEMARCK right section from U.16.D.8½.6. to U.14.o.9½.4. Relief very difficult owing to extreme darkness but was eventually reported complete at 12.30 am. Occasional shelling but situation quiet. Casualties 1 O.R. killed 2 O.R. wounded. Continued repairing and improved trenches where possible. Front line today shelled by our own artillery. Bn Hd Qrs heavily shelled with 5.9" shells at periods during the day. Generally quiet when much movement was in evidence. Casualties 1 O.R. sick evacuated.	
	Aug 26th		Situation quiet – occasional shelling of front. Apparently enemy guns firing at one front, ours on another. Our L.P. Bridges Feeling about and reported our posts in BEAR SUPPORT x RIFLE FARM Casualties 1 O.R. wounded. Lt. P.T. Sadleman + 60 O.R. posted.	

WAR DIARY or INTELLIGENCE SUMMARY

Army Form C. 2118.

226/

Place	Date	Hour	Summary of Events and Information	Remarks and references to Appendices
LANGEMARCK STATION	Aug 27th 1917		Forenoon very quiet. Lewis, a 2/Lt Newig fired very uncomfortably weak MG bursts on our right attacked. 9PM. 55 P.M. Our barrage fell along the enemy line and further on our right attacked. The enemy barrage kept to our lines & even within our own line commenced, and raged for three hours. It was a very Lt cover. Casualties 8 O.R. killed 4 O.R. wounded. 34 O.R. arrived at Batt reinforcement camp and were posted to Coys.	
	Aug 28th		Occupant Barali? Retiring on posts at H.Qrs during Twenty. Noon was very quiet. The Bn was relieved on the front line at 12th. Grenadier Guards Relief was carried out quickly and quietly and was reported complete at 12.35 P.M. On turning to K.30.d Casualties 6 O.R. wounded. 4 O.R reported wounded.	
	Aug 29th		Companies marched back from the line, independently, to DULWICH Camp and rested there until 4 P.M. At 5 P.M. the 73rd Brigade at ELVERDINGE for BANDAGHEM. When they arrived at 9 P.M. and marched to PADDOCK WOOD Camp in the P.L. area. Final 9 Capt M... 11th Lancers arrived and taken 1 O.R.injured. Casualties 1 O.R. wounded.	
PADDOCK WOOD Camp	Aug 30th		Organization of platoons and Companies. Lieut Stephens and 2/Lt Thock granted to W.E. 28 O.R arrived and posted.	
	Aug 31st		Captain Parcels Station Organization and Specialists Training. Casualties A.O.E.	

Attd to Hospital 1. O.E. 16 Bogue (sujt. P. duties an attach music.)

Executed: 4/
Cavalino A.O.E.
[signed] James Waits
Capt 1st KOSB

Narrative of Action
of
16th August 1917.

1st Battalion The Border Regt.

15-8-17

8.30 p.m.   The Battalion marched from bivouac at BLUET FARM and proceeded via BRIDGE ST, SAULES FARM, CAPTAINS FARM, SIGNAL FARM to the place of assembly E. of the STEENBEEK.

10.30 p.m   Battalion Headquarters were established at SIGNAL FARM.

One Section of M.Gs under Lt. PAGE, M.G.C., attached to the Battalion, proceeded with "C" Coy. direct to place of assembly, and one Stokes gun under Lt. WHIGHAM was brought up to SIGNAL FARM.

16-8-17

2.0 AM   The Battalion was formed up E. of the STEENBEEK in rear of the 1st K.O.S.B's on a two Coy. frontage "D" and "B" Coys. in the front line (forming 1st two waves) and "A" and "C" Coys. in support (forming 2nd two waves).

During the approach march the Battalion was shelled intermittently, but the enemy was unable to put down his usual heavy barrage on the CAPTAINS FM. FOURCHE FM. line probably owing to the gas shells our artillery was sending over.

	Previous to the assault W.B. BUTLER, O.C. "D" Coy. was wounded in the foot but after having his wound dressed returned to his company
4.45 AM	Our barrage fell with great precision and the advance started. The enemy put down his usual barrage on the CAPTAIN'S FM. FOURCHE FM. line, and also on RUISSEAU FM. SIGNAL FM. and SENTIER FM but put nothing more than an occasional shell on the line of the STEENBEEK.
6.40 AM	Message received from visual signal station at PASSERELLE FM. saying BLUE LINE had been taken.
7.20 AM	Another message through the same source stated the line was held up by M.G. fire.
7.30 AM	Confirmation of above received from CAPT. J.W. EWBANK, M.C., O.C. "B" Coy. His message stated that K.O.S.B's and S.W.B's were held up by a M.G. in a block-house near MONTMIRAIL FM. The Stokes mortar had been moved from SIGNAL FM, as soon as the BLUE LINE was taken, to PASSERELLE FM., and a message was accordingly sent to Capt Ewbank to get Stokes gun on to the block-house which was holding up the attack & similar orders issued to the O/C Trench mortar.
8.50 AM	Lt R.E.S. JOHNSON O.C. "C" Coy. reported advance had continued and that he had reached his position in gun pits near CANNES FM.

Our own heavy Howitzers, estimated to be 9.2's caused us losses in PANTHER TR. N. of the swamp during the morning and it took some time to get this stopped though the F.O.O. Lᵗ NAPIER. R.A. at WIJDENDRIFT got his messages through with great promptitude.

During the consolidation the enemy Artillery was fairly active between the GREEN LINE and the STEENBEEK, and at times concentrated heavily on WIJDENDRIFT itself but they seemed quite unable to locate our front line, and at any rate made no attempt to shell it.

Enemy aeroplanes were very active all morning and continually flew up and down our line at very low altitude (500'), firing M.G's at the garrison and firing single red very lights.

None of our battle planes appeared to interfere with them, and they had matters pretty much their own way.

One contact plane of ours, which came over unescorted, was promptly brought down by them.

1.0 P.M.	Report from O.C "B" Coy, stating that about 3 or 4 hundred of the enemy were massing in NEY WOOD. The guns were turned on very promptly and with excellent effect, and heavy casualties inflicted by rifle fire from our firing line, many of the men using captured enemy rifles and ammunition. At various times during the afternoon the firing line Coys. reported enemy activity

The opposition from the block-house near MONTMIRAIL FM. had been overcome by an outflanking movement by "B" Coy. which caused the garrison to surrender.

9.10 AM   A/CAPT. W.B. BUTLER. O.C. "D" Coy. reported that RED LINE had been captured and prisoners taken, also that he was in touch with "A" Coy on his right.

9.30 AM   CAPT. EWBANK M.C. O.C. "B" Coy. reported that he had dealt with blockhouse, which had been holding up advance on GREEN LINE, by outflanking it, causing some 40 Germans to surrender and capturing 1 heavy T.M. This had enabled him to push on, and capture his position of the RED LINE. Here he took more prisoners and 2 M.G's.

9.35 A.M.   On receipt of this information. Battalion Headquarters was moved forward from SIGNAL FM. to WIJDENDRIFT, and at the same time the M.G. section was ordered to push forward to PANTHER TRENCH.

After Battalion Headquarters had been established at WIJDENDRIFT situation reports were received from all Coys. enabling me to send to Brigade a map showing accurately the dispositions taken up, a copy of which accompanies this report. The work of consolidation went forward quite smoothly all morning and casualties in the firing line were light, though considerable sniping by the enemy from the E. side of the BROEMBEK was kept up on the WIDJENDRIFT and STEENBEEK lines but only a light and inaccurate one on the front line.

About 8.45 p.m. the 18 pounders withdrew their barrage from the BROEMBEK line onto PANTHER TR from the right Brigade boundary up to the swamp, causing some 10 casualties to my firing line. I don't know the explanation of this as I never asked for the barrage to shift from the BROEMBEK line and as far as I know not a single BOCHE ever got across the stream.

During the afternoon patrols were sent out to the BROEMBEEK and exploited the stream and its crossings.

They encountered no enemy W. of the stream but were sniped by the enemy who appeared to be holding a shell hole line about 200ˣ E of the stream.

The failure of the counter attack finished the enemy's activity, and the relief of my Battalion was carried out during the night. The operation, as far as this Battn. was concerned, was carried out with complete success, and with remarkably light casualties.

The advance was a difficult one owing to the swamp running diagonally across our front from CANNES FARM to the

	E. of the BROEMBEK and this culminated in a definite report from Capt Ewbank received at 7.20 pm that the enemy were massing from NEY WOOD to a point opposite the right boundary of the Brigade Sector, and were already pushing forward in small parties by short rushes.
7.40 p.m	A barrage was at once asked for on the line of the BROEMBEEK from U.16.D.1.8 to U.16.C.1.9*, and this barrage was put down with great accuracy, and just at the right moment.
7.45 p.m	CAPT. and ADJT. A. W. SUTCLIFFE, M.C., who was observing from WIDJENDRIFT, spotted the enemy advancing in large numbers clear of our barrage N.W. of NEY WOOD up to about point U.15.b.2.6. After some little delay I was able to get the battery commander on the phone and got the barrage extended up to this point, turning on both heavy and field guns.

The effect of this barrage was annihilating. It came down just at the right time and in the right place, completely broke up the enemys attack and caused him enormous casualties. All this time a heavy rifle, M.G., and L.G. fire was kept up by our firing line troops, and, as the enemy had practically no real trenches to get into, the losses inflicted by this fire were also very heavy.

Previous to, and during the counter-attack the enemy put down a fairly heavy barrage

BROEMBEEK and I consider the fact that it was carried out so successfully reflects the very greatest credit on the Company Commanders concerned.

They kept touch and direction throughout and arrived at their allotted objectives well up to time.

The endurance displayed by all ranks was beyond all praise as the going throughout was in an appalling state and during the previous 3 days the Battn. had held the firing line for 48 hours and carried out two difficult reliefs under most adverse conditions and suffered considerable casualties from shellfire.

CONFIDENTIAL.

WAR DIARY

OF

1st Batn. The King's Own Scottish Borderers.

From 1st September 1917, To 30th September 1917.

Volume No 38.

Army Form C. 2118.

WAR DIARY
or
INTELLIGENCE SUMMARY.
(Erase heading not required.)

September, 1917.

227

Place	Date	Hour	Summary of Events and Information	Remarks and references to Appendices
PADDOCK WOOD CAMP	1st Sept.		Battalion Parade as strong as possible at 9 a.m. From 10 a.m. to 11 a.m. Companies at disposal of Company Commanders. Specialist Training 11am to 1 p.m. Afternoon – Half holiday. H.O.R. Sick Evac. & Casualties Nil.	
"	2nd Sept.		Sunday – Church Parades & as usual. Sick Evac. & Casualties Nil.	
"	3rd Sept.		Battalion paraded at 9.30 a.m. for Presentation by Maj. Genl. G.A.C. Simpson of ribbons of medals awarded for acts of gallantry on 16/8/17. The following were the honors received:— Captain J. Watt. Bar to M.C. Captain T.J.L. Thompson (M.C.) M.C. 2/Lieut. J. Oliphant M.C. Lieut. J.C. Noel M.C. 10303 Sgt. O'Connor J. "B" Coy. D.C.M. 20853 " Graham W. "D" Coy. D.C.M. 11682 Cpl. Aitkin J. "A" Coy. M.M. 9919 L/Cpl. McTaggart O. "B" Coy. M.M. 19/66 Cpl. Wallace C. "C" Coy. M.M. 18066 Pte. Watson J. "C" Coy. M.M. 20164 " McMillan J. "C" Coy. M.M. 18436 " Bracewell J. "B" Coy. M.M. 10475 Sgt. Smith H. "A" Coy. M.M. 10051 Pte. Johnstone A. "B" Coy. M.M. 24937 " Quinn J. "A" Coy. M.M. 18606 Cpl. Morgan W. (Att. T.M.B.) M.M.	
"	4th Sept.		Companies at disposal of Company Commanders for practising attack, Rapid Trench Digging, Bayonet Fighting & Specialist Platoon in the attack. Training.	

Army Form C. 2118.

WAR DIARY
or
INTELLIGENCE SUMMARY.
(Erase heading not required.)

Instructions regarding War Diaries and Intelligence Summaries are contained in F. S. Regs., Part II. and the Staff Manual respectively. Title pages will be prepared in manuscript.

Place	Date	Hour	Summary of Events and Information	Remarks and references to Appendices
PADDOCK WOOD CAMP	5th. Sept.		Training as on previous day. 1 O.R. joined from 5th. Entrenching Battalion & 1 O.R. from Hospital.	
"	6th. Sept.		Training as on previous day. Draft of 35 O.R. arrived.	
"	7th. Sept.		Training as on previous day.	
"	8th. Sept.		Companies at disposal of Company Commanders from 9 a.m. to 10-30 a.m. Battalion paraded at 2-30 p.m. & marched to HERZEELE (distance 6 miles) arriving about 5-15 p.m. Battalion in Billets.	
HERZEELE	9th. Sept.		Companies at disposal of O.C. Companies. Draft of 5 O.R. arrived.	
"	10th. Sept.		Commanding Officer's Parade as strong as possible - Battalion exercised in the "Attack" on Training Area.	
"	11th. Sept.		Brigade Parade as strong as possible in the Training Area. Practice in the "Attack" carried out.	

Army Form C. 2118.

224

WAR DIARY
or
INTELLIGENCE SUMMARY.

(Erase heading not required.)

Instructions regarding War Diaries and Intelligence Summaries are contained in F. S. Regs., Part II. and the Staff Manual respectively. Title pages will be prepared in manuscript.

Place	Date	Hour	Summary of Events and Information	Remarks and references to Appendices
HERZEELE	12th Sept.		Battalion marched back to PADDOCK WOOD CAMP, moving off at 10 a.m. & arriving in camp about 12-30 p.m. 2.O.R. Sick. Evac. 2.O.R. joined from 9th Entrenching Battalion.	
PADDOCK WOOD CAMP	13th Sept.		Battalion Boxing Tournament for purpose of selecting representatives for Brigade Tournament. Brigade Sports in the afternoon in which Battalion gained second (2nd) in Points. among the chief int[erests] - Battalion event, the Tug-of-War. The following Officers reported for duty :- 9/Lieuts. G.G. THWAITES, J.W. LEES, & A. LAPSLEY.	
"	14th Sept.		Conferences at discretion of O.C. Companies during morning. Brigade Ceremonial Parade in the afternoon.	
"	15th Sept.		Musketry Training & Conferences at discretion of O.C. Companies during morning. Battalion attended Brigade Boxing Tournament in the afternoon. Battalion won 3 out of the 7 Boxing Events. Draft of 31 Other Ranks arrived. 2/Lieut. S.T.C. WRIGHT to England. Sick. 3 O.R. Evac. Sick.	
"	16th Sept.		Presbyterian Service in Camp. Battalion Battering & Manoeuvring what intrenching.	
"	17th Sept.		9th 10 a.m. - A Coy, Advancing under Barrage - B. Coy, B.F. & P.T. - C. Coy, Musketry - D. Coy, Rehearsal of Demonstration. 10 to 11 a.m. - B. Coy. Demonstration of Consolidation of captured position. Remainder of Coys. Arms Drill. 11 to 12-30 p.m. - A. Coy. B.F. & P.T. - B & C. Coys organise "The Attack" - D. Coy. Musketry. afternoon. - Rehearsal for Divisional Exercise Parade by 2 O.R. arrived.

WAR DIARY or INTELLIGENCE SUMMARY

Army Form C. 2118.

Place	Date	Hour	Summary of Events and Information	Remarks and references to Appendices
PADDOCK WOOD CAMP DEPT.	18th Sept.		Official intimation received of award of VICTORIA CROSS to the following N.C.O's of the Battalion for conspicuous bravery in action in the WITBENDRIFT Sector on 16/9/17:- 6895, C/C.S.M. J. SKINNER D.C.M. "A" Coy. 18531, A/C.Q.M.S. GRIM BALDESTON W.H. "B" Coy. Pt. Paraded in the morning. In the afternoon the Battalion took part in a Divisional Ceremonial Parade at which General LA CAPELLE, Commanding 107 French Army Corps made a Presentation of French Honours. The following N.C.O.'s of the Battalion received the CROIX de GUERRE:- 6895, A/C.S.M. J. SKINNER M.C. & 2 Bars D.C.M. "A" Coy. 24353, Sergt. W. from D.C.M. "D" Coy. Presentation followed by Band Concert open to 14th Corps. Battalion Band scored three firsts. Following Officers arrived:- Captain C.H. CRAWSHAW, 2/Lieut. C.M.L. SMITH, 2/Lieut. J.L. GIBSON & 2/Lieut. A.C.D. JOHNSTON. 9 O.R. men. sick.	
PADDOCK WOOD CAMP DEPT.	19th		Raining. A.C. & D. Companies on Rifle Range. "B" Coy. promotions in consolidation. Bathing in afternoon.	
PADDOCK WOOD CAMP DEPT.	20th Sept.		Battalion relieved of Collections Guards in DUBLIN CAMP (A.11.C.4.5) FOREST AREA (Porosting) at 10-15 a.m. & arriving at 3-45 p.m. 2 O.R. men. sick. 10 R. arrived.	
DUBLIN CAMP	21st Sept.		Training continued. Reporting onto a weather made in vicinity of Comp. Battalion run off:- Result:- 1st B Coy. 2nd C. Coy. 3rd D Coy. 4th A Coy. YUKON PACK Competition run off. 2 O.R. men. sick. Following Officers arrived 2/Lieut. G.E. SHARD	

Army Form C. 2118.

23

WAR DIARY
or
INTELLIGENCE SUMMARY.

(Erase heading not required.)

Instructions regarding War Diaries and Intelligence Summaries are contained in F. S. Regs., Part II. and the Staff Manual respectively. Title pages will be prepared in manuscript.

Place	Date	Hour	Summary of Events and Information	Remarks and references to Appendices
DUBLIN CAMP	22nd Sept.		Battalion Training. Work on improvement of Camp continued. Battalion (3 Coys team) won Brigade YUKON PACK Competition. 2 O.R. transferred 6 T.R. 7 M.B.	
DUBLIN CAMP	23rd Sept.		Divine Service. Work on improvement of Camp continued in the afternoon. Officers' Revolver Team Shooting Competition won by A Coy. 2 O.R. Sick evac.	
DUBLIN CAMP	24th Sept.		Battalion Training – Company Inspections. General Parade. Practice Saluting Drill. Specialist Training. Lecture by M.O. on Gas + Tactical Scheme for Officers. Un Comis work by Battalion on improvement of Camp. 1 O.R. accidently wounded (Bombing Practice)	
DUBLIN CAMP	25th Sept.		Battalion Training – Specialist Training. P.T., Lewis Guns on Range & Work on refreshing Utility Track II & on improvement of Huts. 2 O.R. Sick Evac. 10 R. to Base unfit.	
DUBLIN CAMP	26th Sept.		Battalion Training – Company Inspections. Specialist Training. Coys in Musk Formations. Lewis Guns on Range. Work on Huts & Utility Track II.	
DUBLIN CAMP	27th Sept.		Battalion Training – Gas Drill, Inspections. Specialist Training, Lewis Guns on Range. Road & Hut refreshing.	
DUBLIN CAMP	28th Sept.		Battalion Training – Company Inspections. Adjutants General Parade. Specialist Training. P.T. + B.F. Revolver Practice (Officers). Work on Huts + Utility Track II.	

Army Form C. 2118.

232

WAR DIARY
or
INTELLIGENCE SUMMARY.
(Erase heading not required.)

Place	Date	Hour	Summary of Events and Information	Remarks and references to Appendices
DUBLIN CAMP	29th Sept.		Battalion Training – R.S.M's Parade, Specialist Training & Bombing Practice. Work on improvement of Huts & Track. Casualties 2 O.R. killed & 4 O.R. wounded whilst attached to West Riding Field Coy R.E. Sick unevacted 1 O.R.	
DUBLIN CAMP	30th Sept.		Battalion paraded at 2 A.M. & marched to WHITE MILL CAMP in ELVERDINGHE. Accommodated in elephant huts. Transport lines at MICHEL FARM. Transport Lines bombed during night – 1 O.R. wounded. 2 horses & 2 mules killed, 7 horses & 4 mules wounded. Extract from letter to Earl of Cavan, commdg. XIV Corps by Sir Francis Lloyd, G.O.C. London district who personally concerned himself with the arrangements for the investiture of No. 6693, M.C. & R. J. SKINNER V.C. on 26th September:— "I have had your sergeant over to Luncheon at the investiture this morning & had a long talk with him. The King noticed him & told me to take care of him. He is a very fine fellow."	

Dictated sig.
[signature] Capt.
a/Adjt 6 KOSB

30/9/17

S.S. 550B.]　　　　　　　　　　　　　　　　　　　　　Ia/12828.

On His Majesty's Service.

Illustrations to Accompany

NOTES ON THE INTERPRETATION OF AEROPLANE PHOTOGRAPHS.

Series B.

Issued by the General Staff.

CONFIDENTIAL

WAR DIARY

of

1st Batt. The King's Own Scottish Borderers

From 1st October 1917.

To 31st October 1917.

Volume 39.

29 T
9 sheets
1 map

WAR DIARY
INTELLIGENCE SUMMARY

Army Form C. 2118.

October, 1917.

Map Reference
BROEMBEEK Ed. 2 1/10000

Place	Date	Hour	Summary of Events and Information	Remarks and references to Appendices
WHITE MILL CAMP	1st October		Training & preliminary for the line. Coy. Inspection in Fighting Order. See Bill. Repair & maintenance of Cavels. 1 O.R. regimental wounded.	
WHITE MILL CAMP	2nd October		Preparation at disposal of Coy. Commanders during forenoon. Information: Received the job at RIFLE MT. Particulars were sent Bn. in progress. Bn. formed and moved off at 6 p.m. Relief carried out with little difficulty very little shell fire and good moonlight to Report — Relief Completed 01.30 3rd inst. Casualties 3 O.R. wounded, 1 O.R. missing.	
Line	3rd October		Intermittent shelling night & day, SPRING FARM receiving special attention & containing four direct hits. Work on Trenches, rebuilding & repairing carried on with vigor all night. Casualties: 6 O.R. killed, 8 wounded.	
Line	4th October		The Battalion took part in a general advance which commenced at 6 a.m. The disposition of the Battalion prior to the attack was — Firing Line:— A Coy on the Right, C. Coy. on the Left holding line U.17.c.6.1 — U.17.c.1.2 — U.16.a.1.3. B. Coy. was in support in line U.22.d.2.4 — U.22.a.6.6. & D.Coy. in reserve in line U.22.c.4.6 — U.21.d.6.7. (approx) On ZERO Hr. Two Platoons of A.Coy. attached BEAR SUPPORT and Posts in its vicinity. Our barrage lifted without having cleared up all enemy Posts. The garrisons of two at U.17.a.35.70 & U.17.a.15.70 defending their positions stubbornly. Our advance continued by mopping up our approach the Post at V.17.a.35.70 resisted but the other post at V.17.a.15.70 continued to hold out & was holding up the advance of the R. Sussex Fusiliers on our Right. 2nd Lt. 19225 S/C. McKNIGHT & Pte. 19218 E. CHITTENDEN immediately went out & attacked the position from the Left flank & by very creditable work	

Army Form C. 2118.

WAR DIARY
or
INTELLIGENCE SUMMARY.
(Erase heading not required.)

Place	Date	Hour	Summary of Events and Information	Remarks and references to Appendices
Line	4th October (cont.)		succeeded in forcing the enemy to surrender. Three N.C.Os captured 2 M.Gs & 12 prisoners. Consolidation was then in progress & 3 posts were established No I at U.17.d.15.75, No 2 at U.17.c.65.70, & No 3 at U.17.c.55.65. The Third Platoon of A Coy was moved in support at U.17.c.70.25 & one Platoon of B Coy at U.17.c.20.30. The attack was an unqualified success & the G.O.C. 29th Division approved great satisfaction & congratulated all ranks on the great work. 2/Lieut. E.B. WILSON who was wounded in the arm of the attack refused to leave his Platoon until he saw them safely dug in. During the attack the support & Reserve lines were heavily shelled. Battalion H.Q. receiving special attention, several direct hits being registered. Our barrage exact at ZERO + 1 hr. 34 mins lot the enemy artillery was particularly active all day & night. About 2 p.m. the enemy counter-attacked but was repulsed with heavy loss, during the afternoon small parties of the enemy were engaged by our Lewis Gunners & Snipers many casualties being inflicted. Casualties :- KILLED - Officers Nil, O.R. 9. WOUNDED - Officers 1, 2/Lt E.B.WILSON, O.R. 34. MISSING - Officers Nil, O.R. 1.	
Line	5th October		Enemy artillery unusually active all day. Front Line, Supports & Reserve heavily shelled with 5-9's, 4-2's & Field Guns. SPRING FARM again contained a few direct hits.	

WAR DIARY
INTELLIGENCE SUMMARY

Army Form C. 2118.

Place	Date	Hour	Summary of Events and Information	Remarks and references to Appendices
Line	5th October (cont.)		At intervals during the day small parties of the enemy were engaged by our Lewis Gunners & snipers, a number of hits registered. No hostile movement was observed. In the evening the Battalion was relieved by two Companies of the 4th Grenadier Guards & one Company of the 2/Scots Guards. Relief completed at 00.40 when the Battalion marched back to "WHITE MILL CAMP" at ELVERDINGHE. Casualties:- 1 O.R. killed; 1 Off. & 9 O.R. wounded; 9 Off. & 102 shell-shock. The Officer casualties were 2/Lt. G.H.A. SMITH (wounded) & 2/Lieut. J.L. GIBSON (S.S.)	
WHITE MILL CAMP	6th October		Continues not disposal of O.C. Companies for Inspection Baths, etc. With no reply & leaving of Camp continued. E.A. very active all night harassing travel & dropping a large number of bombs. Casualties, 2 O.R. more sick.	
WHITE MILL CAMP	7th October		Preparations for move in progress all morning - especially cleaning of Cooks. Battalion paraded at 12.45 p.m. & marched to DRAGON WOOD CAMP (A.9.a.9.3). Most deplorable state of affairs discovered on arrival. The tents had just been pitched & the ground was one mass of mud, the weather added to the misery of things being bitterly cold & raining heavily. Some arrangements & open & wood anthing which were issued to the men a which were greatly appreciated. Casualties:- NIL.	

Army Form C. 2118.

236

WAR DIARY
INTELLIGENCE SUMMARY.
(Erase heading not required.)

Instructions regarding War Diaries and Intelligence Summaries are contained in F. S. Regs., Part II. and the Staff Manual respectively. Title pages will be prepared in manuscript.

Place	Date	Hour	Summary of Events and Information	Remarks and references to Appendices
DRAGON WOOD CAMP	8th October		Companies at disposal of O.C. Companies. Strenuous endeavours made not only to make the camp more habitable. Battalion received orders to be prepared to move to the line at half hours notice. Battalion busy preparing for the line in case required. Casualties – T/Major T.H. MUIR & accompt struck off strength on proper men proceeding to attend Course at ALDERSHOT.	
DRAGON WOOD CAMP	9th October		Companies at disposal of Coy Commanders for inspection & checking of battle equipment. Preparing for move. Battalion paraded at 2.40pm & marched to International Corner Station, entraining there for PROVEN. Disembarked at PROVEN & marched to PITCHCOTT CAMP (PIEVIA). Battalion had to wait about 5 hours in a field before getting into the camp to take over from the 10/West Yorks. Camp very muddy. Casualties Nil. (2.O.R. Wounded with West Riding R&C)	
PITCHCOTT CAMP	10th October		Companies at disposal of O.C. Companies for cleaning of rifles, equipment & clothing. Platoons reorganized. R.S.M's Class for NCO's. Casualties. Sick. 8 o.r. 2.O.R.	
PITCHCOTT CAMP	11th October		Companies at disposal of O.C. Companies. R.S.M's Class for N.C.O's. Casualties – 2/Lieut. G Pc Proper to U.K. 29/9/17.	
PITCHCOTT CAMP	12th October		At disposal of Coy Commanders. Adjutants Ceremonial Parade. Inspection of Troops. Inspection of Transport by C.O. N.C.O's under R.S.M. The following Officers	

Army Form C. 2118.

WAR DIARY
INTELLIGENCE SUMMARY.
(Erase heading not required.)

Place	Date	Hour	Summary of Events and Information	Remarks and references to Appendices
	12th. October (cont.)		joined for duty:- 2/Lieut. P. REAY; 2/Lieut. P. MILROY; 2/Lieut. S. MORGAN, & 2/Lieut. A.F. CAMPBELL. Details reported from XIVth. Corps Reinforcement Camp. Drafts totalling 101 joined from O.R.C.	
PITCHCOTT CAMP.	13th. October.		Companies at disposal of O.C. Companies. Platoons organised on a minimum strength of 1 N.C.O & 10 O.R. per Section. Lecture on "Smart Feet" by M.O. & on "Discipline on the Line of March." by O.C. Companies. Draft of 3 O.R. joined. 1 O.R. rejoined (sick).	
PITCHCOTT CAMP.	14th. October.		Divine Service. Arms of the Battalion inspected by the Brigade Armourer. Battalion Luther. 1 O.R. Sick unaccounted.	
PITCHCOTT CAMP.	15th. October.		Battalion preparing to move. B, C, & D Coys. paraded at 2-30 A.M. and marched to PESEUHDEK entraining there at 2-30 A.M. Detrained at SAVLTY (on DOULLENS-ARRAS Road) about 2 A.M. on 16th. inst. Marched thence via BAILLEULMONT to Billets in BAILLEUVAL, a distance of about 7 kilometres. A Coy left PESEUHDEN with Train leaving at 6-20 P.M. "C" Coy remained at SAVLTY as an entraining party for Nos. 1, 2, 3 & 4 Trains.	
BAILLEUVAL	16th. October.		Battalion settling into Billets & resting. C. Coy rejoined from entraining duty at SAVLTY. 2/Lieut. T.C. NOEL M.C. transferred to R.F.C.	
BAILLEUVAL	17th. October.		Companies at disposal of O.C. Companies. R.S.M's. N.C.O.s' Class. 1 O.R. Sick unaccounted.	

Army Form C. 2118.

WAR DIARY
INTELLIGENCE SUMMARY.
(Erase heading not required.)

Place	Date	Hour	Summary of Events and Information	Remarks and references to Appendices
BAILLEULVAL	18th October		Companies at disposal of O.C. Companies. Platoon Drill, P.T. & B.F. Specialist Training. Cleaning & improving of Billets. 1 O.R. proc. to 7 M. Bty. 2/Lieut. A.J. HAMILTON joined for duty.	
BAILLEULVAL	19th October		Instruction Platoon Section & Specialist Training. Cleaning corps & arms of Billets & improving drainage system. 2 O.R. sick evac. 2/Lieut. F.W. REES joined for duty. 1 O.R. Trans. to E.F.C.	
BAILLEULVAL	20th October		Parade of Coy Commanders. Inspection. B.F. & P.T. Specialist Training. Commanding Officers Parade as strong as possible. Refitting of Billets during afternoon. 2/Lieut. P. REAY reported to 7/8 K.O.L. Bro. 1 O.R. to U.K. (Munitions)	
BAILLEULVAL	21st October		Divine Service. Informing of Billets in the afternoon. 1 O.R. proc. to 87 T.M. Bty.	
BAILLEULVAL	22nd October		A. & C. Coys. on the Rifle Range. Specialist Training. Company Drill, P.T. & B.F. 6 O.R. evacuated sick.	
BAILLEULVAL	23rd October		Company Drill, Adjutants Parade, P.T. & B.F. Specialist Training. Improvement of Billets continued & erection of new huts standing marquee 2 men per hut marching west opposite. 1 O.R. evacuated sick.	
BAILLEULVAL	24th October		Commanding Officers Parade. Range. Specialist Training. P.T. & B.F. Training of new Horse Lines & Bayonet Fighting Course commenced.	

Army Form C. 2118.

WAR DIARY
or
INTELLIGENCE SUMMARY.
(Erase heading not required.)

Place	Date	Hour	Summary of Events and Information	Remarks and references to Appendices
BAILLEULVAL	25th October		Arms Drill, Shooting Training, B.F. & P.T., Musketry. Work continued on Billets & making of B.F. course & new Lanchot Lines. 11 O.R. arrived.	
BAILLEULVAL	26th October		Commanding Officers Parade. Shooting Training. Arms Drill, B.F. & Musketry. 2 O.R. were sick.	
BAILLEULVAL	27th October		Brigade Ceremonial Parade. Work on Transport Lines continued. 2 O.R. sick, one. 2nd Major SKINNER J. V.C. rejoined from sick leave to some Tr WK.	
BAILLEULVAL	28th October		Church Parade. Work on B.F. course & Transport Lines. Casualties, NIL	
BAILLEULVAL	29th October		Shooting Training. Trench to Trench Attack. C & D Coys. Work on Transport Lines. 3 O.R. rejoined sick & 1 O.R. rejoined wounded.	
BAILLEULVAL	30th October		Shooting Training, P.T. & B.F., C & D Coys on the Ranges. Trench to Trench Attack by A & B Coys. Work on Transport Lines. Official information received of the award of decorations to the undermentioned Officers & O.R. for acts of gallantry on 4th October, 1917:— Captain & Qt. Mr. W. SIMPSON } M.C. Lieut. E.B. WILSON } 19122. L/C. McKNIGHT & Coy } 19218. " CHITTENDEN & Coy } D.C.M. 7780. L/Cpl. ST. PARKINSON (D. Coy), 20932, D.LISYME (D. Coy), 8403, Cpl. R. FALCONER (A Coy) & 15055. Pt. G. ROBBINS (A Coy) Military Medals	

Army Form C. 2118.

WAR DIARY
INTELLIGENCE SUMMARY.
(Erase heading not required.)

Place	Date	Hour	Summary of Events and Information	Remarks and references to Appendices
BAIZIEUX VAL	9/10		Brigade Ceremonial Parade. Officers to Parade for remainder. Work continued on new Infantry Lines. 2/Lieut. J.L. GIBSON to U.K. Sick 20/10/17. 1 O.R. transferred to 87th. T.M. Bty.	

Dictated by.

Ennerdale-Eagle

Alan SKSB.

November 1917
M.G. to 38th Dn.

MESSAGE FORM.

To: No.

1. I am at........................ Note. — Either give Map Reference or mark your position by a 'X' on the Map on back.

2. My Line runs..

3. My Platoon / Company is at........................and is consolidating.

4. My Platoon / Company is at........................and has consolidated.

5. Am held up by (a) M.G. (b) Wire at.................(Place where you are).

6. Enemy holding strong point..................................

7. I am in touch with....................on Right/Left at..........

8. I am not in touch with..................on Right/Left.

9. Am shelled from................................

10. Am in need of :—

11. Counter Attack forming at..................................

12. Hostile (a) Battery (b) Machine Gun (c) Trench Mortar active at..................

13. Reinforcements wanted at..................................

14. I estimate my present strength at................rifles

15. Have captured..................................

16. Prisoners belong to..................................

17. Add any other useful information here :—

Time................m. Name..................
Date................1917. Platoon..................
  Company..................
  Battalion..................

(A). Carry no maps or papers which may be of value to the Enemy.
(B). Give no information if captured, except the following, which you are bound to give :—
  Name and Rank.
(C). Collect all captured maps and papers and send them in at once.

87/29 1 KOSB 24!
Army Form C. 2118.

WAR DIARY
INTELLIGENCE SUMMARY.
(Erase heading not required.)

November, 1917.

Vol 23

Instructions regarding War Diaries and Intelligence Summaries are contained in F. S. Regs., Part II. and the Staff Manual respectively. Title pages will be prepared in manuscript.

Place	Date	Hour	Summary of Events and Information	Remarks and references to Appendices
BAILLEUVAL	1st Nov.		Battalion Training. "A" & "D" Coys on the Range. "B" Coy repairing Bn. Cinecoond Parade Ground. "C" Coy. French to Trench Attack. Specialist Training & Interior Economy. Snipers under the I.O., N.C.Os & Offrs under the R.S.M. at 2.15 p.m. Company Commanders' Tactical Scheme at 2 p.m. Work on new Lewisgun Lewis & B.F. Course.	
"	2nd Nov.		Brigade Ceremonial Parade for inspection by G.O.C. Division & presentation of Medal Ribands. The following Officers & Other Ranks were presented with ribands:- Capt. W. SIMPSON, M.C.; 9/122, L/Cpl McKNIGHT "A" Coy, D.C.M.; 9/216, L/Cpl. CHITTENDEN, "A" Coy, D.C.M.; 10475, Sgt. SMITH A. "A" Coy, M.M.; 8108 Cpl. FALCONER R. "A" Coy, M.M.; 24497, Pte. QUINN T. "A" Coy, M.M.; 7760, Sgt. T. ST. PARKINSON "D" Coy, M.M.; 20422, Pte. SYME T "D" Coy, M.M. Companies at disposal of O.C. Companies for inspection of billets etc. Bayonet Fighting Course completed. 1 O.R. to Base for disposal (unfit). Battalion attended Divine Service. Work continued on new Trenchfoot Lines.	
"	3rd Nov.			
"	4th Nov.		2 O.R. sick evacuated.	
"	5th Nov.		A & B Coys on the Range. B & C Coys. B.F. & P.T. & Specialist Training. D Coy. French to Trench Attack. Throwing of live bombs & firing rifle grenades (all Subalterns Officers). 2/Lieut. G.E. SHARD to U.K. sick 26-10-17. 1 O.R. unevacuated sick.	

Army Form C. 2118.

WAR DIARY
or
INTELLIGENCE SUMMARY.
(Erase heading not required.)

Instructions regarding War Diaries and Intelligence Summaries are contained in F. S. Regs., Part II. and the Staff Manual respectively. Title pages will be prepared in manuscript.

Place	Date	Hour	Summary of Events and Information	Remarks and references to Appendices
BAILLEUL VAL	6th Nov.		A Coy - Cross Country Route March practicing Advanced & Flank Guards. B.Coy - On Range. C. Coy - Sand Tactics, Advanced & Flank Guards. D.Coy - Digging of Platoon Strong Points. Work on new Transport Lines. 3 O.R. evacuated Sick.	
BAILLEUL VAL	7th Nov.		A Coy - Digging Platoon Strong Points. B.Coy - Cross Country Route March with Advanced & Flank Guards. C.Coy - On Range & at O.C. Coys disposal. D.Coy - Cross Country Route March with Advanced & Flank Guards. Work on new Transport Lines. 7 O.R. arrived.	
"	8th Nov.		A Coy - Cross Country Route March with Advanced & Flank Guards. Outposts - B. Coy - Jan 2. Tactics, Protection on the move & at rest. C. Coy - Digging of Platoon Strong Points. D. Coy - On Range. At disposal of O.C. Companies. 2 O.R. Sick Evacuated.	
"	9th Nov.		Battalion Route March, no strong as possible, practicing Advanced Guards. Work on new Transport Lines.	
"	10th Nov.		Companies at the disposal of O.C. Companies. Commanding Officer's inspection of Billets. 3 O.R. Sick Evacuated.	
"	11th Nov.		Divine Service. 1 O.R. to Base unfit.	
"	12th Nov.		Battalion Parade as strong as possible for Brigade Field Day. Battalion acting as Advance Guard to Brigade. 7 O.R. Transferred to 226 Employment Coy.	

243/

WAR DIARY
or
INTELLIGENCE SUMMARY.
(Erase heading not required.)

Army Form C. 2118.

Instructions regarding War Diaries and Intelligence Summaries are contained in F.S. Regs., Part II. and the Staff Manual respectively. Title pages will be prepared in manuscript.

Place	Date	Hour	Summary of Events and Information	Remarks and references to Appendices
BOISLEUX		13th cont.	2/R. Q. & L/. A. FRANKLIN to England as candidates for Infantry commissions. Battalion paraded through open weather. C. & D. Coys open weather parties.	
			A. Coy on Range. C. Coy. Bayonet fighting. 3. O.R. evacuated sick.	
		14th Mor.	A. C. & D. Coys open weather parties, positions, fire & movement with Lewis gun "watching out" to Stokes Mortars, fire & movement.	
			G. Skirmishing, supports. B Coy at School of O. C. Company.	
		15th cont.	Battalion paraded as strong as possible for Divisional field day at 9-30 a.m. Battalion acted as Enemy towards the Bde in above attack in the village of RANSART. Field Marshal Sir Douglas Haig watched the operations. Battalion marched to billets about 5.45 p.m. 2 O.R. evacuated sick. G.O.C. thought it to establishment of XVIII Corps School.	
		16th cont.	Company at the School of O.C. Companies for Lectures & scheme etc.	
		17th cont.	Preparing for move. Battalion paraded at 1-15 p.m. & marched to BOISLEUX-AU-MONT (8 miles). Entrained at BOISLEUX Station leaving at 7-15 p.m. Disembarked at PERONNE about 2 a.m. on	

Army Form C. 2118.

WAR DIARY
or
INTELLIGENCE SUMMARY.
(Erase heading not required.)

Instructions regarding War Diaries and Intelligence Summaries are contained in F. S. Regs., Part II. and the Staff Manual respectively. Title pages will be prepared in manuscript.

Place	Date	Hour	Summary of Events and Information	Remarks and references to Appendices
HAUT ALLAINES	17th		Brigade marched thence the units at village of HAUT ALLAINES. Distance about 8 miles.	
	18th Sept.		Preparing to move. Battalion marched at 6.30 A.M. & marched to FINS (distance 15 kilos) arriving about 2 P.M. and bivouacked in huts in DESSART WOOD.	
DESSART WOOD	19th Sept.		Battalion known properly for the line. Battle Stores & Kits issued. Battalion paraded at 1.30 A.M. 19/20 Sept. – Fighting Order with packs.	
"	20th 20th		Battalion left DESSART WOOD about 2 A.M. & marched to GOUZEAUCOURT, Brigade Assembly Point. At 6-20 A.M. (ZERO HOUR) the barrage opened & the Battalion advanced through VILLERS PLOUICH to take part in a general attack on the BLUE, BROWN, & RED LINES by the 12th, 20th, 6th, & 29th Divisions. About 9 A.M. a message was received that the 1st & 2nd Objectives had been taken & the Battalion was ordered to advance to MARCOING which was its objective. The Battalion advanced in Artillery Quarter Column being preceded by Tanks, a very little opposition was met with except at The Railway Bridge beyond MARCOING where several M.G's had to be put out of action before the	

245
Army Form C. 2118.

WAR DIARY
INTELLIGENCE SUMMARY.
(Erase heading not required.)

Place	Date	Hour	Summary of Events and Information	Remarks and references to Appendices
	20th Nov. (continued)		Bridge sends its escort. A & D Coys. in support "mopped-up" the Village. C Coy went through over the Railway Bridge & B Coy. captured the canal lock on the left of the Village. B & C Coys then formed a Bridgehead across the front of MARCOING. Part of the 1/Bn. R.I. Regt. then advanced through the Battalion to capture FLOT FARM at the 3rd Objective but they were not supported by the 1st Cav. Division Squadrons on the Right & had to retire. One squadron of the 5th Dragoon Guards arrived on the scene but did not take any part in the action. Casualties:- 2/Capt. H.G. WILLOCK wounded. O.R. killed 3, wounded 23.	
MARCOING (line)	21/08 Nov.		In conjunction with the 2/5 W. Ridg & 7/The Yorks Shire Battalion was ordered to attack & capture the RED LINE from G.7.c. to G.14.c. At 11am the Battalion was drawn up in two lines — Front Line, C & D Coys with C Coy on the left. Support Line — B & A Coys with B Coy on the left. The attack did not commence at 11 a.m. firstly because the Tanks were not ready to move & secondly the 2/6 W. Ro. rushed on ahead. The advance & engage some M.G.'s known to be in the house at about G.20.b.6.7. Finally the Tanks got into position & advanced on the first system of the RED LINE. They were immediately met with very	

Army Form C. 2118.

216

WAR DIARY
INTELLIGENCE SUMMARY.
(Erase heading not required.)

Instructions regarding War Diaries and Intelligence Summaries are contained in F. S. Regs., Part II. and the Staff Manual respectively. Title pages will be prepared in manuscript.

Place	Date	Hour	Summary of Events and Information	Remarks and references to Appendices
	21st Nov. (Continued)		Heavy M.G. fire. The Tanks got on to the first system of trenches & as far as the enemy were over to run back into the wood. Meanwhile the front line had advanced about 40 yds. The Tanks proceeded on to the 2nd system of the RED LINE & immediately the enemy again opened very heavy M.G. fire from his original front line & from the slopes of the hill 6.7.6. & 6.8.c. which directly held up the advance of the front line & from this point onward it was quite impossible to advance a yard without every gun fire from enemy M.Gs in front & on the right. the first three of night being exceedingly effective. At 6 p.m. the Battn. received orders to reassume their original positions & consolidate them. The night was spent in making a extensive line around the Bridge Head. About 50 prisoners taken.	
			Casualties – 2/Lieuts A.H. CURRIE & J.C. HOWIE wounded. O.R. Killed 2 – Wounded 55	
MARCOING 22nd (Ser.)			Consolidation of position continued. Trench journal of with that of 10th Br. R. Regt. on the left. Communication Trench dug. "C" Coy dug Strong Point. Casualties – 2/Capt. N.C. WILLOCK died of wounds. 1 O.R. died of wounds. 3 wounded.	
MARCOING 23rd (Ser.)			Strengthening Trench. Some enemy artillery activity. 1 O.R. to U.K. for Tank Commission. Casualties – 2 O.R. Killed – 4 Wounded – 2 sick of wounds.	

Army Form C. 2118.

WAR DIARY
or
INTELLIGENCE SUMMARY.
(Erase heading not required.)

Instructions regarding War Diaries and Intelligence Summaries are contained in F. S. Regs., Part II. and the Staff Manual respectively. Title pages will be prepared in manuscript.

Place	Date	Hour	Summary of Events and Information	Remarks and references to Appendices
MARCOING (Line)	24th		Battalion moved out to the Right & took over the Right Sector of the Brigade front from 2/S.W.Bo. Eng. fire trench. Casualties - 2 O.R. killed, 3 Wounded, 1 Missing.	
MARCOING (Line)	25th & 26th November		Still in MASNIERES Sector, front of position extensively wired. Casualties, 25th - 20 O.R. Wounded; 26th - 10 O.R. killed, 4 Wounded.	
MARCOING	27th Nov.		Relieved by 2/Herts Regt. & went into Reserve in MARCOING VILLAGE no recruits attacking Battalion of the 67th Bde. Casualties - 10 O.R. killed, 2 Wounded, 2 Sick Evacuated.	
"	28th & 29th November		Resting. Enemy bombardment with gas shells. Casualties - 28th, 4 O.R. Sick Evacuated. 29th 2 O.R. Wounded, 3 Sick Evacuated.	
MARCOING	30th Nov.		At 9 a.m. a message was received from Bde. H.Q. that the enemy had attacked heavily on our Right & broken through part of the line held by the 20th Division, & that this Division was at that moment retiring over the field on our Right. The Battn. was ordered to take up a position forming a defensive flank on the Right of the Division with the left of the Battalion resting on the road South of MARCOING COPSE. Orders were at once issued to Coys.	

WAR DIARY
or
INTELLIGENCE SUMMARY.
(Erase heading not required.)

Army Form C. 2118.

Place	Date	Hour	Summary of Events and Information	Remarks and references to Appendices
	30th Nov. (Continued)		a Battalion H.Q. proceeded in advance to reconnoitre the new position on approaching the cross at the Chapel of the Virgin figures were seen on the hill in front & immediately rifle & M.G. fire was opened on the H.Q. party. It was obvious that the enemy were in possession of the ground which was to have been occupied by the Battn. As it was impossible to proceed further along the edge of MARCOING-COPSE, Battn. H.Q. worked further south & up a sunken Road (running through L.26.c.3.0) which it was found possible to organise the Battalion for a counter-attack. The remainder of the position of "A" Coy & "B" Coy were placed in position & at about 11 a.m. these Coys attacked the enemy who were advancing round the Right of MARCOING, & drove them back some 600 yards, enabling the Battalion to occupy a line running from L.35.a.a.3 to L.35.a.a.7 by midday. At 12.30 p.m. the Battalion was reinforced by 2 Coys of The Worcestershire Regt. of the 88th Bde. Touch was obtained with the 20th Division on the Right by 2.30 p.m. & thus a advance & practically continuous line was established on the Right Flank of the 29th Division. This was consolidated	

Army Form C. 2118.

WAR DIARY
INTELLIGENCE SUMMARY.
(Erase heading not required.)

Place	Date	Hour	Summary of Events and Information	Remarks and references to Appendices
	3/4 9pm		as am no much fell. Casualties - Killed, Lieut. F.G. CARSON, Lieut. W.R.D. MEIKLE. 11 CR. Wounded, Major J. WATT M.C. (slightly), 9/Capt. E. GILES, 9/Lieut. G.Y. MENAT, Lieut. R. McDONALD (not duty), 79 C.R. Missing, 9/Lieut. R. MILROY, 40 CR.	

W. Agen Capt
A/adjt. 1/K.O.S. Borderers

Confidential

War Diary

of

1st Battalion King's Own Scottish Borderers

From 1st December 1917.   To. 31st December 1917

Folio 41.

Army Form C. 2118.

WAR DIARY
INTELLIGENCE SUMMARY.

December 1917

(Erase heading not required.)

Instructions regarding War Diaries and Intelligence Summaries are contained in F. S. Regs., Part II. and the Staff Manual respectively. Title pages will be prepared in manuscript.

Place	Date	Hour	Summary of Events and Information	Remarks and references to Appendices
Line (MARCHING)	1st to 5th December		Battalion holding defensive line on Right Flank of Division. On night of 5th/6th orders were received to withdraw to the main HINDENBURG Support line in front of which a protective line of Outposts was to be dug. The withdrawal was effected without casualties & when the move was completed the Battalion was relieved by the 2/R. Irish Rifles (36th Division)	
	6th Dec.		On relief Battalion marched through RIBECOURT & FINS to ETRICOURT & entrained there at 12 midnight. Casualties from 1st to 6th = 1st O.R. 1 killed. 16 Wounded. 2nd. O.R. 6 Wounded. 3rd. O.R. 6 killed. 8 Wounded. 4th. OR 1 killed. 5th. N.K. 6th. N.K. Battalion detrained at MONDICOURT & marched to Billets at BEAUDRICOURT arriving about 7 p.m. Casualties - 2/Lieut. A.G.D. JOHNSTON to U.K. sick 20/11/17.	
BEAUDRICOURT	7th Dec.			
	8th Dec.		Settling into Billets. Cleaning up, refitting & reorganising. Motor Parade.	
"	9th Dec.		Battalion attended Divine Service. Casualties - Nil.	
"	10th Dec.		Battalion Training. Platoon & Ceremonial Drill. Draft of 35 O.R. arrived.	

Army Form C. 2118.

WAR DIARY
INTELLIGENCE SUMMARY.
(Erase heading not required.)

Place	Date	Hour	Summary of Events and Information	Remarks and references to Appendices
BEAUCOURT.	10th December		Platoon Drill & Specialist Training. 2 O.R. sick Evacuated.	
"	12th December		A & B Coys on the Range. Company Drill & Marching Drill & Specialist training. Instruction to Company Officers in working Vickers M.G. by M.G. Officers. 2 O.R. sick Evacuated. Draft of 5 O.R. arrived.	
"	13th December		C & D Coys on the Range. Company Drill & Specialist training. Saluting Drill. 6 O.R. sick Evacuated.	
"	14th December		All Coys on the Range. Company Drill & bath. on Marching Order. Battalion inspected by G.O.C. Division. 6 O.R. sick Evacuated.	
"	15th December		Strenuous Drill by Companys. Inspection of Billets by Commanding Officer. 3 O.R. sick Evacuated. Following Officers joined for duty:- Lieut. K.M. SANDISON. Lieut. G.H.H. BELL, 2nd Lieuts. D.C.B. SMITH, F. MARTIN, F.E. LAWSON, T.E.S. PASLEY, A. FROST, G.E. DOUGHTY & E.C.L. CROFT.	

Army Form C. 2118.

WAR DIARY
or
INTELLIGENCE SUMMARY.

(Erase heading not required.)

Place	Date	Hour	Summary of Events and Information	Remarks and references to Appendices
BEAUDRICOURT	16th Dec.		Divine Service. Casualties NIL.	
"	17th Dec.		Battalion paraded in fighting order at 10-30 a.m. & marched to FILLIEVRES. A heavy overnight snowfall made marching difficult. Arrived at FILLIEVRES (distance 12½ miles) at 4-30 p.m. Billeted by 5 p.m. O.C.R. billet requisitioned.	
FILLIEVRES	18th Dec.		Battalion paraded at 9-30 a.m. (fighting order) & marched to WAMBERCOURT CAYRON ST. MARTIN, a distance of 12 miles. Snow very deep in parts and marching heavy. Arrived 2-30 p.m. & settled in billets by 3 p.m. Casualties - 9 Lieut. G.R. LAMB to F.A.	
WAMBERCOURT	19th Dec.		Battalion paraded in fighting order at 11 a.m. & marched to HERLY via N stowe. a 10.3 miles. Road trying march, hilly country & road drifted impassable in many parts by snowdrifts. Arrived about 3-30 p.m. In Billets about 3-50 p.m. Casualties – NIL.	
HERLY	20th Dec.		Battalion cleaning up & reorganising. Casualties – NIL.	

Army Form C. 2118.

WAR DIARY
or
INTELLIGENCE SUMMARY.
(Erase heading not required.)

Instructions regarding War Diaries and Intelligence
Summaries are contained in F. S. Regs., Part II.
and the Staff Manual respectively. Title pages
will be prepared in manuscript.

Place	Date	Hour	Summary of Events and Information	Remarks and references to Appendices
HERLY	21st December		Company Inspection. Platoon Drill & Handling of Arms. Ceremonial Drill. Casualties – 1 O.R. injured accidentally. Draft of 111 O.R. arrived.	
"	22nd December		Companies at disposal of O.C. Companies. Inspection of C & D Coys. Billets by Commanding Officer. Casualties – Sick Evacuated 11 O.R.	
"	23rd December		Divine Service. 2.O.2. Sick Evacuated. 2 O.R. attend I.B. refresher courses.	
"	24th December		Company & Ceremonial Drill. March to Trench & Counter-attack. Musketry & Range Practice. 2 O.R. Sick evacuated.	
"	25th December		Christmas Day – Holiday. Voluntary Church Services. Impromptu Parade for meal & speech by Lt. General Hunter Weston, Commanding VIII Corps, which consisted the	
"	26th December		March to Trench & Counter-attack. Platoon & Ceremonial Drill. Gas Drill. Specialist training & open Warfare. Musketry. Casualties nil.	

Army Form C. 2118.

WAR DIARY
or
INTELLIGENCE SUMMARY.

(Erase heading not required.)

Instructions regarding War Diaries and Intelligence Summaries are contained in F.S. Regs., Part II. and the Staff Manual respectively. Title pages will be prepared in manuscript.

Place	Date	Hour	Summary of Events and Information	Remarks and references to Appendices
HERLY	27th December		Heavy enemy air onslaught. Battalion chiefly made of prisoners the majority of villages & the attack.	
"	28th December		Lunch to Front Attack. Musketry & Specialist training. "A" Company continued work of clearing roads of snow. Enemailles N.F.	
"	29th December		Battalion working on roads. Orders for move received. Lieut. J.W. REES to the Base for dispersal on night. Draft of 60 Other Ranks arrived.	
"	30th December		Move postponed for 24 hours. Work on roads continued. Major J.H. HULSE 17th Lancers attached 10th O.K. Regt, expired from Senior Officers Course at Aldershot.	
"	31st December		Battalion paraded at 10 a.m. & marched to ASSINGHEM, via Pihem, Fauquembergues-Wicquin. Battalion in billets at ASSINGHEM about 3-45 p.m.	

Dictated by C Hamlyn Captain
a) Adjutant 1/K.O.S.B.

WAR DIARY
or
INTELLIGENCE SUMMARY.
(Erase heading not required.)

Army Form C. 2118.

1 K O S B

Vol 25

JANUARY 1918

Place	Date	Hour	Summary of Events and Information	Remarks and references to Appendices
HAZEBROUCK	1st		Bath for whole Bat. 9.15 a.m. to whole to HAZEBROUCK	HAZEBROUCK map
			Hygienic Cinema for troops. Band went with m.m. Light Infantry	
			returned to B.E. billets 2nd-1217.	
LE NIEPPE	2nd		Battalion hospital at 11 a.m. & marched to RIETVELD via	
			ZUIDPEENE. Numbers cleared. Arriving about 2 p.m. Conditions...	
RIETVELD	3rd	9am	Battalion hospital at 9-30 a.m. & marched to BOLLEZEELE arr.	
			6.30 pm EN ROUTE are ZUIDPEENE. LEDZEELE WATTEN...	
			at 2.30 p.m. Battalion into bivouac into Conditions N.R.	
BOLLEZEELE	4th		Settling into billets & cleaning up. Conference everything...	
			...BOLLEZEELE to...	
			Battalion.	
PROVEN	5th	5H.	Bn marched to 550 M.R. th. this Battalion marched at 8 a.m. & marched to	
Camp	Jan		PROVEN entraining there for 80E sidings. Remainder of Battalion...	

Army Form C. 2118.

WAR DIARY
or
INTELLIGENCE SUMMARY.
(Erase heading not required.)

Place	Date	Hour	Summary of Events and Information	Remarks and references to Appendices
CANAL BANK (BOESINGHE)	6th Jan.		Heavily bombarded during the Battalion in huts on the Canal Bank. Major BIESINGER Inspected & O. Mr Hove at EILHOEK Battalion to be employed providing Fatigue Parties for construction of dugouts & work in Army line. Sustained indir. orders: 250 Eindhoven Leg & 61 West Course Battalion drowned with. 1 O.R. Sick Evacuated.	
"	7th Jan.		450 men working on construction of huts & carrying material. Headquarter personnel engaged in improving interior of existing huts. Draft of 4 O.R. arrived.	
"	8th Jan.		Work as on previous day. 18.2 Slightly Wounded by Shrapnel on Canal Bank. Following Officers arrived :— 2nd Lts. W.F. STEWART, D.A. GLENDINNING, G.K. BROWN, W.C. TAYLOR, A.W. ROBB, & W. Mc. SMITH. 230 men working at huts on Canal Bank. 180 men carrying material forward from CORMORANT DUMP. 2 O.R. Sick Evacuated.	
"	9th Jan.		280 men working at CORMORANT DUMP & 230 on Canal Bank. 1 O.R. Sick Evacuated.	

Army Form C. 2118.

WAR DIARY
or
INTELLIGENCE SUMMARY.
(Erase heading not required.)

257

Instructions regarding War Diaries and Intelligence Summaries are contained in F. S. Regs., Part II. and the Staff Manual respectively. Title pages will be prepared in manuscript.

Place	Date	Hour	Summary of Events and Information	Remarks and references to Appendices
CANAL BANK BOESINGHE	10th July	9am.	Work on for 9th inst. Permanent Wiring Parties at 10th + 18 UR. 1 Coy. 20 UR established at CORMORANT & RUGBY Dumps respectively. *Lieut. C.R. LAMB struck off strength on being invalided over to U.K. Captain W.K. INNES " " " " " on appointment as Staff Captain, 87th Bde. Lieut. R.R. MacBRYAN, 10th/2 U.R. PHQ joined 10.R. sick komentils.	
"	11th July		Work continued. Sanitary Parties of work - HET SAS Loeb, CANAL BANK, J. Canal. RUGBY & CORMORANT Dumps. 1 UR Bttln. U.U.R. Wanted by A.E. Gnd. CORMORANT Dump. 2 U.R. sick komentils. Official intimation received of the following awards :- MILITARY CROSS - Lieut. F. DAKE, Capt. H.J. HARVEY, Lieut. E. GILES, Lieut. H.R. ECHUN, & Lieut. W. BARNARD. D.C.M - 9635 Cpl. S.M. STEVENSON P. 9. 14447 Pte WAITE T "B" Coy. 2 Lights Az. BUGLERS H. C. Coy.	
"	12th July		Work continued on HET SAS Loeb & Canal Bank. Lieut. R. McDONALD, sick on hent to U.K. & struck off strength. 10.R. to U.K. for Lemp. Commission.	

Army Form C. 2118.

WAR DIARY
or
INTELLIGENCE SUMMARY.
(Erase heading not required.)

Instructions regarding War Diaries and Intelligence Summaries are contained in F. S. Regs., Part II. and the Staff Manual respectively. Title pages will be prepared in manuscript.

Place	Date	Hour	Summary of Events and Information	Remarks and references to Appendices
CANAL BANK BOESINGHE	13th July		Work as on previous day. Casualties Nil.	258
"	14th July	"	1 O.R. sick evacuated.	
"	15th July	"	"	
"	"	"	Following O.R. mentioned in Sir Douglas Haig's Despatches of 7th Nov 1917 — 5272 A/Sgt Hemsley J, 1867 Cpl Boling L, 1102 Pte J McCulloch. Craft of 4 O.R. arrived.	
"	16th July		Work as on previous day. Official intimation received of death of: 18044 Pte to M Maple Cpl L.G. M.M — 7466 Pte Gallier G, 22902 Cpl Roberts R, 17440 Pte Crampton G.A, 16522 Pte Morgan J.E, 16584 Cpl Dyson H, 6554 Pte Sanderson W, 28146 Pte Smith H, 27082 A/L/Cpl Cooper H, 28526 Pte Darnell W (4th T.M.B). 2 O.R. sick evacuated.	
"	17th July		Work as on previous day. Casualties Nil.	

Army Form C. 2118.

WAR DIARY
or
INTELLIGENCE SUMMARY.
(Erase heading not required.)

Instructions regarding War Diaries and Intelligence Summaries are contained in F. S. Regs., Part II. and the Staff Manual respectively. Title pages will be prepared in manuscript.

252

Place	Date	Hour	Summary of Events and Information	Remarks and references to Appendices
CANAL BANK BOESINGHE	18th. Jany		Battalion paraded at 10-30 a.m. & marched via ELVERDINGHE, DRONDRE CORNER & DIRTY BUCKET CORNER to RED ROSE Camp, nr Mt BRANDHOEK. Here took over from 2/ Hampshire Regt. In billets at 3 p.m.	Reference Map 28 N.W.
			Remarks Nil	
RED ROSE Camp	19th. Jany		Battalion stood to & settling into billets. Lectures & Gymnastics for all Specialist Training. Letters to Csg. Inf. of 2 Prov. Inf. Bn Somali Reg. Gazette No 14 Nil	
RED ROSE Camp	20th. Jany		Divnl. Service. One of the Battalion inspected. Captain G.M.H. OGILVY, 1/R.O.S.B. reported for duty & took over "D" Coy. vice of Captain A. BROWN. Strafl. at 25 I.R. joined. 2 O.R. Sick evacuated.	
RED ROSE Camp	21st. Jany		Battalion Training. Drill & Gas Drill, Specialist Training. Lectures &c. 1 O.R. Sick evacuated.	
RED ROSE Camp	22nd. Jany		Battalion Parade (Ceremonial) as strong as possible. Specialist Training. Lectures	

Army Form C. 2118.

260

WAR DIARY
INTELLIGENCE SUMMARY.
(Erase heading not required.)

Instructions regarding War Diaries and Intelligence Summaries are contained in F. S. Regs., Part II. and the Staff Manual respectively. Title pages will be prepared in manuscript.

Place	Date	Hour	Summary of Events and Information	Remarks and references to Appendices
RED ROSE CAMP	23rd July		On "Consolidation of Battn." by 2/Major T.H. MUIR, to all Officers. Remainder Nil	
			Elementary Musketry & Drill; Specialist Training; Lewis Gunnery; Gas Helmet for Subaltern Officers; Kit & Hut Inspection by C.O. 10/R.S. Brie unfit	
	24th July		Duties for Brigade General Parade; Specialist Training + Drill. Rigging Practice. 1 O.R. Sick Present.	
	25th July		Brigade General Church Parade for inspection by the C.O.C. 29th Division. Following Officers & O.R. of the Battn. received extd. ribbons:— M.C.:— 2/Capt. H.R. CUFFLEY; Lieut. W. BARNARD M.C. Serjeants! Recognition Cert:— 2/Capt. H.R. CUFFLEY; Lieut. W. BARNARD M.C.; Lieut F. DALE M.C.; 8634 A.S.M. R. STEVENSON D.C.M.; 18162 R.S.I. WAITE D.C.M.; 18646 E/C. J.F. CAPE M.M. (with bar); 27363 Cpl. MCCREANOR M.M.; 28655 Sjt. QUINN J (Bars); 11110 Oz. MCCULLOCH R (Bars); 17870 Cpl. JOHNSTON E (Bars); 40423 L/C. WALLOCH (Bars); 22706 Pte. DAVIDSON (Bars); 20144 Pte. CAMPBELL (Bars); 41091 Pte. HERRIOT (M.M.). 2 O.R. Sick Present.	

Army Form C. 2118.

WAR DIARY
or
INTELLIGENCE SUMMARY.
(Erase heading not required.)

Place	Date	Hour	Summary of Events and Information	Remarks and references to Appendices
				25/1 Reference Map 26 N.W.
RED ROSE Camp	26th Jany		Battalion paraded & marched to BRANDHOEK Light Railway Siding & Coy. leaving Camp at 1.30 p.m. Battalion entrained about 2.40 pm for WIELTJE. Entrained WIELTJE about 4.30 A.M. & marched to ENGLISH Camp, taking over from the 2/Hampshire Regt. Battalion in billets by 5 p.m. 2 O.R. wounded.	
ENGLISH Camp	27th Jany		Battalion working on Divisional Defence Line. Permanent party of 33 O.R. working at WIELTJE Dug-outs, Battalion parties at work erecting NISSEN huts in the Camp. 3 O.R. Sick Evacuated.	
"	28th Jany		Battalion working on Divisional Defence Line. Permanent party of 14 N.C.Os & Men sent for work under "A" Works Company at SALVATION Corner. 2 O.R. Sick Evacuated.	
"	29th Jany		Battalion working on Divisional Defence Line. 2 O.R. Sick Evacuated.	
"	30th Jany		Proceed to INDIA as Instructor & struck off strength	" 7.20 hrs Sgt. R.M.E. selected to "

Army Form C. 2118.

WAR DIARY
or
INTELLIGENCE SUMMARY.

(Erase heading not required.)

Place	Date	Hour	Summary of Events and Information	Remarks and references to Appendices
	3/3/17		Battn. working on trenches above the C.R.S. [illegible] in of [illegible]	
			[illegible] Point NEW [illegible] 33 S.R. arrived.	

O.H. [illegible signature]

1 KOSB 263

Army Form C. 2118.

WAR DIARY
of
FEBRUARY 1916 INTELLIGENCE SUMMARY.
(Erase heading not required.)

Place	Date	Hour	Summary of Events and Information	Remarks and references to Appendices
ENGLISH FM 109.	1st February		Battalion working on Divisional Defence Line. Casualties Nil.	
"	2nd February		" " " " " 2 O.R. Sick evacuated.	
"	3rd February		Battalion preparing for the Line. Battalion paraded about 3 a.m. & marched to Goof by 5 a.m. Relieved 4/Worcester Regt (Left Battalion) as under:-	
			"A" Coy - Right Front Line Posts from V.29.d.9.5. to V.23.d.0.2.	
			"B" " - Centre " V.23.d.0.2 " V.29.a.20.5	
			"C" " - Left " V.29.a.20.5 " V.28.b.30.1.	
			"D" " - In support at Pillboxes at V.28.c.5.1 (2 Platoons & by H.Q) & 1 Platoon at INCH Havors.	
			Battalion H.Q at Pillbox 83. Relief complete 10 a.m. Casualties Nil. Details marched to dute in BRAKE Camp.	
Firing Line	4th Feb		A. B+ C. Coys. at work priming up Posts. Deepening trenches & laying duckboards. German aircraft shot down near Battn. H.Q. O.R. wounded.	

Army Form C. 2118.

26A

WAR DIARY
~~INTELLIGENCE SUMMARY.~~
(Erase heading not required.)

Instructions regarding War Diaries and Intelligence Summaries are contained in F. S. Regs., Part II. and the Staff Manual respectively. Title pages will be prepared in manuscript.

Place	Date	Hour	Summary of Events and Information	Remarks and references to Appendices
Living line	5th February		Work same as on previous day. Practically no shell fire but German M.Gs firing occasionally at night. Reconnoitring Patrols sent out by A, B, & C Coys (1 each). 2 O.R. killed.	
"	6th February		Work on linking up Posts resulting in continued. Little activity on this side. "A" Coy sent out an offensive patrol. 3 O.R. wounded. Lieut. J. OLIPHANT M.C. to England for 6 months tour of duty. Struck off strength.	
"	7th February		Work as on previous day. Artillery normal. "B" Coy sent out an offensive patrol. 1 O.R. wounded.	
"	8th February		Work continued. Activity normal. "C" Coy sent out an Offensive Patrol. 1 O.R. killed. 1 O.R. wounded.	
"	9th February		Work as on previous day. Battalion relieved by 1st Border Regt. (D Coy by 1 Coy of 2/S.W.Borders). Relief completed without casualty at 4 a.m. on 10th February. Battalion entrained at MERTTE Siding & detrained at	

(A893) D.U.&L.,London,E.C. Wt W30/M1677 53,000 4/17 Sch. 32a Forms/C/2118/14

WAR DIARY
INTELLIGENCE SUMMARY.
(Erase heading not required.)

Army Form C. 2118.

265

Place	Date	Hour	Summary of Events and Information	Remarks and references to Appendices
				Reference Map Sheet 27.
"B" Area (WATOU)	10th February		ABEELE, marching to Billets in "B" Area (WATOU Sector). Rain bty of Battalion in Billets about 7 a.m. Billets consisted mainly of isolated farmhouses scattered over a wide area. 2 O.R. Sick Evacuated.	
"	11th February		Settling into Billets. Resting. 1 O.R. Sick Evacuated.	
"	12th February		P.T. & Recreational Training. Reorganisation & general cleaning up. Inspection. 1 O.R. Sick Evacuated.	
"	13th February		P.T. & Recreational Training. Reorganisation, Inspections etc. Casualties NIL.	
"			Parades & work as detailed at Coy Commanders Conference. Baths. 4 O.R. arrived.	

Army Form C. 2118.

266/

WAR DIARY
or
INTELLIGENCE SUMMARY.
(Erase heading not required.)

Place	Date	Hour	Summary of Events and Information	Remarks and references to Appendices
"B" Coy (WATOU)	14th February		P.T. & Recreational Training. Musketry & Drill. Baths.	
			Notification received of the following awards:- Belgian CROIX de GUERRE. Lieut. Colonel C.A.C.O. MURRAY; 10303 Sgt. McCANNON J. D.C.M; 19216 L/C. CHITTENDEN W. D.C.M.; 19123 Pte. McKNIGHT J. D.C.M; - MILITARY MEDAL:- 20194 Pte. CAMPBELL R.; 18494 2/Cpl. HANDLEY J. 1 O.R. reported Sick.	
"	15th February		Ordinary Instructions. Platoon & Saluting Drill. Musketry. Wiring. 6 O.R. Sick Evacuated. Lieut. J.H. MAXWELL to U.K. for 6 months tour of duty.	
"	16th February		Platoon Close & Open order Drill. Saluting Drill. Musketry. Range Firing. Wiring. Bayonet fighting. Specialist Training. Draft of 34 O.R. arrived. 4 O.R. Sick Evacuated.	
"	17th February		General Parade as strong as possible followed by Parade Divine Service. 2 O.R. Sick Evacuated.	

Army Form C. 2118.

WAR DIARY
INTELLIGENCE SUMMARY.
(Erase heading not required.)

Place	Date	Hour	Summary of Events and Information	Remarks and references to Appendices
"B" Coy (WATOU)	18th February		Company Extended Order & Saluting Drill. Musketry & Wiring Lecture by G.O.C. 29th Division in Cinema Hall, STEENVOORDE. 60 Officers & N.C.O's attended. Inspection of his subaltern. 3 O.R. Sick evacuated.	
"	19th February		Parades & Training same as on previous day. M.O's Lecture to 'A' Coy. 5 O.R. Sick evacuated. 1 O.R. rejoined Bn.	
"	20th February		Brigade Manoeuvre Parade. Battalion paraded at 9 a.m. 2 O.R. Sick evacuated.	
"	21st February		Practice for Brigade Ceremonial Parade for Presentation of medals by G.O.C. 29th Division. Casualties Nil.	
"	22nd February		Brigade Ceremonial Parade & Presentation of medals & ribbons by G.O.C. 29th Division. Lieut Genl Sir Aylmer Hunter-Weston K.C.B, D.S.O, was present. 2 O.R. Sick evacuated.	

WAR DIARY
or
INTELLIGENCE SUMMARY.

Army Form C. 2118.

26/

Remarks and references to Appendices: Sheets 27 & 28 N.W.

Place	Date	Hour	Summary of Events and Information
"B" Camp (WATOU)	23rd February		Divisional Field Day. Battalion paraded at 5 am Proceeding Worth at
		8 am	Battalion had billets. Men mess celebrations in the evening. N° of church dinner are provided & each Company styped a concert. 15 O.R. evacuated sick. Rev. D. LAMONT, Chaplain to ENGLAND.
"	24th February		Sunday. Voluntary C. of E. Service. 5 O.R. to Base as medically unfit. 5 O.R. to 226 Employment Coy. temporarily unfit. 6 O.R. sick evacuated.
"	25th February		Companies at disposal of O.C. Companies. Battn Training School allotted to A & B Coys. Captain G.H.M. OGILVY struck off strength to U.K. sick 16/2/18. 6 O.R. sick evacuated.
"	26th February		Battalion preparing to move. Battalion paraded at 10.30 a.m. a marched to main road POPERINGHE by the STEENVOORDE - POPERINGHE Battalion in Billets in the "KLOISTERS" Rue de Michel at 12.10. 8 O.R. sick evacuated. 3 O.R. to 67th I.W. Coy.
POPERINGHE	27th February		Battalion employed working under R.E. on Army Zone Defences thro' Corps

269
Army Form C. 2118.

WAR DIARY
or
INTELLIGENCE SUMMARY.
(Erase heading not required.)

Place	Date	Hour	Summary of Events and Information	Remarks and references to Appendices
POPERINGHE	28th Feb.		at work & on in Billets daily. Left POPERINGHE huts at 7.30 am for train entraining at WIELTJE Siding & then marching to Westoutre. Brought back by train leaving WIELTJE siding at 3.45 pm. Returned on return 2 O.R. injured from hospital.	
			West on Army Foot trip. 2 H.R. sick remitted	

Dictated by Captain
Offrancher
a.a.g. 1st S.L.B.

1st KOSB 27/
Army Form C. 2118.

WAR DIARY
or
INTELLIGENCE SUMMARY.
(Erase heading not required.)

MARCH 1918

Place	Date	Hour	Summary of Events and Information	Remarks and references to Appendices
PIPERINGHE	1st March		A, B & C Coys working on Army line. D Coy in Billets & Bathing	Sheet 28 N.W.
"	2nd March		B & D Coys working on Army line. A Coy in Billets & Bathing	
			2/Lt. ... Sick	
"	3rd March		A, C & D Coys working on Army line. B Coy in Billets & Bathing	
			20R rejoined unit & 10R to Hotel	
"	4th March		A, B, D Coys working on Army line. C Coy on Billets — Inspection of the Bn.	
			2/Lieut. N.E.N. HENDERSON & servant transferred to 87th T.M.B. 20R rejoined Bch & 10R wounded	
"	5th March		Battalion entrained at POPERINGHE Station at 12 noon, detraining at WESTRE Siding at 1 pm. A, C, D Coys accommodated in CALIFORNIA Camp. & B Coy H.Q. in ENGLISH Farm Camp. 30R sick evacuated. 10R rejoined from R.E.	
ENGLISH Fm. CALIFORNIA Camp	6th March		Battalion preparing for the line. Battalion marched off at 5pm via Inch 6.	

Army Form C. 2118.

WAR DIARY
or
INTELLIGENCE SUMMARY.
(Erase heading not required.)

Ref Map Special C2.1/10000

Place	Date	Hour	Summary of Events and Information	Remarks and references to Appendices
Firing Line	7th March		Battalion took over Firing Line from 2/NORTHANTS & 2/EAST LANCS (8th Division). Disposition of Coys:- D Coy Right; B Coy Centre; C Coy Left; A Coy Right Support. B.H.Q. Two Companies of 2/S.W.Borderers attached to Battalion, one Coy in Support & the other in Reserve. Relief completed without casualty at 10-30 p.m. 1 O.R. transferred to 226th Employment Coy.	P14.807 83
"	8th March		Quiet, little activity on either side. Work on connecting up of posts continued. Wiring Each Coy sent out an Officers Patrol of 1 Officer & 10 O.R. with the object of securing a prisoner but without success. 3 O.R. wounded, M.G. fire. Activity normal. "B" Coy. H.Q. dugout blown in. Stench & Patrols as on 7th inst. 3 O.R. shell shock.	
"	9th March		Battalion H.Q. heavily shelled between 2 p.m. & 2-30 p.m. by high velocity gun. Tracks swept by M.G. fire at intervals. Battalion relieved. Right 2 Coys relieved by 2/S.W. Borderers & Left 2 Coys	

Army Form C. 2118.

WAR DIARY
or
INTELLIGENCE SUMMARY.
(Erase heading not required.)

Place	Date	Hour	Summary of Events and Information	Remarks and references to Appendices
				Ref map - Special C.2. N/10000
			hy 11 Cndn. Regt. Relief completed without casualty to Battn. at 11pm. Battalion marched back to Billets in JUNCTION Camp (St JEAN). 2 O.R. wounded. M.G. fire. H.U.R sick evacuated. 4 Captain A. BROWN & Lieut D. ARMSTRONG to U.K. for 6 months tour of duty	
JUNCTION CAMP	10th March		Battalion resting & cleaning up. 5 O.R. sick evac. 1 man to Base unfit. Lorries transferred to 29th Div. Signal Coy.	
"	11th March		Battalion working on the Divisional Line. 3 O.R evacuated Sick. 1 O.R. returned from F.M. Bty.	
"	12th March		Preparing for the Line. Battalion heavily shelled about 5 p.m. Lorries out. Right Sub-sector of Zyft Bde. from 2/8 St Broderick. Disposition — A & C. Coys in firing line, B & D in support. H.Q. at BELLEVUE. Relief completed without casualty at 11-45 p.m. S.O.S calls sent up on our Right about 12-55 a.m. 3 O.R. wounded.	
ZUYDCOOTE Trench H.Q	13th March		"Broodseinde" by 9pr shells from 12 a.m. to 10-45 a.m. Quiet on front	

WAR DIARY
INTELLIGENCE SUMMARY

Army Form C. 2118.

273

Place	Date	Hour	Summary of Events and Information	Remarks and references to Appendices
			line. 3/O.R. wounded. 2/O.R. sick evacuated. Lieut. H.C. ROOKE, 3/15 O.S.B. wounded (gas).	
Firing Line Trench	14th		H.Q. changed from BELLEVUE to PUCHARY further forward. New H.Q. especially good. MUIR LODGE after 2 or 3 or. in forward position in improvement on H.Q. making shelters etc. 10 O.R. wounded. 1 O.R. sick evacuated. 1 O.R. Trans. to XVIII Corps H.Q. 1 O.R. gunner sick	
"	15th	Noon	Practically no activity on either side. 3 O.R. wounded (accidental).	
"	16th	inst.	Companies changed over, B&D to firing line & A&C to support line. 2 O.R. wounded.	
"	17th	inst.	C.S.M. SKINNER V.C., D.C.M., killed by sniper. 1 O.R. killed & 1 O.R. wounded by sniper. 2 O.R. wounded (gas). 2/Lieut. R.J. SANDEMAN 1/2nd G wounded (gas).	

Army Form C. 2118.

274

WAR DIARY
or
INTELLIGENCE SUMMARY.

(Erase heading not required.)

Place	Date	Hour	Summary of Events and Information	Remarks and references to Appendices
	1917			
Firing Line Trench	18th March		Battalion relieved by 1st Border Regt. Relief complete by 11-30 p.m. "D" Coy heavily shelled coming out. 3 O.R. killed, 5 O.R. wounded. 10 O.R. sick evacuated. 1 O.R. rejoined sick. 2/Lieut. F.W. VEES, 3/R.O.L.B provided to join Machine Gun Centre, GRANTHAM.	
HASLER Camp	19th March		Battalion resting & cleaning up. Funeral of late C.S.M. SKINNER, V.C., D.C.M. in the afternoon to VLAMERTINGHE Cemetery. Camp heavily shelled during day & in the evening, with H.E. & shrapnel. 4 O.R. wounded. 4 U.R. Sick evacuated.	
"	20th March		Battalion working forward on Bn. Support line. Camp again shelled. 1 O.R. wounded.	
"	21st March		Battalion working forward as on previous day. Camp shelled. Direct hit on one of H.Q huts. 1 O.R. killed & 2 O.R. wounded returning from work. Lieut. W. BARNARD M.C., 3/R.O.L.B to England for 6 mths Tour of	

275

Army Form C. 2118.

WAR DIARY
INTELLIGENCE SUMMARY
(Erase heading not required.)

Place	Date	Hour	Summary of Events and Information	Remarks and references to Appendices
HASLER Camp	22nd March		Duty. 5 O.R. train to 29th M.S. Coys. Battalion entrained at WIEITZE at 1pm & detrained at BRANDHOEK at 2.15 pm & marching thence to Billets in "B" Camp, BRANDHOEK.	
"B" Camp BRANDHOEK	23rd March		2 O.R. sick evacuated. Battalion refitting.	
"	24th March		Battalion working on the Army Line. Engaged by them casualties Nil.	
"	25th March		Companies at the disposal of O.C. Coys. for reorganisation etc. Battalion working. Nothing to disclose. Draft of 109 O.R. joined from 29th Divisional Wing.	
"	26th March		Battalion working on the Divisional Reserve Line. Casualties Nil.	
"	27th March		B & C Companies working on the Divisional Reserve Line. A & D Coys. at disposal of O.C. Coys. Draft of 22 O.R. joined from 29th	

Army Form C. 2118.

276

WAR DIARY
INTELLIGENCE SUMMARY.
(Erase heading not required.)

(Reference Map C.2 1/10,000) Special

Place	Date	Hour	Summary of Events and Information	Remarks and references to Appendices
"B" Camp BRANDHOEK	28th March		Divisional Wing. Lieut. C.C. ROOKE rejoined from attach.	
			Companies at disposal of O.C. Companies. Inspections etc. Buttos.	
			Companies & H.Q. put through half hours No drill by Bn ho Staff	
	29th March		2/Lieut. D.A. GLENDINNING & servant pro. to 87th T.M.B. 2/Lieut. H.E.H. HENDERSON & servant rejoined from 87th T.M.B.	
			Companies inspected in "Jurisdiction"- B&D by C.O. & A&C by 2nd in Command.	
			Divine Service. Pres. & C.O.E.	
"	30th March		Battalion preparing for the line. Battalion entrained at HASSLE SIDING at	
			7-31 a.m. & detrained at SPREE F.M. Took over Right sector of Firing line	
			from 2/R. Inniskins as follows:- B Coy. from X Coy. in Right Firing Line; C Coy.	
			from Z Coy. Left Firing Line; A Coy. from Y Coy. in Support; & D Coy. from W Coy.	
			in Reserve. Relief complete about 1 a.m.	
			Details in Billets at BRAKE Camp.	
			Draft of 4 O.R. arrived. 3 O.R. rejoined from Hospital.	
Firing Line Trench	31st March		Very quiet on line. Coys. at work improving trench system.	
			2 O.R. wounded.	

87th Brigade.
29th Division.

1st BATTALION

KING'S OWN SCOTTISH BORDERERS

APRIL 1918.

Army Form C. 2118.

WAR DIARY
or
INTELLIGENCE SUMMARY.

APRIL, 1918

Special Map C.2. 1/10000
(PASSCHENDAELE)

Place	Date	Hour	Summary of Events and Information	Remarks and references to Appendices
Firing Line	1st April		Little activity on either side. Work on improvement of line. 1 O.R. returned from hospital.	
"	2nd April		Battalion relieved by 2/S.W. Borderers. Marched back to rest in JUNCTION & CALIFORNIA Camps. H.Q, A, B, & D Coys in JUNCTION & C Coy in CALIFORNIA. 1 O.R. wounded.	
JUNCTION & CALIFORNIA Camps	3rd April		Battalion resting & cleaning up. Battn. sick evacuated. 7 O.R.	
"	4th April		D Coy any working forward on WATERLOO line. A Co D Coys at Inf Drill Platoon Drill & afternoon Bombing Instruction. Inspection of into by Co. Bn Hos. 2Lieut. S.K.BLOUNT, 3/K.O.S.B. struck off strength on being invalided etc. U.K. Lieut. G.K. Smith. 7 O.R. evacuated sick. 1 O.R. returned sick.	
"	5th April		Battalion preparing for the line. Battalion paraded about 7.30 p.m. & marched via PLANK ROAD, WATERLOO & TRACK 5. Taking over the Left Sub-Sector from the 1/Border Regt. in the following order :- D Coy front	

Army Form C. 2118.

WAR DIARY
INTELLIGENCE SUMMARY.
(Erase heading not required.)

Place	Date	Hour	Summary of Events and Information	Remarks and references to Appendices
			A Coy., Border Regt. on Right Flk.; A Coy. from B Coy. in Left Flk.; B Coy. from D Coy. in Support; & C Coy. in E Coy. in Reserve. Battn. H.Q. in BELLEVUE Pillbox. Relief complete about 1-45 a.m. Lieut. R.B. MACBRYAN, 1/KOSB. struck off strength, sent to U.K. 27/3/18	
FIRING LINE	6th April		Little or no activity. Working on improvement of trench system & supply up. R.E. material. 2 O.R. Killed. 2/Lieut. H. LAPSLEY & 6 O.R. wounded.	
"	7th April		Situation normal. Front line companies wiring & Lewis gun posts. 1 O.R. Killed. 2 O.R. wounded.	
"	8th April		Battalion relieved by 26th Royal Fusiliers. Brought by train to POPERINGHE & marched thence to billets in ROAD CAMP ST. JAN TER BIEZEN. Battalion in billets at 9 a.m. 9/4/18. Troops 1/9 AA guard.	
ROAD CAMP	9th April		Battalion under orders to entrain at ROUSBRUGGE on night of 9/10th. 9 Wiltshires	

279

Army Form C. 2118.

WAR DIARY
or
INTELLIGENCE SUMMARY.
(Erase heading not required.)

Instructions regarding War Diaries and Intelligence Summaries are contained in F. S. Regs., Part II. and the Staff Manual respectively. Title pages will be prepared in manuscript.

Place	Date	Hour	Summary of Events and Information	Remarks and references to Appendices
			at TINCQUES. Orders cancelled & Battalion detailed to proceed to NEUF BERQUIN, proceeded by buses leaving junction of WATOU - POPERINSHE & PROVEN - POPERINSHE Roads at 2 a.m. 10/4/18.	
NEUF BERQUIN	10th April		Sich recruits I.O.R. & Pers. unfit G.S.R. Arrived NEUF BERQUIN about 11 a.m. Proceeded on Billets. Rose until 5 P.m. During stay an enemy plane was brought down by D Coy L.G. Team. Battalion moved off shortly after 5 pm to take up position between ESTAIRES & STEENWERCKE where the enemy had broken through. Disposition of Battn :- A, D, B & 2 Platoons of C Coy (from left to right). S.W.96 on left by Battn. 2/Lieut. J. MAITLAND, 2K.O.S.B. & 10 O.R. joined.	
FIRING LINE	11th April		The enemy attacked in overwhelming force about 6 a.m. B, C, & D Coys met the attack with A Coy in reserve. The units on the right fell back & B.C. & D Coys more practically surrounded. The remnants of the Companies were compelled to retire & did so fighting stubbornly. During the night A Coy made a total n member of Prisrs. Casualties :- W/Major T.H. MUIR 17th Lancers 2nd in Command; Capt. C.H. CRAWSHAW M.C.	

WAR DIARY
or
INTELLIGENCE SUMMARY.

Army Form C. 2118.

280/

Place	Date	Hour	Summary of Events and Information	Remarks and references to Appendices
			Adjutant: 2/Lieut. W. McB. SMITH; 2/Lieut. J.H. LAWSON; 2/Lieut. S. MORGAN; 2/Lieut T.E.S. PASLEY & 2/Lieut. W.E. STEWART, wounded – Lieut. H.C. ROOKE, 2/Lieut. G.S. DOUGHTY, 2/Lieut. E.L. CROFTS, killed – Captain R.M. SHORTER wounded & missing – 2/Lieut. N.E.N. HENDERSON, 2/Lieut. W.C. TAYLOR, 2/Lieut. U.A. BOND & 2/Lieut. A.W. ROBB, missing. Other Ranks – KILLED 17; WOUNDED 207; MISSING 249.	
FIRING LINE	12th Mid.		Conforming to the retirement "A" Coy left their posts about 2-30 a.m. Reported at 87th Bn. H.Q., & then took up a position which they were called to evacuate shortly afterwards on account of the heavy shell fire. Asked back to dig a support line behind the 86th Bde. Casualties – Lieut. G.G. THWAITES, 2/Lieut. A.E. CAMPBELL, & 2/Lieut. W.E. STEWART wounded.	
"	13th		The line was further withdrawn & eventually "A" Coy got to BORR.E & they stayed overnight. Lieut. J.J. PARSONS M.O.R.C. Medical Officer wounded. Lieut. G.S. LOVE M.O.R.C. joined for duty.	

Army Form C. 2118.

281

WAR DIARY
or
INTELLIGENCE SUMMARY.
(Erase heading not required.)

Instructions regarding War Diaries and Intelligence Summaries are contained in F. S. Regs., Part II. and the Staff Manual respectively. Title pages will be prepared in manuscript.

Place	Date	Hour	Summary of Events and Information	Remarks and references to Appendices
BORRE	14th April		Battalion marched to billets on the Ebblinghem near SYLVESTRE-CAPPEL.	
			The roll call was answered by 1 Officer + 152 O.R - Officers Major D.C.	
			BULLEN-SMITH O.C A Coy. 10th reinforcements arrived.	
SYLVESTRE-CAPPEL	15th April		Resting & reorganising. Further reinforcements joined from BULL CAMP (ST JUNTIN) attd. M.M.	
BLEZEN			Lieut. D.T. HOLMES reported for duty.	
"	16th April		Remnants of Brigade organised into a composite Battalion under the command of Lieut Colonel C.A.C.O. MURRAY, comdg. 108 K.O.S.B.	
			At 2-30 p.m. Battalion paraded & marched to Billets in BURRE, being in reserve to the 1st Australian Division. Casualties - Nil. Enemy attacked Australians during night but were repulsed.	
BORRE	17th April		About 3-30 a.m. the Battalion moved into support to the 1st Australian Division. Battalion heavily shelled during enemy bombardment commencing at 4 a.m. & moving to house. Battalion dug in. Relived by the Reserve	

Army Form C. 2118.

WAR DIARY
or
INTELLIGENCE SUMMARY.
(Erase heading not required.)

Sheet 27 Belgium & France.

Place	Date	Hour	Summary of Events and Information	Remarks and references to Appendices
			Brigade of the 1st Australian Division & moved back to former billets on farm-houses near SYLVESTRE-CAPPEL. Casualties - Lieut. T.J. GLOVER, 3/K.O.S.B., joined for duty; 2/Capt. H.R. COLLIER M.C. killed, 2/Capt. D.C. BULLEN-SMITH wounded, C.S.M. A. MUIRHEAD & 10 O.R. killed, 12 O.R. wounded.	
SYLVESTRE CAPPEL	18th April		Composite Battalion disbanded. 1/4 K.O.S.B. moved to billets on farm buildings near SYLVESTRE-CAPPEL. Lieut. G.H.H. BELL rejoined from sick; Lieut. G.L. BROWN, M.C. joined for duty. Draft of 61 O.R. joined.	
"	19th April		Resting & reorganizing.	
"	20th April		Party working on 2nd Zone Support Line. Bttn. H.Qrs. & C. & D. Coys joined A. & B. Coys in Billets at LA BREARDE. Captain C.H. CRANSHAW M.C. rejoined from wounds.	
LA BREARDE	21st April		Party working on 2nd Zone Support Line. Remainder of Bttn. reorganizing, cleaning up etc.	

Army Form C. 2118.

WAR DIARY
or
INTELLIGENCE SUMMARY.
(Erase heading not required.)

Instructions regarding War Diaries and Intelligence Summaries are contained in F. S. Regs., Part II. and the Staff Manual respectively. Title pages will be prepared in manuscript.

Place	Date	Hour	Summary of Events and Information	Remarks and references to Appendices
LA BREARDE	23rd April		Furnishing parties for work on 2nd Zone Support Line. Inspection etc.	
"	24th April		2Lieut. A. FROST, 3/K.O.8.B. rect. to U.K. 13/4/18. Draft of 80 O.R. joined 23/4/18. Draft of 5 O.R. joined 23/4/18. I. O.R. to Employment Base depôt 23/4/18.	
"	25th April		Companies at disposal of Coy. Commanders for inspection, musketry etc. Drafts inspected in the afternoon by S.O.C. 87th Bde.	
"	26th April		Four hours training in the morning. Battalion inspected by the C.O. in the afternoon.	
"	27th April		Battalion preparing for the Line. Battalion marched off at 6 p.m. 1nd ordr from 11th EAST YORKS in the Centre Sub-sector. No 2 Coy. in the Firing Line; 2 Platoons of No 1 Coy. in Support & 1 Platoon in Reserve. Relief complete 11.30 p.m.	Firing Line from E.11.c.1.1. to E.16.d.9.4. on attached Map.
FIRING LINE	28th April		Battalion working on improvement of Line — eavesdropping Posts & thickening Parapets. Casualties NIL.	
"	29th April		Working on consolidation of Posts & deepening trench Support Coy. rebuilding shelters; 40 yds. new trench dug connecting Coy. H.Q. with Reserve Trench. 2 O.R. wnd. 25th Tunnelling Coy. R.E.	

283

Army Form C. 2118.

WAR DIARY
or
INTELLIGENCE SUMMARY.
(Erase heading not required.)

Place	Date	Hour	Summary of Events and Information	Remarks and references to Appendices
FIRING LINE	30th April.		3 O.R. Sick Evacuated, 1 O.R. wounded. No. 2 Coy. wiring of Posts 1, 2 & 3. Parapets thickened. No.1 " wiring & deepening of trench. 1 O.R. wounded. 2 O.R. Sick evacuated. Capt. L.M. SANDISON & Lieut. T.J. GLOVER to Base unfit.	

285
1/KOSB

Army Form C. 2118.

WAR DIARY
INTELLIGENCE SUMMARY
MAY, 1918
(Erase heading not required.)

Place	Date	Hour	Summary of Events and Information	Remarks and references to Appendices
FIRING LINE	1st May		No 1 Company in support relieved No 2 Company in firing line & working on improvement of line. All quiet. 1O.R. killed. Lieut D.T. HOLMES wounded at duty	(Reference Map 36A. NE Square E 17)
"	2nd May		Situation normal. Practically no activity. Work as usual. 2 Lieut W.C. BROWN, 2/KOSB & 2 Lieut A.L. CRANSTON, 3/KOSB joined for duty. Decorations as under awarded for action on 11th-14th April – Bar to M.M. 17268, Pte. O'REILLY P, 2nd Envy; M.M. 29553 Sgt GRAHAM W, DCM 15726 Cpl BROWN J, 16282 Sgt WILSON W, 16716 Pte DITCHBURN J, 20279 Pte WARD JS, 28681 Pte DUNLOP W.	
"	3rd May		Very quiet. Work as usual. 1.O.R. wounded (gas).	
"	4th May		Enemy artillery active. Work as normal. 1.O.R. wounded. Draft of 23 O.R. joined.	
"	5th May		Enemy artillery again active. Battalion relieved by 4th WORCESTERS & 2nd HANTS. Relief complete 11-25 a.m. Marched back to Camp at LEGRANDE HASARD 6.O.R. marched to 24th Div. M.G.C.	36 T 10 May

Army Form C. 2118.

WAR DIARY
or
INTELLIGENCE SUMMARY.
(Erase heading not required.)

Instructions regarding War Diaries and Intelligence Summaries are contained in F. S. Regs., Part II. and the Staff Manual respectively. Title pages will be prepared in manuscript.

Place	Date	Hour	Summary of Events and Information	Remarks and references to Appendices
LE GRANDE HASARD	6th May		Battalion resting & cleaning up. Following officers joined :- Lieut. J.B. STANTON, 2nd Lts. Lieut R.D. SMITH, Whites, J.B. VANSAGNEY, T.B. NICHOLAS, J.A.D. RENWICK, W.C. SCHAAB, M.C. SLATER, J.H. BRUCE, M.T. McGREGOR & J.C. HOWIE - all 8 killed. Draft to the O.R. joined. 2 O.R. rejoined duty. 4 O.R. sick evacuated. 2/Lieut. A.W. WYLIE rejoined from duty at Bn. H.Q. as I.O.	
"	7th May		Party digging on forward area. Corps at disposal of R.E. Corps for training from 9 a.m. to 1 p.m. All carrolling officers paraded under Adjutant. 2/Lieut. A.W. WYLIE appointed Bn.Tn. I.O. 10 O.R. wounded. 2 O.R. Sick evacuated.	
"	8th May		Party digging on forward area. Musketry & Specialist Training. 1 O.R. Sick Evacuated.	
"	9th May		Party digging & Wiring etc. on forward area. Musketry and Specialist training. Lieut. Adams C.F. 82nd Bn. joined D.S.O. Br.Lt. Bgt. assumed command of the Battalion vice Lieut. Colonel C.A.C. MURRAY, Highland Light Infy. (T.F.) to ENGLAND 9/5/18. Lieut. A.C. ROBERTSON Highland Lt Infty Bn (T.F.) & 2/Lt. D. DUNKEY 5th H.L.I (T.F.) joined for duty. Captain J.McLIR C.F. joined. 8 O.R. joined.	

WAR DIARY
or
INTELLIGENCE SUMMARY.
(Erase heading not required.)

Army Form C. 2118.

Place	Date	Hour	Summary of Events and Information	Remarks and references to Appendices
LE GRAND HASARD	10th 9/17		Battalion employed on trench work. Draining, Braking & Revetment	
			Battalion inspected by Commanding Officer. 1 O.R. reported	
	11th 9/17		Digging & setting in trench area. Inspection Weekly Roll & Returns 2nd Lieut S. MORGAN transferred (SS) strength P. strength	
	12th 9/17		Battalion present in the Colony	
			Divine Service. Digging in front area. Athend intimation received of the award of the M.C. to the following — 2/Lieut D.C. BULLEN-SMITH Lieut. G.G. TWWATES & 2/Lieut A.E. CAMOSELL. Casualties—NIL	Ref Map. 36A N.W.S 9/7
	13th 9/17		Battalion preparing for the line. Parades about 8.h.m & relieved C2 of WORCESTER & 9 HAMPSHIRE Regts in the left sector of the Divisional Front. No 2 Coy took over from 2 Coy WORCESTER Regt in strong pts & No 1 Coy from W Coy HAMPSHIRE Regt in support line. Relief complete. 11.45 a.m. Strgth of 20 O.R. attached Lieut D.H. DEVALES trophies system	
			Battalion joined for duty.	

Army Form C. 2118.

WAR DIARY
INTELLIGENCE SUMMARY.
(Erase heading not required.)

Instructions regarding War Diaries and Intelligence Summaries are contained in F.S. Regs., Part II. and the Staff Manual respectively. Title pages will be prepared in manuscript.

Place	Date	Hour	Summary of Events and Information	Remarks and references to Appendices
FIRING LINE	14th May		Situation quiet. Little activity. Work commenced on repair & improvement of trench system. Wiring & Patrols. M.R. mounted 242 och. mounted. S.C.R. tho. to 22D left bn.	
"	15th to 19th May		Activity actual with the front. Working mightily on improvement of trench system. Wiring & Patrols. Casualties :— 15th — Dupt. of 6.C.R. attived. 16th — Dupt. of 12 B.C. attived. 17th — Dupt. of 16 C.R. attived. 18th OR. 19th — Dupt. of 8.C.R. attived.	
"	20th May		Battalion relieved by 2/S.W. Bers. & went into Brigade support, taking over the PETIT SEC BOIS defence system. Battalion H.Q. removed in our position. Casualties NIL	
PETIT SEC BOIS	21st May		Working on improvement of Reserve line. Little hostile activity on either side. Major A. GORDON, 2/5 K.O.S.B. joined for 1 months attachment. Capt. A.H. AITON, 2/5 H.L.I, & Lieuts. H.A. HENRY & T.M. WELSH, 7/H.L.I. joined for duty. Dupt. of 6.C.R. attived. 2 O.R. sick.	

Army Form C. 2118.

WAR DIARY
or
INTELLIGENCE SUMMARY.
(Erase heading not required.)

Instructions regarding War Diaries and Intelligence Summaries are contained in F. S. Regs., Part II. and the Staff Manual respectively. Title pages will be prepared in manuscript.

Place	Date	Hour	Summary of Events and Information	Remarks and references to Appendices
PETIT BOIS	22nd Aug.		wounded, 2 O.R. wounded. Working on Posts & Wire. Situation quiet. 2 O.R. sick evacuated, 3 O.R. attached Bn. wounded (gas).	
"	23rd Aug.		Work as on previous day. Situation normal. 3 O.R. wounded, 1 O.R. sick evacuated.	
"	24th & 26th Aug.		Working on improvement of line. Patrols sent out nightly. Casualties: - 24th. 4 O.R. sick evacuated. 25th. 2/Lieut. T.G.R. gassed, 1 O.R. wounded, 1 O.R. reported sick & 1 O.R. reported from Div. H.Q. 26th. 2 O.R. sick evacuated. 4/Lieut. H/L 85th to HAYLING ISLAND for course.	
"	27th Aug.		The Battalion carried out a highly successful raid against two enemy Machine gun positions at E.17.a.90.60 and E.17.a.96.70. The Raiding Party consisted of 2/Lieut. J.C. HOWIE (O.C. Raid); 2/Lieut. R.C. SLADE (2nd in Comd.); Sgt. J. WILSON, "A" Coy & 32 Other Ranks. An incentive to the capture of Prisoners (the raison d'être of the Raid being to obtain identifications) was the promise of monetary reward by the Brigadier-General and the Commander. Ubique	See special Map attached

WAR DIARY
or
INTELLIGENCE SUMMARY.

Army Form C. 2118.

Raid Continued

The Raiding Party went out & took up position at 1.45 a.m. Jumping off position was in the BECQUE about E.17.a.45.58 to E.17.a.65.75. The Raiders were surprised in 3 parties with a snowy party producing L.G. On artillery barrage descended at 2.15 a.m. the moment the barrage lifted up the objective the Raiders rushed the position. "A" Party SLADE with "B" Party went for the southern gun. The enemy gun team were caught before they could get their gun in action & three of the team were taken prisoners unwounded & Lieut. SLADE shot other two men. The M.G. opened out of the light but not high. The Raiders were unable to reach the other gun. It having been removed from the position in which reconnoitring parties had located it.

Our casualties consisted of 3 O.R. slightly wounded by a shell from our own artillery which opened up for the attack.

The Raiding Party were back in their own line within 25 minutes after jumping off.

The prisoners taken belonged to the 132 I.R. 39th Division and stated that the prisoners crossed off the Raid were members

Army Form C. 2118.

WAR DIARY
or
INTELLIGENCE SUMMARY.
(Erase heading not required.)

Place	Date	Hour	Summary of Events and Information	Remarks and references to Appendices
			Sept continued	
PETIT SEC BOIS	27th May (Night)		Upon Corps, Divisional & Bde Commanders (Exclusive of Bns attached) Circ. I. & DRMN 212 H21 issued for duty. Lieut. T. SARSFIELD + 61 Signallers from I.B. Battalion relieved by the 1/R. DUBLIN FUSILIERS (3 Platoons) & 2/R. FUSILIERS (1 Platoon). Battalion marched back to Bivouac Camp on Dunkerque side of HAZEBROUCK. Most antiste that time. Relief complete abt	
HAZEBROUCK	28th May		Battalion resting & cleaning up. Warning issued that Bde was in Divisional Reserve. 4 O.R. Sick evacuated. Draft of 73 O.R. arrived. Capt W. SIMPSON M.C. to U.K. for 6 mths tour of duty.	
"	29th May		Party digging in Forward area. Conferences at Headqrs of O.C. Companies for training, inspections etc. Specialist Training. Lecture to Battalion Officers on Gas & Emplacements, Relieving by 2/Lieut. A.W. WYLIE I.O. 10 O.R. sick evacuated. 40 O.R. joined from Sick & Wounded. 2/Lt CARR J.H. to U.K. for Junior Commission.	
"	30th May		Party working in Forward area. Conferences at Headqrs of O.C. Companies for training. 1 O.R. wounded S.I. Draft of 5 arrivals arrived.	
"	31st May		Party digging in Forward area. Training as in Previous day. Lecture to Battalion Officers by the Important Special instruction in the M.36 Grenade. Lieut. A.A. WEST On B.D. 1/R.DB. arrived.	

Checked by Captain
Acts L R/home adjutant 1/R.DB
as Adjutant 1/R.DB

ACCOUNT OF RAID CARRIED OUT BY THE 1st KING'S OWN SCOTTISH BORDERERS
ON THE MORNING OF THE 27th MAY 1918.
****

The Raiding Party, which consisted all told of 2 Officers commanding (2/Lieut.HOWIE and 2/Lieut.SLADE) and 33 Other Ranks, 1st KINGS OWN SCOTTISH BORDERERS, crawled out into position in the BECQUE about E.17.a.45.58 to E.17.a.60.75. On arrival here, the Officer Commanding decided to utilise a deep ditch, which ran from their position in a South-easterly direction parrallel to the road and about 150 yards from it. He, therefore, left Party "A" where they were and decided conducted Parties "B" and "C" down this ditch in order to get them opposite their objectives.

The barrage fell punctually at 2.15 a.m. and, in the bright moonlight, the lifts forward and back could be clearly distinguished.

When the barrage reached the green line, 2/Lieut. SLADE and the raiders crawled forward some 30 yards, and the moment the barrage lifted out to the red line, the party rushed forward, "B" Party, under 2/Lieut. SLADE making straight for the southern gun, reaching the position before the enemy gun team were able to get the gun running, and the entire gun team, consisting of 3 men, and the gun were captured.

Party "C", consisting of the Lewis Gun Team, took up their position in one of the unoccupied Posts about E.17.a.82.55, as previously arranged to cover the operation. As no hostile fire came from the South, this Lewis Gun did not open fire, but remained out until the other Raiding Parties had withdrawn.

Party "A", which was detailed to capture the most northern of the hostile Machine Guns, was unable to do so, as the gun had been moved to the East side of the road, was therefore not clear of our barrage.

While the Raiders were lying in the assembly position, fire was opened on them in bursts from the Northern gun, and from a sniper located somewhere behind the gun. This fire, however, ceased immediately our first barrage went down.

While the raiders were rushing the Southern gun position, the enemy fired one green Very Light from the Northern gun position, and about 10 minutes after our barrage had fallen, the enemy put down a heavy barrage on our Front Line about E.17.a.10.80, and behind our Front Line to the South of this point and down the road. This had been anticipated and the Trench accordingly, practically cleared at this point. This barrage, for the most part, fell about 80 yards in rear of our Trenches, and was continued until about 2.45 a.m.

Our casualties consisted of 3 other ranks slightly wounded by shell-fire when in the assembly position. Captures – 3 of the enemy, belonging to the 132nd I.R., 39th Division, and one light machine gun. *2 of the enemy were also shot by 2/Lieut SLADE as they were running away.*

NOTES

1. It is the opinion of the Raiding Officers that casualties were avoided by the rapidity with which they *party* charged the gun position. This is also borne out by the prisoners' statements, who say that they were overwhelmed immediately the barrage had lifted.

   The value of creeping forward and getting close up under our barrage before it lifts was again proved. Also, the absolute necessity of having an ample supply of aircraft photographs to study. It was largely due to the study of these photographs that the raid was so successful.

2. The special signalling arrangements worked well, and information was received at Brigade Headquarters of the result of the raid at 2.55 a.m.

   2 Message-carrying dogs were also liberated from left company Headquarters in the firing line. These returned to Brigade Headquarters in half an hour and 25 minutes respectively.

H N Festing

CAPTAIN,
BRIGADE MAJOR 87th INFANTRY BRIGADE.

Copies to :-
1. O.C.Raid
2. S.W.D.
3. K.O.S.B.
4. Border.
5. M.G.Battn.
6. C.R.A.
7. 2/Royal Fusrs.
8. 88th Bde.
9. 86th Bde.
10. 1st Austn.Bde.
11. G.O.C.
12. B.M.
13. S.C.
14. 29th Divn.
15. War Diary
16. File
17. ...

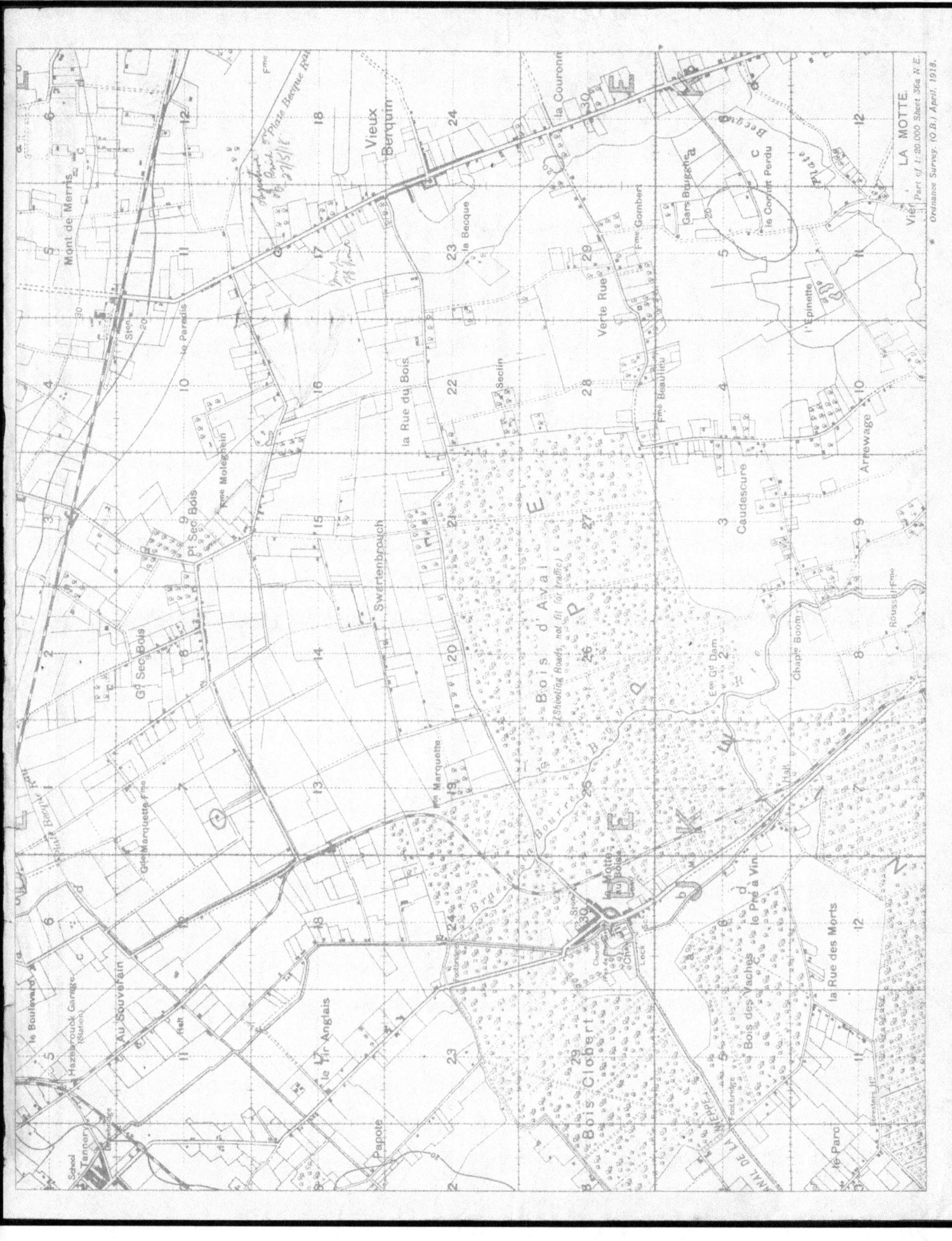

VOLUME NO 17

1 KOSB Vol 30

Army Form C. 2118.

WAR DIARY
or
INTELLIGENCE SUMMARY.
(Erase heading not required.)

JUNE, 1918.

Reference Map 36A. 1/40,000   37T 7 sheets

Place	Date	Hour	Summary of Events and Information	Remarks and references to Appendices
HAZEBROUCK	1st June		Battalion Training. 2nd Lieut. & Specialist Training. Special instruction in the No. 36 Grenade. Party working at night on Forward Area. 10 R sick evacuated.	
"	2nd June		Divine Services. Working party in Forward Area at night. 10 R. N.J. wounded	
"	3rd June		Training & work as on 1st inst. Lieut. D. SLOAN. 3/Lieut B joined for duty. Draft of 27 O.R. arrived. Lieut. Colonel CASO. MURPHY awarded D.S.O. (Birthday Honours).	
"	4th June		Battalion preparing for the line. Took over Right Brigade Sector from 2 Coys of 2/LEINSTER & 2 Coys of 1/WORCESTER REGTS. B Coy on the Firing Line & A Coy in support. C & D Coys occupied LA MOTTE DEFENCES. Battalion H.Q. at E. 26 a. 90.20. Relief complete at 2-15 a.m. By arrangement the 2nd Bn. K.O.S.B. were on our immediate Right. The first night time was quiet. Battalion working on improvement of Line. Reconnaissance patrols out. 1 O.R. wounded. 3 O.R. to U.K. for Infantry Commissions.	
FIRING LINE	5th June		10 R joined for duty.	

Army Form C. 2118.

WAR DIARY
or
INTELLIGENCE SUMMARY.
(Erase heading not required.)

Place	Date	Hour	Summary of Events and Information	Remarks and references to Appendices
FIRING LINE	6th June		Work as on 5th inst. Reconnoitre Patrols 2/O.R. Killed. 2/O.R. wounded. 1/O.R. to U.K. for Company Commander. 20458 A/CSM QUINN T. "C" Coy. marked D.C.M. C Billeting Hounds.	
"	7th June		Work & Patrols as usual. 1 O.R. wounded. Official intimation received of the award of the M.M. to the following :- 240767 W.C.S.M. WILSON T. "B" Coy; 40452 A/Sjt MALLOCH F.W. "A" Coy; 92187, Sjt Bell C. "A" Coy.	
"	8th June		Battalion H.Q. heavily shelled & moved back to FETTLE FM. Draft of 5 O.R. arrived. 1 O.R. rejoined from hosp.	
"	9th June		Battalion H.Q. heavily shelled with Gas from 12 midnight to 2 am. Companies changed over - C Coy taking taking our Front Line; D Coy, Close support; A Coy, LA MOTTE Defences; & B Coy, Reserve. Draft of 5 O.R. arrived. 1 O.R. to U.K. for Company Commander. 4 O.R. sick evacuated.	
"	10th June		Work & Patrols as usual. Draft of 3 O.R. joined.	

Army Form C. 2118.

WAR DIARY
INTELLIGENCE SUMMARY.
(Erase heading not required.)

Ref. Map Sheet 36 A 1/40,000

Place	Date	Hour	Summary of Events and Information	Remarks and references to Appendices
FIRING LINE	11th June		Battalion was relieved by 1st Scottish Rifles & 1st Lancashire Fusiliers (that Coys. each). Relief complete about 2 am. 12/6/16. Battalion marched back to billets North of MORBECQUE. 2/Lieut. S. HARGAN rejoined from Sick Leave. Draft of 69 O.R. joined	
MORBECQUE	12th June		Resting & cleaning up. 10 R sick evacuated. Draft of 80 R arrived.	
"	13th June		Company Officer's Parade. Practice in Platoon in the Attack & in the tactical handling of a Coy. Specialist Training. 30 R. Sick evacuated.	
"	14th June		Battalion Practicing the Attack. Sudden orders received to proceed to the Line. Battalion preparing for the Line. Took over Right Sub Sector from 2 Coys 1st Scottish Rgt & 2 Coys 1st Lancs Fusiliers. C Coy. in Front Line; D Coy. in close support; B Coy. in Reserve; A Coy. in LA MOTTE Defences; Battn. H.Q. FETTLE FM. Relief complete at 1 am 15/6/16. 3 O.R. Sick evacuated. 1 O.R. wounded.	
FIRING LINE	15th June		LA MOTTE village heavily shelled with Gas & H.E. Several horses set on fire & 'A' Coys' cookhouse burnt down. Enemy attacked on Right Bde. & our Left in the morning	

WAR DIARY or INTELLIGENCE SUMMARY.

Army Form C. 2118.

Place	Date	Hour	Summary of Events and Information	Remarks and references to Appendices
FIRING LINE	16th June.		(88th. Bde.) a captured 3 turns. Attack expected on our front the following morning & preparations made to meet it. An advanced Battn. H.Q. was established. 2/Lieut. J.B. NICHOLAS to hospital sick.	
"	17th June.		Expected attack did not materialise. Situation throughout the day normal. BOIS D'AVAL heavily shelled during the night. Working Party digging firing off front. 2 O.R. were wounded (with 29th. Div. Eng. Er.) 2 O.R. sick evac. 1 O.R. to Base unfit.	
"			New kind of Gas discharged from our front by Special R.E. Coy, in early morning. Patrols sent out at night to investigate effect of Gas. Battalion relieved by the 1/Rl. DUBLIN FUSILIERS. Relief complete 2.45am. 2 O.R. wounded. 7 O.R. sick evac.	
HAZEBROUCK	18th. June.		Battalion marched back to Camp formerly occupied near HAZEBROUCK. 1 O.R. Sick evac. Official intimation received of death of M.S.M. Pte (8275) Sgt A DRYLIE, E Coy.	
"	19th June.		Battalion preparing for the line. Battalion took over same part of Right Sector pro previously occupied. Hrs 1st Rl. Dublin Fusiliers. A Coy in Front Line: B Coy in Support: C Coy in Reserve: D Coy LA MOTTE 8 Coy in Support line: 8 Coy in Brouffart (Lent from 5 O.R., 2 O.R. joined). DEFENCES.	

245

Army Form C. 2118.

WAR DIARY
or
INTELLIGENCE SUMMARY.
(Erase heading not required.)

Instructions regarding War Diaries and Intelligence Summaries are contained in F. S. Regs., Part II. and the Staff Manual respectively. Title pages will be prepared in manuscript.

Ref. Map. 36A. 1/20,000.

Place	Date	Hour	Summary of Events and Information	Remarks and references to Appendices
FIRING LINE	20th June		Situation normal. Little activity on either side. Shell morning fire two enjoyed on improvement of ground system. Patrols. Ranks A. HOLDAN G. E. McVEAN & H. J. FORBES, 3/KOSB joined for duty. 3 O.R. joined. 7 O.R. sick evacuated.	
"	21st June		Coast during the night. Battalion relieved by 10th EAST YORKS, 22nd Left Bde. Finished back to camp at EECK-HOUT-CASTEEL. Relief complete about 2 a.m. 1 O.R. killed. 3 O.R. wounded. 4 O.R. sick evac.	
EECK HOUT CASTEEL	22nd June		Battalion turned out at 2.25 am & marched via BEHINGHEM to RECQUINGHEM, distance of 10 kilometres. Battalion in Billets about 5 a.m. 2 Lieut. W. F. STEWART struck off strength. 10 O.R. joined.	
RECQUINGHEM	23rd June		Church Parades. Gpl. BOWYER, C.Coy. to U.K. for Cadet Commission. 5 O.R. sick evac. 10 O.R. joined.	
"	24th June		Work of reorganising Battalion commenced. Lecture to all Officers & NCOs by commanding Officer. Lecture by Brigadier Genrl. JACKSON to all officers & NCOs. Specialist training. Lgt. SUTTIE, Signalling Offr. to DUNSTABLE to attend Course. 1 O.R. Lieut. LOVE S.S. No. 12 R. U.S.A.	

D.D.&L., London, E.C. Wt. W1771/M2911 750x50 5/17 Sch. 52 Forms C2-8/4
(A504)

Army Form C. 2118.

WAR DIARY
or
INTELLIGENCE SUMMARY.
(Erase heading not required.)

Instructions regarding War Diaries and Intelligence Summaries are contained in F. S. Regs., Part II, and the Staff Manual respectively. Title pages will be prepared in manuscript.

Place	Date	Hour	Summary of Events and Information	Remarks and references to Appendices
			M.O. 4c Battery for duty with U.S. Army. Capt. H.B. SHERLOCK, R.A.M.C. joined for duty as M.O. 2 O.R. sick unevacuated.	
BROUCHES	25th June		Battalion Training. Companies practising the "Attack". Specialist Training. Lecture to subaltern officers by the Major. All N.C.O's with the R.S.M. 7 O.R. sick unevac. 1 O.R. joined.	
"	26th June		Battalion Training. Companies under O. Coys. Practising the "Attack". Steady Drill; Specialist Training etc. 3 O.R. rejoined from hospital sick.	
"	27th June		Battalion Ceremonial Parade. 2 O.R. sick unevac.	
"	28th June		Brigade practising for Brigade Ceremonial Parade. 3 O.R. sick unevac. 2 O.R. rejoined from hospital.	

Army Form C. 2118.

WAR DIARY
or
INTELLIGENCE SUMMARY.
(Erase heading not required.)

Place	Date	Hour	Summary of Events and Information	Remarks and references to Appendices
RECQUINGHEM	June 29th.		Brigade Ceremonial Parade. Medal ribbons presented by Brigadier General CAREY. Crombs. 29th Division. Lieut-General Sir 1.5.5. Gough XV th. Corps present. Sick evac. 3 O.R. 2 O.R. rejoined from hospital.	
"	June 30th.		Church Parade. Capt. J.S.R. HIGGINS to BOULOGNE for 7 days rest. 2 Lieut. S. MORGAN rejoined from sick. Sick evac. 5 O.R. 1 O.R. joined from Base.	

Dictated by

Geo A Brown, Captain,
a/Adjt. 1/KRRC

WAR DIARY or INTELLIGENCE SUMMARY

Army Form C. 2118.

1.K.O.S.B.

JULY 1918

Place	Date	Hour	Summary of Events and Information	Remarks and references to Appendices
RACQUINGHEM	1st JULY		Battalion training. Companies practising "The Attack". Specialist training. Special instruction in B.F. & P.T. Lecture to Sno N.c.o's by Divisional Sno Officer. 5 O.R. rejoined from hospital.	Reference Map Sheet 36 A. 1/40,000.
"	2nd JULY		Battalion Method of Advance at BLARINGHEM. Training in accordance with S.S.143. Patrols & Sentries, musketry. 1 O.R. rejoined from hospital.	
"	3rd JULY		Brigade Tactical Exercise for Officers. Companies at disposal of O.C. Coys. for training. Special Classes commenced for instructors in P.T. & B.F. 2 O.R. evac. wounded. 5 O.R. rejoined from hospital.	
"	4th JULY		Battalion Initiating for Brigade Sports. Sports to take place on Olt. present at B.Q. & Central. Sports treated in Battno being placed in platoons:- 1 Coy – K.O.S.B. 2 Coy – Border Regt. 3rd – S.W.Bs., 2 O.R. rejoined from hospital.	
"	5th JULY		Companies on the attack. Specialist training. Lecture to Battalion on RECREATION AT TRAINING by Colonel CAMPBELL illustrated by Sonny & wrestling demonstrations. Inspection of Rifles by R.B.Bs. 1 O.R. rejoined from hospital.	

Army Form C. 2118.

WAR DIARY
or
INTELLIGENCE SUMMARY.
(Erase heading not required.)

Instructions regarding War Diaries and Intelligence Summaries are contained in F. S. Regs., Part II. and the Staff Manual respectively. Title pages will be prepared in manuscript.

Place	Date	Hour	Summary of Events and Information	Remarks and references to Appendices
RAEQUINGHEM	6th July		Battalion carried out Tactical Schem (Defence). Sick evacuated 5 O.R. Rejoined from sick, 1 O.R.	
"	7th July		Divine Service. Draft of 30 O.R. joined. 2 O.R. rejoined from sick. 10 R. sick evac.	
"	8th July		Brigade Memorial Parade for inspection by GENERAL PLUMER, Commdg. Second Army. Presentation of medal ribbons. Draft of 2 O.R. joined. 2 O.R. sick evac.	
"	9th July		Holiday. Battalion attended 24th Divl. Horse Show & Band Contest. 2/Capt. F. DALE M.C. to U.K. to attend Course at ALDERSHOT, & struck W.C. strength.	
"	10th July		Inter-Company Scheme; Attack & Defence; A & B Coys v C & D Coys. Draft of 18 O.R. joined. 3 O.R. sick evacuated.	

WAR DIARY
INTELLIGENCE SUMMARY.

(Erase heading not required.)

Army Form C. 2118.

Sheets 27 & 36A.

Place	Date	Hour	Summary of Events and Information	Remarks and references to Appendices
RACQUINGHEM	11th JULY		Inter-Company Schemes; Attack & Defence; B & A Coys. & D & C Coys. A Coy on Range. 1O.R. sick evac. 2 O.R. rejoined from sick.	
"	12th JULY		Battalion in Billets on account of rain. Lectures, kit inspection etc. 10.R. sick evac. 1 O.R. rej. from sick.	
"	13th JULY		A & B Coys - Inter-Coy Scheme - Attack & Defence. C & D Coys. Musketry. Live Grenade Practice, & Rapid Wiring. 1 O.R. rej. from sick.	
"	14th JULY		Battalion paraded at 10 a.m. & marched via BLARINGHEM - SERCUS - EECK HOUT CASTEEL & HAZEBROUCK, to a Camp at VIEUX (on the outskirts of Hazebrouck). Dinner on line of march. Battn. in camp at 3-30 p.m. ½ Lieut. A.W. WYLIE to Bde. as I.O. 1O.R. sick evac.	
HAZEBROUCK	15th JULY		Battalion paraded at 2 p.m. & marched to BORRE. Taking over Reserve Line from the 4th Australian Infy. Battn. Battalion accommodated in Farm-	

Army Form C. 2118.

WAR DIARY
or
INTELLIGENCE SUMMARY.
(Erase heading not required.)

Sheet 36.A.

Place	Date	Hour	Summary of Events and Information	Remarks and references to Appendices
Reserve Line.	16th July.		Reliefs complete about 5 p.m. Battalion working at night improving trenches & tunnels in Support & Reserve Lines. Casualties NIL.	
"	17th July		A & C Coys working on construction of dugouts at Btn H.Q. & at BD.R.E. D Coy on Bays during frames & improving trenches in Reserve Line. 2/Lieuts. A.S. GARDINER, R. KENNEY, 3rd K.O.S.B. joined. Strgth of 20 O.R. attend. 1 O.R. sick evac. 2 O.R. rej. from sick.	
"	17th July		Working on improvement of Line. Battalion relieved in the afternoon by 13th. EAST LANCS. & marched to Camp at V.13.d (on the outskirts of HAZEBROUCK). 2 O.R. sick evac.	
HAZEBROUCK	18th July		Battalion paraded at 4 p.m. & marched to "C" Camp, BLARINGHEM (9 miles). 2 O.R. sick evac.	
"C" Camp.	19th July		Inspections of Equipment, Clothing etc. Battalion under orders to move at shortest possible notice. 1 O.R. transferred to 87th T.M. Bty.	

Army Form C. 2118.

WAR DIARY
INTELLIGENCE SUMMARY.
(Erase heading not required.)

Instructions regarding War Diaries and Intelligence Summaries are contained in F. S. Regs., Part II. and the Staff Manual respectively. Title pages will be prepared in manuscript.

Place	Date	Hour	Summary of Events and Information	Remarks and references to Appendices
"C" Camp	20th July		Battalion out on Tactical Exercise March. Theoretical Training. Captain C.H.V. CRICHTON-BROWNE reported for duty & assumed Command of "B" Coy vice A/Captain C.H.M. BELL. 1 O.R. sick evacuated.	Sheets 36A & 27.
"	21st July		Divine Services. Baths. Brawlers nil.	
"	22nd July		Battalion paraded at 9 a.m. & marched via WALLON CAPPEL to Billets on outskirts of HONDEGHEM. Dinner en route. 2 Billets about 3.30 pm. 12 O.R. sick evac. 20 O.R. refd. from sick. 10 R. to base unfit.	
HONDEGHEM	23rd July		Battalion resting. Inspections etc. 6 O.R. sick evac. 1 O.R. transferred to R.E.Sig.	
"	24th July		Battalion paraded at 9 a.m. & Companies marched independently to Billets in & around ST. MARIE CAPPEL. Batt. H.Q. & "B" Coy in Village. Right of 1 S.O.R. joined. 1 O.R. sick evac.	

Army Form C. 2118.

WAR DIARY
INTELLIGENCE SUMMARY.
(Erase heading not required.)

Instructions regarding War Diaries and Intelligence Summaries are contained in F. S. Regs., Part II. and the Staff Manual respectively. Title pages will be prepared in manuscript.

Place	Date	Hour	Summary of Events and Information	Remarks and references to Appendices
ST. MARIE CAPPEL	25th JULY.		Four hours' training carried out under Co. Commanders. G.O.R. sick unwanted. Pr. 9385, Pte. T.H. JACKSON (sentenced to DEATH, commuted to 10 yrs. P.S. - Houston) to No. 7 Prison, LES ATTAQUES, CALAIS.	
"	26th JULY.		Four hours' training under O.C. Coys. Party of officers reconnoitring forward area. 3 O.R. sick unwanted. 10 R. rejoined sick.	
"	27th JULY.		Training as on previous day. Inspection of Battalion L.G.R. Specialist training. 6 O.R. sick unwanted.	
"	28th JULY.		Divine Service. Pipe Bands of the 1st, 2nd, & 6th Battns. of the Regt. played programme in field outside Village. Most enoyable concert. Sgts. Johnson & Cox to U.K. for Lewis Gun Course. 2 O.R. sick.	
"	29th JULY.		Companies at musketry at O.C. Coys. for training. Specialist training. Special B9 P.T. class for N.C.Os. commenced. 4 O.R. sick once. 10 R. rejoined from Hospital.	

Army Form C. 2118.

WAR DIARY
or
INTELLIGENCE SUMMARY.
(Erase heading not required.)

Instructions regarding War Diaries and Intelligence Summaries are contained in F. S. Regs., Part II. and the Staff Manual respectively. Title pages will be prepared in manuscript.

Place	Date	Hour	Summary of Events and Information	Remarks and references to Appendices
ST. MARIE CAPPEL	30th JULY		4 hours' training under Company Commanders. Musketry Training. 1 O.R. wounded accidentally. 2 O.R. sick come.	
"	31st JULY		Owing to anticipated move on 1st August the Battalion celebrated MINDEN DAY. Highly successful sports were held at Bde H.Q. followed by a Concert in the evening. 2 O.R. rejoined from sick.	

Initiated by

Geo. F. Brown
Captain,
Adjutant

Army Form C. 2118.

WAR DIARY
INTELLIGENCE SUMMARY.

AUGUST, 1916.

Sheet 27, 1/40,000.

1 KOSB

Place	Date	Hour	Summary of Events and Information	Remarks and references to Appendices
ST. MARIE CAPPEL	1st August		Companies at disposal of O.C. Coys for training. Specialist training. 2 O.R. Sick evac.	
"	2nd August		Battalion Tactical Scheme commenced but abandoned owing to rain. 1 O.R. rejoined from hospital.	
"	3rd August		4 hours training under O.C. Coys. Battalion paraded at 9 a.m. & marched to Camp at V.23.a.3.7 (Sheet 27) on the outskirts of HAZEBROUCK. Battalion in Camp at 11.15 a.m. 2 O.R. Sick evac.	
HAZEBROUCK	4th August		Divine Services. 1 O.R. evac sick.	
"	5th August		Reorganization of Camp & training under O.C. Coys. 2 O.R. Sick evac.	

Army Form C. 2118.

WAR DIARY
INTELLIGENCE SUMMARY.
(Erase heading not required.)

Instructions regarding War Diaries and Intelligence Summaries are contained in F. S. Regs., Part II. and the Staff Manual respectively. Title pages will be prepared in manuscript.

Place	Date	Hour	Summary of Events and Information	Remarks and references to Appendices
HAZEBROUCK	6th August		Training in a.m. O.C. Corps. Battalion marched to LA BREARDÉ in the afternoon, this being the King moving the first entrant is for I.O.R. one sick.	
"	7th August		Specialist Training. Baths. 2 O.R. sick one.	
"	8th August		Battalion working parties burying cable. Lieut. D.L. KERR, 3/KRRB. joined for duty. Casualties Nil.	
"	9th August		Comprises at disposal of O.C. Corps for training in accordance with Lieut. General IVOR MAXSE'S notes. Specialist training. E.O. Second in Command & Lieut. H.A. HENRY visited Second Army Central School to witness demonstration by students. 5 O.R. one sick.	

Army Form C. 2118.

WAR DIARY
INTELLIGENCE SUMMARY
(Erase heading not required.)

Place	Date	Hour	Summary of Events and Information	Remarks and references to Appendices
HAZEBROUCK	10th August		Training as in previous day. Night Operations. Casualties Nil.	Reference Map - Sheet 27.
"	11th August		Divine Services. Lecture by C.O. to all Officers & N.C.Os. 3 O.R. men. Lieh. 10.R. rej. from Hos. 10.R. Lt. 87% T.M. By. 7% Officers under Major E.H. CRANSHAW M.C., gave a demonstration in the "Platoon attacking a Strong Point".	
"	12th August		Training as for 10th inst. Casualties Nil.	
"	13th August		Companies on the Range. Battalion inspected by N.O.	
"	14th August		Battalion preparing for the Line. First Brigade moved off at 7.40 p.m.	

WAR DIARY or INTELLIGENCE SUMMARY.

(Erase heading not required.)

Army Form C. 2118.

Instructions regarding War Diaries and Intelligence Summaries are contained in F. S. Regs., Part II. and the Staff Manual respectively. Title pages will be prepared in manuscript.

Place	Date	Hour	Summary of Events and Information	Remarks and references to Appendices
SIRAUS + N.6	15th August		Relieved 2/LEINSTER REGT. in the Left Sector of the Brigade Front. Disposition of Battalion:- C Coy. & 2 Platoons D Coy. in Front Line; 2 Platoons D Coy. in Close Support; A Coy. in Left Support; & B Coy in Right Support. Battalion H.Q. at W.16.6.10.50 (Gunpowder). Relief complete 12-30 a.m. 15/8/16. B Coy took over part of the front line from 6th K.O.S.B. (9th Division) & pushed in an immediate life & part of the enemy gave themselves as prisoners & 1 U.P. man wounded. 10 O.R. to F.A.	
	15th August		Heavy enemy bombardment to our position in the early morning which was kept up through the day on our artillery & ammunition from the point crossing to SINST & I. JOHNSTON replied. Lt. STEVENSON, D Coy. all prisoners taken by 1st Batt. 5/th I.R. 4th Division. Another prisoner (Officer) was captured by D Coy. Lieut. A.L. CRANSTON was seriously wounded during the patrol & after several unsuccessful attempts had been made to bring him in, this was accomplished by the Secretary Captain H.B. SHERLOCK M.O. & Lieut. Crowstow. List of wounded same day. Further casualties:- Lieut. D.M. O'STOKE, wounded; 3 O.R. killed & 16 O.R. wounded	

WAR DIARY or INTELLIGENCE SUMMARY

Army Form C. 2118.

Attack continued.

By 11-40 am the RIDGE was in our hands & the attack on OUTERSTEENE progressing satisfactorily. At 12-30 pm Battn H.Q. moved forward to C Coys former H.Q. at X.25.b.2.9. At 1-30 pm the village of OUTERSTEENE had been captured & completely cleared of the enemy. Consolidation was commenced forthwith on a line centred hundred yards in front of the village.

At 2.30 pm the advancing Officer moved forward & established a forward Battn H.Q. in a small portion of trench at F.2.b.2.2. Very little resistance was experienced during the whole progress of the advance.

Prisoners & material captured by this Battalion:—

Prisoners (including several Officers) 300.
Machine Guns   60
Trench Mortars   2

Battalion casualties:— 2nd Lts. A. MACLEAN & H.T. FORBES killed. 2 Lts.
J.A. RENWICK, J.B. NICHOLAS & W.C. SELLAR wounded.
Other Ranks — Killed 15. Wounded 105. Missing 6.

WAR DIARY
—or—
INTELLIGENCE SUMMARY.
(Erase heading not required.)

Army Form C. 2118.

Instructions regarding War Diaries and Intelligence Summaries are contained in F.S. Regs., Part II. and the Staff Manual respectively. Title pages will be prepared in manuscript.

Place	Date	Hour	Summary of Events and Information	Remarks and references to Appendices
FIRING LINE	17th August		Conference at Battalion H.Q. with regard to attack to be made on 18th August, against the HOEGENACKER SPUR. Battalion preparing for the advance. Batt'n. H.Q. moved forward from IONIC HOUSE to "A" Coys H.Q. Brigade H.Q. a 1st. Border Regt. H.Q. moved up to take over IONIC HOUSE about 9 P.m. Lieut. J.B.M. STANTON, 1st. K.O.S.B., attd. 87th. T.M. Bty. wounded & several Casualties.— Lieut. C.A. MORETON 1st. K.O.S.B. joined for duty. killed.- 2 O.R. wounded.	See Special Map Attached
"	18th August		Battalion participated in an attack on the HOEGENACKER RIDGE, THE RIDGE on the Battalion front being the objective with the capture of the village of OUTERSTEENE as an interim & gradual objective. Jumping off point was the frontline the Battalion was then strongly trusted in readiness in rear of "A" Coy. who moved at 1.a.m. the AFRICAN TRENCH in rear of 6th. K.O.S.B. (9th Division) & in support to them. Battalion attacked in conjunction with 6th K.O.S.B on the LEFT & 2/S.W. BORDERERS on the RIGHT. There was no artillery preparation. Promptly at 11 a.m. the Barrage fell & the Battalion went over the Top as one man. We were on the enemy before they realized that an attack was taking place & their anxious & recoiling garrison rendered purposeless enemy. The attack was never one momentarily held up. the isolated M.G. Posts which did that at no times being speedily & effectively dealt

WAR DIARY or INTELLIGENCE SUMMARY.

Army Form C. 2118.

Place	Date	Hour	Summary of Events and Information	Remarks and references to Appendices
			Attack Continued.	
			About 3 A.m. our own Grenadiers were heavily shelled. Enemy appeared to be massing for a counter-attack & we sent up the S.O.S. The counter-attack did not develop, the enemy troops being dispersed by our artillery fire. Enemy continued to bombard our line heavily & at 9 A.m. the S.O.S. was again sent up but no counter-attack was made.	
FIRING LINE	16th August		Villages, RIDGES, & Supports heavily shelled during the rest of morning. About 11 A.m. enemy were again seen massing for a counter-attack which did not materialise in consequence of a very effective barrage put down by our Artillery. About 5 P.m. The 86th Bde. Machine on our Right, being relieved by putting down a heavy barrage all along the Ridge. Shelling slackened considerably about 6 P.m. Situation much quieter towards night. Battalion relieved by 1st Border Regt. & went into Reserve in the old front line. 4 O.R. killed, 5 O.R. wounded.	

Army Form C. 2118.

WAR DIARY
or
INTELLIGENCE SUMMARY.
(Erase heading not required.)

Instructions regarding War Diaries and Intelligence Summaries are contained in F. S. Regs., Part II. and the Staff Manual respectively. Title pages will be prepared in manuscript.

Place	Date	Hour	Summary of Events and Information	Remarks and references to Appendices
RESERVE LINE	20th August		Situation quiet. Battalion relieved by 21 Hampshire Regt. & move out to former Camp on outskirts of HAZEBROUCK. 1 O.R. wounded. 1 O.R. Sick evac. Draft of 6 O.R. arrived. 1 O.R. rej. from Hospital.	
HAZEBROUCK	21st August		Battalion resting & cleaning up. Checking of Battle Stores, etc. 5 O.R. Sick evac. 1 O.R. to Conv: unfit. 5 O.R. # Convalescent Camp, CAYEUX, unfit.	
"	22nd August		Companies at disposal of O.C. Coys for re-organization. 5 O.R. Sick evac.	
"	23rd August		Companies at disposal of O.C. Coys for small tactical schemes. Patrols, use of Lewis Guns, etc. Camp Inspection by Brigade Officer, Baths. Lieut. T.O.H. PHANT. M.C. graded "B" & struck off strength. 1 O.R. rejoined wounded.	
"	24th August		Battalion at Inspection by the Commdg. Officer & Medical Inspection by the M.O. 5 O.R. Sick evac. 5 O.R. joined, transferred from 6/K.O.S.B.	

Army Form C. 2118.

WAR DIARY
or
INTELLIGENCE SUMMARY.
(Erase heading not required.)

Place	Date	Hour	Summary of Events and Information	Remarks and references to Appendices
HAZEBROUCK	25th August		Divine Service. Drafts of 38 O.R. joined. Lieut. J.M. WELSH & 2/Lieut. J. MAITLAND to U.K. for employment with the R.A.F.	
"	26th August		Preparing for the Line. Battalion paraded & marched off about 7.30 p.m. relieving the 2/LEINSTER REST in support in the left sector of the DIVISIONAL Front. Relief complete about 10.30 p.m. 2/7th CANASTER N14.	
SUPPORT LINE	27th August		Battalion relieved 18/D.L.I. & 1 Platoon YORKS & LANCS in Front Line. Relief complete 1.30 a.m. 28/8/18. Capt. F. DALE M.C. rejoined from Senior Officers Course at CAMBRIDGE. The following officers joined for duty:- Lieut. R.G. MOIR, 3/K.O.S.B.; 2/Lieuts. J. MARTIN, & J.W. RENWICK, 3/K.O.S.B.; J.O. CALLANDER & J.W.M. JAMIESON, 4/K.O.S.B.; G.G.B. MACKENZIE & F. MILLER, 5/K.O.S.B. 2/Lieut. J.B. YANS AGNEW, 1/K.O.S.B. wounded.	
FRONT LINE	28th August		Artillery active on both sides. Vicinity of Battalion H.Q. heavily shelled. 1 O.R. wounded.	
"	29th August		Situation quiet. Little activity on either side during the day. 2/Lieuts. E. HUNTER &	

Army Form C. 2118.

WAR DIARY
or
INTELLIGENCE SUMMARY.
(Erase heading not required.)

Instructions regarding War Diaries and Intelligence Summaries are contained in F. S. Regs., Part II. and the Staff Manual respectively. Title pages will be prepared in manuscript.

Place	Date	Hour	Summary of Events and Information	Remarks and references to Appendices
FIRING LINE	30th August		7. W.L. BIRRELL, 3/K.O.S.B. joined. Draft of S.O.R. arrived.	
		About 2-30 a.m. information was received from Brigade that the enemy had retired on our Divisional Front & Battalion was ordered to push forward & get in touch with the enemy. A, B, & D Coys. moved forward, C Coy. remaining in their original position. The Battalion pushed on towards BAILLEUL without meeting with any serious opposition. 2/Lieut. A.G. STOREY, 5/K.O.S.B. joined. 10 R. rejoined from sick. 2/Lieut. J.O. CALLADER wounded.	
"	31st August		Battalion continued to push forward & met with little opposition. Battalion relieved by 1st Border Regt. in line immediately in advance of BAILLEUL & returned to 'Y' (OUTERSTEENE) LINE. Draft of S.O.R. joined. 2 O.R. rejoined sick. 20 O.R. transferred to R.E.	

Dictated by
Pro L. Ryan
for L. Ryan Captain
Adjutant

SECRET.   29th Div. No. I.G. 106/16.

29th DIVISION INTELLIGENCE SUMMARY
from 6 a.m. 18th to 6 a.m. 19th August 1918.

I. OPERATIONS.

The attack against the HOEGENACKER SPUR, launched yesterday at 11 a.m., in conjunction with the 9th Division, was completely successful; not only were the original objectives obtained, but the line was pushed considerably beyond, the village of OUTTERSTEENE falling into our hands. There was no artillery preparation, the barrage opening practically at the same time as the launching of the attack; the enemy in the front line was therefore over-run before they knew that the attack had commenced.

The line now runs as given on the map attached. The total number of prisoners taken by this Division is 10 Officers, 349 unwounded O.R's., and 41 wounded O.R's., making a total of 400 prisoners. The 9th Division had captured, up to yesterday evening, 8 Officers and 227 O.R's unwounded. The material is not yet counted.

The enemy has since heavily shelled our new positions, and also apparently attempted a small counter-attack on the front of the Division on our left at 9.0 p.m. last night; it is doubtful whether he will make a counter-attack in any strength; most of the higher N.C.O's. captured yesterday were of the opinion that none would be made, and the weak state of his reserves behind the front would make it extremely difficult for him to find the troops, as it can safely be reckoned that at least 3 Battalions have been rendered useless in yesterday's attack, and these would have to be replaced by other troops to hold his new front line.

The enemy barrage in reply to ours opened up at 11.5 a.m. on our front line; at 11.36 a.m. it dropped about 400 yards and became less intense; his counter-battery reply and shooting in back areas generally was very weak.

II. IDENTIFICATIONS.

The following Regiments were identified on this Divisional Sector:- 62 I.R., 12th Division, 49th I.R. 140th I.R., 4th Division, 53rd Field Art.Regt., 45th Foot Arty.Bn. The identifications were all normal, but it was found that all regiments had side slipped considerably to the South.

III. PRISONERS' STATEMENTS.

The Attack.
From prisoners, it appears that the 12th Division were fully alarmed and expected an attack, but did not think that it would take place in the middle of the day; the 4th Division, on the other hand, was not in a state of readiness - it would appear therefore that the enemy did not think that the 29th Division would take part in the attack.

Barrage.
Our barrage was reported by prisoners to be very heavy, and in consequence the troops in the front line had no chance of escaping rearward. The smoke barrage also appears to have been very effective.

Losses.
According to a reliable prisoner in one Company of the 62nd I.R., the Company Commander, one of the Platoon Commanders, and about 25 O.R's. were killed by our barrage to-day; according to him the whole Company was practically accounted for.

P.T.O.

(2)

Intentions.

One or two N.C.O. prisoners were of the opinion that it was their intention to gradually withdraw troops from the line in this sector, and evacuate a large part of the salient; their Companies had taken over larger sectors the previous evening, which would mean that either a Regiment or a Division has been withdrawn further South; the prisoners were of the opinion that the 14 I.R. had been withdrawn, but this Regiment may actually have been taken out and put in further South; it seems clear from yesterday's identifications that the sector of the 140 I.R. extends to the railway and perhaps South of it.

IV. INFORMATION FROM OTHER SOURCES.

Fifth Army Front.

Our patrols have entered the enemy's line South of the LYS Canal, capturing 4 prisoners and inflicting casualties.

Enemy observed retreating South of MERVILLE.

General.

A British force has marched through PERSIA from BAGDAD to ENZELI (on the CASPIAN Sea). A detachment has gone to BAKU to help the Armenians and Russians against the Turks.

In N.E. PERSIA British forces have been brought round the southern and western side of AFGHANISTAN and are working up the Trans Caspian Rly.

A French report estimates the German casualties from August 1914 up to the 17th June at 6,000,000 killed, wounded, and missing, of which 1,520,000 have been killed.

There are now nearly 1,400,000 American troops in France.

J. Turvill
for Lieut

Lieut.Colonel, G.S.,
29th Division.

19th August 1918.

P.

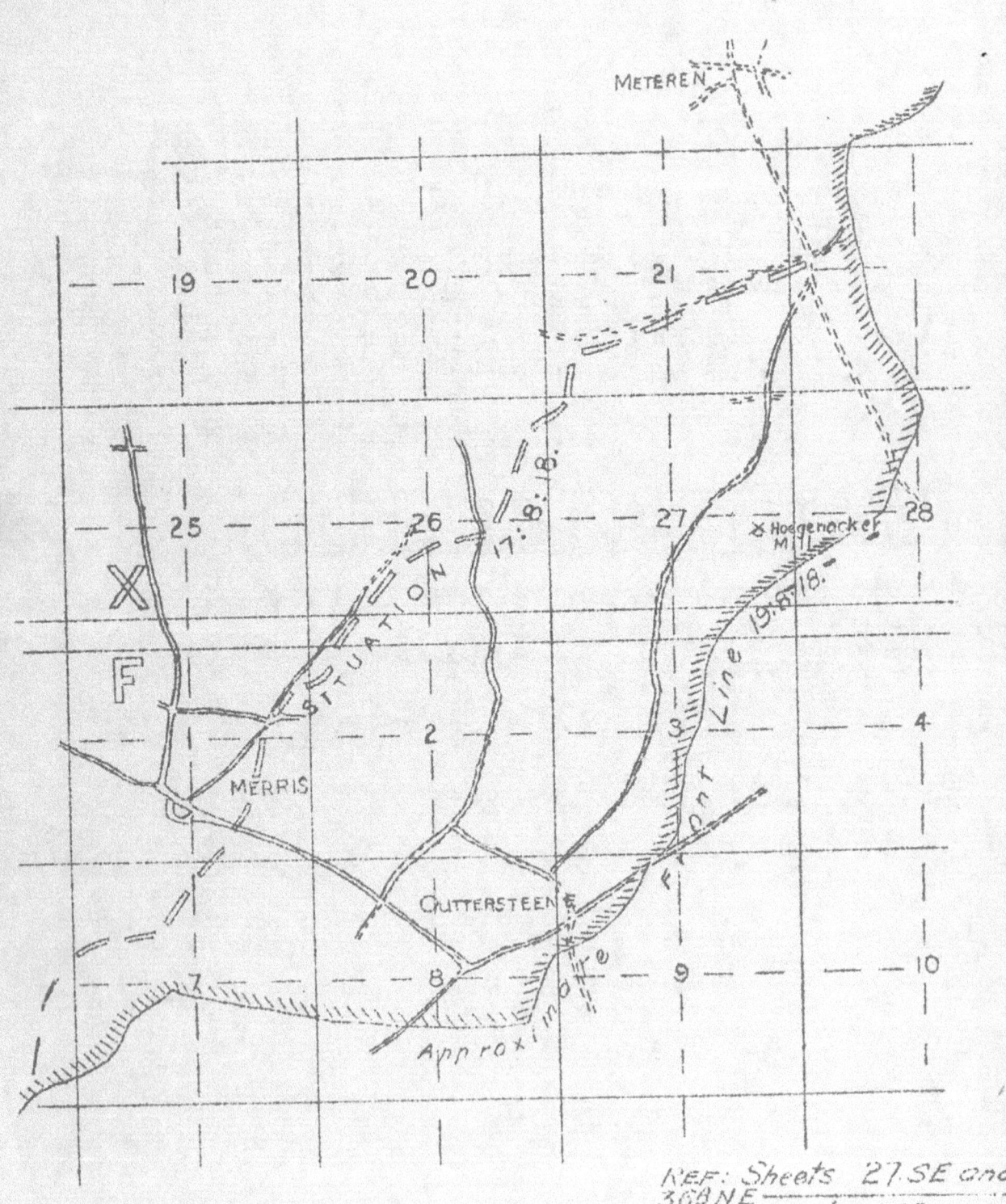

WAR DIARY
INTELLIGENCE SUMMARY

SEPTEMBER 1918

Army Form C. 2118.

Place	Date	Hour	Summary of Events and Information	Remarks and references to Appendices
Reserve Line.	1st Sept. 1918		Quiet watch. 1st London Left Battalion remained in "J" (OUTERSTEENE LINE). Casualties 4 O.R's killed, 4 O.R's wounded. 2/Lt. Renwick rejoined. 1 O.R. sick evac.	
"	2nd Sept. 1918		During the day Companies prepared to move into the line, when in the evening they relieved the 2/4 Londoners in the firing line. Casualties – 1 O.R. wounded. 3 O.R's sick evac. 6 O.R's joined from base.	
Firing Line.	3rd Sept. 1918		At 5.30 a.m. Companies commenced to advance to objectives and by 10 noon they had reached the outskirts of NIEPPE. During the afternoon, Companies continued the pursuit of the enemy, finally digging in about 1000 yards in front of NIEPPE VILLAGE. In the evening the Battalion was relieved by the 11th London Regt, and moved into OULTERSTEENE. Quiet bombardment at 11 p.m. lasting 1/2 hour. Casualties – Lts. Thickett, Ryan, R.A.M.C. gassed on duty. Quiet watch. 1 O.R. sick. 1 O.R. wounded.	
Reserve Line.	4th Sept. 1918		Battalion resting and cleaning up. Burying of horse corpses, etc. Casualties – 2 O.R's sick evac.	
"	5th Sept. 1918		Companies at the distance of 0.6 days. Battalion by Divine Officer. Battalion bathing in the afternoon. Casualties – 2/Lieut. R.D. Wyles + Servant despatch into hospital. 1 O.R. sick, 1 O.R. struck off strength of 8th Bn. taken on battalion.	

Army Form C. 2118.

WAR DIARY
or
INTELLIGENCE SUMMARY.
(Erase heading not required.)

Sheets 36d. 1/40000 & 36. 1/40000.

Place	Date	Hour	Summary of Events and Information	Remarks and references to Appendices
RESERVE LINE.	6th Sept 1918.		Battalion moved into forward area and occupied camp at NIXON FORK (A.2.c.8.2) South of BAILLEUL. Casualties - nil.	
"	7th Sept 1918.		"A", "B" & "C" Companies on Working Parties. "D" Company as divisional D.b Company for fitting of equipment, etc. Casualties - 3 O.R's transferred to 6th M.G.B.	
"	8th Sept 1918.		Companies at the disposal of D.b Companies till 12 noon for re-organization, fitting of equipment, etc. Officers and N.C.O's on map reading nd the use at the Compass. Casualties - 14 O.R's sick.	
"	9th Sept 1918.		Companies at the disposal of O.b. Coys for preliminary instruction firing of equipment, etc. Casualties - 3 O.R's reinforcement.	
"	10th Sept 1918.		Battalion moved to camp at V.19 b.3.a (NEVADA FARM). Afternoon devoted to cleaning of kit, stacking of latter stores, etc. Casualties - 1 OR wounded.	
NEVADA FARM.	11th Sept 1918.		From 6.15 a.m. to 9 a.m., Companies engaged on the cleaning of camp & billets. 9 a.m. till 12 noon - battalion to be at disposal of Company Commanders, patrols and small fatigue parties being carried out.	

D. D. & L. London, E.C.
W't. W. 17178 M 2931 750,000 5/17 **Sch. 52** Forms C 2118/14
(A'00)

Army Form C. 2118.

WAR DIARY
or
INTELLIGENCE SUMMARY.
(Erase heading not required.)

Instructions regarding War Diaries and Intelligence Summaries are contained in F. S. Regs., Part II. and the Staff Manual respectively. Title pages will be prepared in manuscript.

Remarks and references to Appendices: Sheet 27. - 1/4 a.a.a.o.

Place	Date	Hour	Summary of Events and Information
NEVADA FARM.	11th Septr 1918. (contd)		Battalion relieved by the Natural Rifles in "Invictous". Casualties - 5 O.R.'s wounded. 5 O.R.'s rejoined sick.
"	12th Septr 1918.	6.15 a.m. to 7.15 a.m.	Battalion on the morning of shoots and bombing practice.
		10 a.m.	The Battalion march to billets and previous bombing at H. 30. a. 8. 8 near WALLON CAPPEL. Casualties - 1 O.R. sick. 5 O.R.'s rejoined sick.
WALLON CAPPEL.	13th Septr 1918.		Inspection of kits & equipments by the Commanding Officer. Letters to all officers who had to by the Commanding Officer re "Divisions' Esprit de Corps". Lieut. W.B. James M.C., transfer the military medal by X.th Corps he 16244 Pte R.Y. Hart transferred to 52nd Division. Casualties - 1 O.R. killed. 1 O.R. wounded. 3 O.R.'s sick. 13 O.R.'s rejoined.
"	14th Septr 1918.		Inspection of Lewis equipments by the Commanding Officer. M[?] & tough of Stretcher Bearers & Cyclists Battalion joined for duty. 3 O.R.'s rejoined sick. Casualties - 2 O.R.'s sick.
"	15th Septr 1918.		Major Ll. Bruceland M.C. assumed temporary command of the Battalion vice Lt. Col. Batty-Parnell D.S.O. in hosp. to sick. Battalion attended Divine Service. Casualties - 4 O.R.'s rejoined sick. 1 O.R. rejoined wounded.

Army Form C. 2118.

WAR DIARY
or
INTELLIGENCE SUMMARY.
(Erase heading not required.)

Instructions regarding War Diaries and Intelligence Summaries are contained in F. S. Regs., Part II. and the Staff Manual respectively. Title pages will be prepared in manuscript.

Place	Date	Hour	Summary of Events and Information	Remarks and references to Appendices
WALLON CAPPEL	17th Sept 1918.		Bn. Later. moved to a new area received tents at F.25.a.2.9. St JAN TER BIEZEN. Casualties - Nil.	Sheets 27 & 28. 1/40,000
ST JAN TER BIEZEN	18th Sept 1918.		Battalion at the disposal of O.C. bgd. HQ Personnel under the Sig. Sig. Officer under the Bttn. Intelligence Section. Parties to all Officers by the Commanding Officer. Casualties - 2 O.R. sick evacuated.	
"	18th Sept	10.10	Rendezvous on the rifle range from 9 a.m. to 12.30 p.m. also for training, lunch. H.Q. Officers, M.O.'s, C.S.M.'s to talk from Intelligence with C.A.B. Officer. Casualties - 1 O.R. sick evacuated. 1 O.R. trans. to T.M.B.	
"	19th Sept		Battalion at the disposal of O.C. bgd. for musketry at Cattle Green, equipment etc. Headquarters Personnel under the Sig. In the evening the Bttn. marched into the line, relieving the 29th B.I. and 10. Yorkshire Brigade Group, arriving the Menin Road System. Relief complete - 12.30 a.m. 20/9/18. Casualties - 1 O.R. sick evacuated. Draft of 5 O.R. joined. Disposition of Battn. in Line - B, C, & D Coys. from YPRES - MENIN Road to	

Army Form C. 2118.

WAR DIARY
or
INTELLIGENCE SUMMARY.
(Erase heading not required.)

Place	Date	Hour	Summary of Events and Information	Remarks and references to Appendices
FIRING LINE	20th September		ZILLEBEKE Lake. A Coy. in Reserve in YPRES ECOLE. Battalion H.Q. in YPRES Ramparts at I.14.d.1.8.	
			Little activity on either side. Town of YPRES shelled intermittently during day. Patrols sent out at night & 4 forward Posts were established. Casualties - NIL.	
"	21st September		"D" Coys Patrol captured 3 prisoners in the early morning. Work on improvement of trenches. Situation normal. "B" Coy. established a L.G. Post in front of their line, at I.16.c.2.6. "D" Coy. sent out party at night to recruit the TUILERIE. Casualties:- 1 O.R. wounded. Draft of 7 O.R. joined.	
"	22nd September		"D" Coys Post at the TUILERIE was attacked early in the morning & resulted in casualties to our garrison of 7 O.R. killed, 20 O.R. wounded, & 10 O.R. missing. Lieut. D.M. DOUAVIE rejoined from remount. A & C Coys & 1 Platoon of B Coy. were relieved by 1st LANCS. FUSILIERS. Relief complete at 1-45 a.m. 23-9-18. Companies relieved took up a position in Close Support	

Army Form C. 2118.

WAR DIARY
or
INTELLIGENCE SUMMARY.
(Erase heading not required.)

Instructions regarding War Diaries and Intelligence Summaries are contained in F.S. Regs., Part II. and the Staff Manual respectively. Title pages will be prepared in manuscript.

Place	Date	Hour	Summary of Events and Information	Remarks and references to Appendices
SUPPORT LINE	29th September		YPRES & vicinity heavily bombarded during early morning. Situation normal during day. Casualties - 1 O.R. to U.K. for Perm. Commission. 1 O.R. attached Batt. as candidate for Perm. Commission.	
"	24th September		1 Aviator taken during early morning. Battalion relieved by the 1/Worcester Regt. & moved by Tram Tr. ROAD CAMP ST. JAN TER BEZIEN. Battalion all in camp by 5.30 a.m. 25-9-18. 2/Lt. A.S. GARDINER struck off strength 2 wound. 3 O.R. sick evac.	
ROAD CAMP	25th September		Battalion resting & cleaning up. Casualties:- 1 O.R. to U.K. for Perm. Commission. 6 O.R. sick evac. 9 O.R. to Base unfit. 1 O.R. rejoined Sick.	
"	26th September		Battalion preparing to move. Battalion paraded at 8 p.m. & marched to POPERINGHE taking over Billets in the RHOISTERS. Town slightly shelled. Lieut. N.D. KENNEDY proceeded to join 1/4 K.O.S.B. Lieut. A.W. WYLIE rejoined from 87th Bde. H.Q. 6 O.R. sick evac. 2 O.R. trans. to T.M.B.	

WAR DIARY or INTELLIGENCE SUMMARY

Army Form C. 2118.

Ref. Maps - YPRES 1/40.000
GHELEVELT 1/10.000

Place	Date	Hour	Summary of Events and Information	Remarks and references to Appendices
POPERINGHE	27th SEPTEMBER		Battalion ordered to take part in a general advance on the 28th. Sept. Battn. Paraded at 4 p.m. & moved by motor buses & light railway to place of assembly in S.11.d.3. Rd. YPRES. Scheme of operations & objectives as per attached Battn. O.O. No. 70.	
FIRING LINE	28th SEPTEMBER	About 1 a.m.	Battalion moved forward to CARAVAN TRENCH - jumping off point. After a preliminary bombardment lasting 5 minutes our barrage came down at 5.30 a.m. & the Battn. commenced the advance in artillery formation. The 2/5 W. Sur. & 1/4 Bord. Regt. captured their objectives without much opposition & the Battn. passed through these units to the assault of TOWER HAMLETS & JED TREN. By approximately 9.40 a.m. the Battalion had gained their objectives. No enemy opposition was met with being principally by M.Gs trained on DULLONS. When the Battalion had gained their objective the 85th Bde. passed through & continued the advance. About 5.30 p.m. C. & D. Coys. moved forward to protect right flank of 88th Bde. At 7.30 p.m. the distribution of the Battalion was - C & D Coys in P.35 &	

Army Form C. 2118.

WAR DIARY
or
INTELLIGENCE SUMMARY.
(Erase heading not required.)

Instructions regarding War Diaries and Intelligence Summaries are contained in F. S. Regs., Part II. and the Staff Manual respectively. Title pages will be prepared in manuscript.

Place	Date	Hour	Summary of Events and Information	Remarks and references to Appendices
FIRING LINE	29th SEPTEMBER		A. & B. in TOWER HAMLETS — VELDHOEK line. Situation during night very quiet. Casualties to Battalion during 24 hours:— Captain AHATON, 4 o.R. killed; Captain B.C. ROBERTSON Highland Cyclist Batn. wounded; 1 o.R. killed; 10 o.R. wounded. Prisoners & material captured by Battn. during 24 hours:— Prisoners 250; 10 & 77 c.m. guns; 12 Machine Guns; 2 Trench Mortars & ant:- Trench rifles; 5 Aerophot anguns; & 3 horses.	
"	30th SEPTEMBER		65th Bn. continued the advance. A & B Coys. changed into with Cd. Engrs. Casualties:— 8 o.R. wounded; 22 R. missing. Proportion of Battalion remained the same. Casualties:— 1 o.R. wounded. Colonel G.E. BEATY-PWNFALL D.S.O. returned from leave. Dictated by [signature] Captain, 1/KOSB	

Secret   Copy No. 4

Operation Order No 40
by Major C. H. Crawshaw M.C.
Commanding 1st Battn. The K.O.S.B.
In the Field ... 26:9:18

Ref. Sheets :—   Ypres   1 : 10,000
                      Ghelevult   1 : 10,000

1. The 87th. Infantry Bde. will attack on a date and at a zero hour to be notified later.

2. Boundaries and objectives are marked on map already issued.

3. The 87th. Bde will attack on a <u>one</u> Battalion front. The 86th. Bde will be on the left, the 35th. Division on the right. The 88th. Inf. Bde. will be in Reserve.

4. The plan of attack will be as follows :—
   (a) 2nd S.W.B. will attack up to the RED LINE
   (b) 1st Border Regiment will pass through this line & make good the GREEN LINE marked "Approximate Objective".
   (c) It is essential that the STIRLING CASTLE — CLAPHAM JUNCTION Ridge be taken.
   If hostile resistance is easily overcome the 1st K.O.S.B. will be used to capture TOWER HAMLETS and VELDHOEK and the 2nd Royal Fusiliers on the left will be used to capture the POLDERHOEK SPUR — CAMERON HOUSE
   (d) The 88th. Inf. Bde. will be used to exploit success by capturing GHELEVULT.

5. The day will be known as J day

6. On I/J night the Battn. will move to assembly positions in CARAVAN TRENCH — from Gordon House Siding on left to the Zillebeke Stream on the right.

7. Companies will occupy CARAVAN TRENCH as follows:— A. B. D. C. (from the Right).
Battn. H.Q. will be in ARCADIA VILLA.

8. <u>Method of advance</u>:—
Shortly after zero the Battn. will on receipt of orders move out from CARAVAN TRENCH in 2 lines of 2 coys. with platoons in artillery formation. In the 1st line, A will be on the right
C will be on the left
In the 2nd line, B will be on the right
D will be on the left.
The approximate inter-company boundary will be a line running immediately S of MOATED GRANGE to TULERIE CHIMNEY thence due East through YEOMANRY POST — JASPER DUGOUTS.
A Coy. will be responsible for keeping direction. Its right will be on the N side of ZILLEBEKE LAKE & will follow that line until the ZILLEBEKE — HELLFIRE CORNER road is reached. On reaching this road the advance will be made on a bearing of 102° magnetic.

9. <u>Barrage</u>.— The barrage will fall on the Blue line at zero and will lift at zero + 4.
Jumps will be 100 yards per 3 min.
Every 500 yds. it will dwell for 6 min. (This will be distinguished by Thermite shell being fired which gives a most brilliant flash.)
At the Red line it will dwell for 12 minutes after which there will be no more halts until the Black line is reached.
East of the Black line the attack will be supported by heavies. The creep will be 1000 yards in 45 minutes. The halt on the Black line will be 3 minutes.

(3)

10. Signals:—

(a) The S.O.S. will be inoperative until the barrage ceases.

(b) Contact Planes will be called for by Planes at (1) Z + 2 hours 15 min.
 (2) Z + 4 hours.

All means of establishing contact with planes will be taken and must be shown whenever a plane calls. For this purpose Discs and America cloth Flaps on S.B.R.s will be carried.

A contact plane will sound its Klaxon Horn & drop white Very lights when calling for flares &c. The contact planes will be marked with TWO BLACK RECTANGULAR FLAPS (2 feet by 1 ft. 3 ins.) attached to the lower planes. Each plane will also have a streamer. All ranks must be warned how to recognise a contact aeroplane.

(c) Counter attack aeroplanes will be in the air from Zero + 1 hour onwards to give warning of an impending hostile attack. This warning will be given by the plane dropping a Red Parachute light over the locality. It will also call for artillery by Wireless.

(d) Dropping S.A.A. from Aeroplanes:—

A certain number of planes have been detailed to drop S.A.A. on parachutes should it be required. Two kinds of S.A.A. will be dropped.
 (a) Bundle packed (b) M.G. ammn. in belts.

Battn. H.Q. will signal that S.A.A. is wanted as follows:—

N = M.G. S.A.A. required

△ = Bundle S.A.A. required

Each signal will be made up of white cloth 12 feet by 1 foot, and in each case attention will

(4)

Signals (continued)

be called by firing a white Very light from the ground.

As the amount a plane can carry is limited, this method should only be adopted in cases of extreme urgency.

All parachutes must be collected & returned.

11. Rations :— 1 day's extra rations will be carried in addition to the Emergency Ration.

12. Water :— All water bottles must be filled on I/T night and must not be used. All water required for use during the night will be sent up in Petrol Tins. 50% will carry an extra water bottle.

13. Prisoners of War :— These will be sent down to Prisoners of War Cage at the Barracks, Ypres. O.C. Coys must see that only the smallest possible escort is sent down, otherwise fighting strength is depleted.

14. Medical Arrangements :—

The R.A.P. and bearers will move forward with Battn. H.Q.

    Aid Posts - - - - - - - Ramparts
    A.D.S. - - - - - - - - Prison, Ypres.
    Embussing Point
    for Walking Wounded - - - - near Ypres Station
    Main D.S. - - - - - - Hop. Factory.

(5.)

15. <u>Battn. H.Q.</u> will be in ARCADIA HOUSE
The probable jumps will be to
(1) KENNEDY'S PILLBOX at L 16 c. 2.7.
(2) RIDGE ST. TUNNELS
(3) JASPER DUGOUTS

16. <u>Dress</u> :— <u>Fighting order.</u> (No spades or picks will be carried)
(a) Each man will carry 1 Mill's Grenade.
(b) Each man will carry a Red Aeroplane Flare.
(c) All riflemen will carry 170 rounds.

17. <u>Dump</u> :— The Bde Dump is at I 9 d 15.10 (near the School, Ypres) from which arrangements have been made to send up supplies of S.A.A. and water as soon as possible by Pack Mule Train which will probably come up the Warrington Plank Road.

(Sd.) C. H. Crawshaw, Major
Cmdg. 1/K.O.S.B.

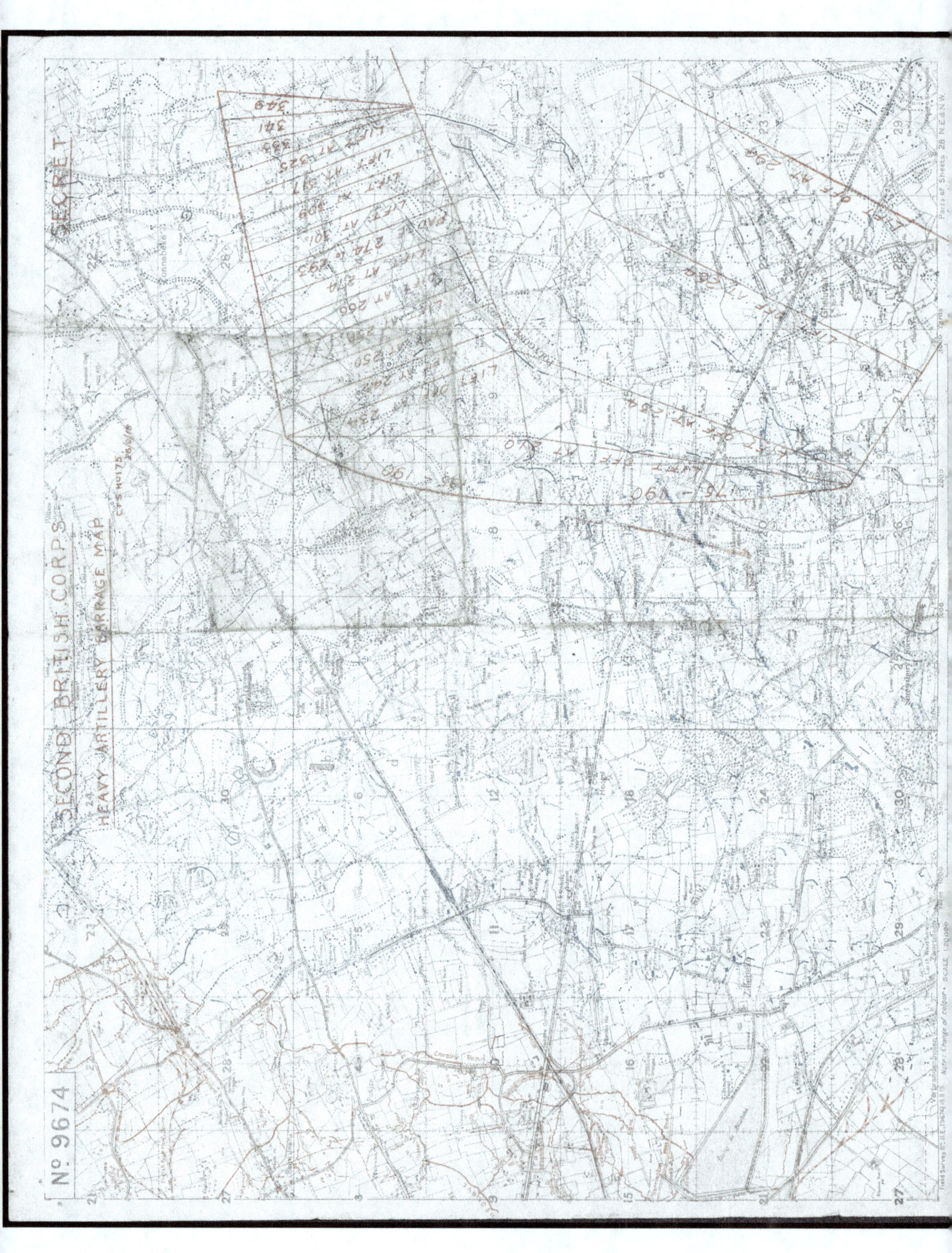

Army Form C. 2118.

WAR DIARY
or
INTELLIGENCE SUMMARY.
(Erase heading not required.)

VOLUME No. 51
1 KOBR
OCTOBER 1916.

Reference Map Sheet 20.

Place	Date	Hour	Summary of Events and Information	Remarks and references to Appendices
LHQ	1st October		Revd. H.Q.; Lt. W. Harris, & draft joined C & D Companies in Tower Hamlets - Valdhoek Line. Colonel B.S.H. PONHALL D.S.O. went forward to join A & B Companies. Casualties - Nil.	
	2nd October		Orders received for Battn. H.Q. & C & D Coys. to move forward to join A & B Coys. Battalion took over line from 2/HAMPSHIRE REGT. Casualties :- 6 O.R. sick evacuated; 1 O.R. missing.	
	3rd October		Quiet day. Battalion relieved by the 20TH D.L.I. & marched to a former enemy Pill Camp at KRUISEIKE (nr. GHELUVELT). Camp heavily shelled as Battalion was marching in & orders were issued for Companies to carry on to the old camping area - the TOWER HAMLETS - VELDHOEK Line. Battalion in camp by 5 am on 4/10/16. 2/Lieut. J.A.P.RENWICK, 3/K.O.S.B. 9 wounded ;- 3 O.R. killed ; 10 O.R. wounded. 2/Lieut. H.L. PURDOMS H.K.O.S.B. struck off strength to U.K. sick 28.9.16. 1 O.R. rejoined sick.	

Army Form C. 2118.

WAR DIARY
or
INTELLIGENCE SUMMARY.
(Erase heading not required.)

Place	Date	Hour	Summary of Events and Information	Remarks and references to Appendices
			Reference Map, Sheet 28.	
VELDHOEK LINE in the Trenches.	5th October		Battalion handed at 2 pm & marched to the WESTHOEK area. Battalion accommodated in Pillboxes & Dugouts. Casualties - 1 O.R. sick evacuated.	
WESTHOEK	5th October		Battalion resting & cleaning up. Casualties - 3 O.R. sick evacuated. 2/Lieut. T. SIMPSON, 3rd K.O.S.B. & draft of 40 O.R. joined. Lt. BROWN M.N. to U.K. for Temp. Commission. 3 O.R. sick evacuated.	
"	6th October		Divine Service. Companies at disposal of O.C. Companies for reorganization. Casualties - 10 O.R. sick evacuated.	
"	7th October		Battalion paraded at 2 pm & marched to Billets in YPRES - Ramparts & vicinity. Casualties - 6 O.R. sick evacuated.	

Army Form C. 2118.

WAR DIARY
INTELLIGENCE SUMMARY.
(Erase heading not required.)

Reference Map - Sheet 28.

Place	Date	Hour	Summary of Events and Information	Remarks and references to Appendices
YPRES	8th October		Battalion intended an Battle Drill for inspection by the Commanding Officer. Thought Lines heavily shelled during night - 3 O.Ranks killed & 3 wounded. I.O.R. wounded. Draft of 10 O.R. joined. 2/Lieut. W.C. BROWN, 9/ R.I.S.B. for B'n. as attd.	
"	9th October		Bde. Gymnal Parade for inspection by II Corps Commander. 8 O.R. sick evac. I.O.R. rej. from hospital.	
"	10th October		Battalion preparing for move. Lieut-Colonel G.E. BEATY-POWNALL D.S.O. wounded in the head by H.E. about 1130 & died in 10th C.C.S. 2 hours later. Major C.H. CRAWSHAW M.C. assumed command of the Battn. Battalion marched to former Camping Area at WESTHOEK. 2 O.R. sick evac.	
WESTHOEK	11th October		Battalion preparing for the Line. Battalion marched off at 1430 & relieved the 4/WORCESTER REGT. in the Right Sub-Sector of the Divisional Front. Disposition of Battalion:- A Coy Right Firing Line; B Coy Left Firing Line; D Coy in support; C Coy in Reserve. Battalion H.Q. at L.S.E.E.T. Relief complete at 2230. 3 O.R. sick evac.	

Army Form C. 2118.

WAR DIARY
or
INTELLIGENCE SUMMARY.
(Erase heading not required.)

Reference Maps Sheets 28 & 29.
(See Operation Orders & Narrative attached).

Place	Date	Hour	Summary of Events and Information	Remarks and references to Appendices
FIRING LINE	12th October		Forward Area heavily shelled in the early morning. Situation quiet during forenoon. About 2300 three hundred Gas Projectors were fired from our line between L.9.a.5.6 & L.8.C.7.6. D & A Coys furnished working parties at night - D Coy carrying bridges from Bttn. H.Q. to forward dumps, & A Coy digging small trench at L.9.d.6.2. 1 O.R. sick evac.	
"	13th October		Patrols from A & B Coys were sent out to secure an identification but were unsuccessful. Front Line slightly shelled about 04.30. Orders issued for Battn. to take part in a general advance on morning of 14th inst. Battalion moved back at 2000 to assembly positions near SCORER CORNER. Gas shell set H.Q. Billets on fire. Lieut. J.K.DRON, H.L.I. 2 O.R. killed, 2 O.R. wounded, 1 O.R. accid. wounded. 9 O.R. sick evac.	
"	14th October	0530.	Forward Area heavily shelled between 0400 & 0500. Our Barrage opened at 0530. At 0730 the Battalion moved forward through LEDEGHEM. Halt made East of the village about 0930. Forward move resumed at 1500, the Battalion marching in Diamond formation to a point about 3000 yds the East. Battalion accommodated in houses. 2nd Lieut. R.C.SLADE M.C. 3/K.O.S.B. wounded. 1 O.R. wounded.	

Army Form C. 2118.

WAR DIARY
INTELLIGENCE SUMMARY.
(Erase heading not required.)

Place	Date	Hour	Summary of Events and Information	Remarks and references to Appendices
				Ref. Map Sheet 29.
FIRING LINE	15th October		Battalion assembled at 0600 no Battalion in Bde. Reserve. Barrage opened at 0900. Bde. moved forward about 0930. Enemy put down heavy barrage. 87th Bde. moved through 88th Bde. about 1020. Battalion halted East of SAINES about 1130 moving forward again at 1300 to the outskirts of HEULE. About 1600 the Battalion set out to exploit along railway running North of HEULE. A, B, & D Coys. made good bridgeheads over the HEULEBEEK at WATERMOLEN, OLD MILL & CUERNE, and opposition being met with from Machine Guns. A. Coy. captured 2 M.Go. during this operation. During the night Posts were established on the River LYS. 2.O.R. killed. 2/Lieut. J.W.M. JAMIESON, 4/K.O.S.B. wounded; 18 O.R. wounded. 30 R. sick one.	
"	16th October		Enemy active on the opposite side of the LYS - M.Gs, Snipers & Sniping guns. Battalion area heavily shelled. In the afternoon & evening the Battalion was relieved by the 2/HAMPSHIRE REGT. & marched back 8th Billets on the outskirts of HEULE. One 5.9, 2 Field Pieces & 2 M.Gs were captured by the Battalion during the operations from 10th to 16th October. 1.O.R. killed. 2/Lieut. J. ROUGH, Argh. & Suth. wounded, 7 O.R. wounded.	

Army Form C. 2118.

324

WAR DIARY
or
INTELLIGENCE SUMMARY.
(Erase heading not required.)

Ref. Map Sheet 29.

Place	Date	Hour	Summary of Events and Information	Remarks and references to Appendices
HEULE (SH.10.C)	17th October.		Battalion resting & cleaning up. Induction of Battle Stores, etc. 1 O.R. accid. wounded. 7 O.R. sick evac.	
"	18th October.		Companies at disposal of O.C. Coys. for reorganization etc. Major C.H. CRAWSHAW M.C., commanding Battalion presented Divisional Cards of Honour to recipients on parade. 2 O.R. wounded. 10 O.R. sick evac. Draft of 20 O.R. joined.	
"	19th October.		Lieut. Colonel W.T. WILKINSON D.S.O., K.O.S.B., arrived & resumed command of the Battalion. Brigade at half hour's notice to move forward to take part in further operations. 1 O.R. sick evac. 2 O.R. rej. sick. 1 O.R. rejoined wounded.	
"	20th October.		Battalion paraded & marched off at 1300. Battalion crossed the LYS & went into scattered Billets about TINGE FM (I.26 central). Billeting difficult as most of the buildings were already occupied by other units. Own ermamt heavily shelled as a precaution this not day. Casualties – NIL.	

Army Form C. 2118.

WAR DIARY
or
INTELLIGENCE SUMMARY.
(Erase heading not required.)

Remarks and references to Appendices:

Reg. Map Sheet 29.
(See Narrative of Operations attached.)

Place	Date	Hour	Summary of Events and Information	Remarks
LINE	21st October		Day spent in resting & preparing for the advance. Casualties NIL.	
"	22nd October		At 0230 the Commdg. Officer attended conference at 1st Border Regt. H.Q.'s where the Brigadier issued orders for the attack. At 0630 the Battalion moved to assembly positions behind ridge at WOLFSBERG - B Coy. on Right & C Coy. on Left in First Line - A Coy. Right & D Coy. Left in Second Line. Owing was slow & it was impossible to assemble close to our Front Line. At ZERO hour, 0900, the barrage opened & the Battalion moved forward under slight enemy shelling. In touch on Right with 1st. Border Regt. & on Left with 9th. Division. In spite of heavy M.G. fire the Battalion captured several farms with 176 prisoners, 28 M.G.s & 2 Trench Mortars. The advance on the Right was held up by M.G. fire from the direction of KATTESTRAAT & OOTEGHEM. Battalion relieved by 2 Battn. 2/S.W.B. & moved back into Billets about RAPPAART. Relief complete by midnight. Lieut. J.H. MAXWELL & 2/Lieut. T.W.L BIRREL wounded. 8 O.R. killed; 58 O.R. wounded & 1 O.R. missing.	
RAPPART	23rd October		Resting & cleaning up. At 1900 Battalion paraded & marched to Billets in HARLEBEKE. 1 O.R. wounded, 5 O.R. sick evac.	

Army Form C. 2118.

WAR DIARY
or
INTELLIGENCE SUMMARY.
(Erase heading not required.)

Ref. Maps - Sheet 29 & TOURNAI 5.

Place	Date	Hour	Summary of Events and Information	Remarks and references to Appendices
HARLEBEKE	24th October		Companies at the disposal of O.C. Coys for cleaning up, inspections, etc. Casualties Nil.	
"	25th October		Reorganisation of Companies. I.O.R. (Confirmd) at Div H.Q. killed. Notification received of the award of the Military Medal to the following:- 17575, Sgt. Stringfellow W. B Coy; 21302, Pte. Buarley E.C. D Coy; 12243, Pte. Bryson J. C Coy; 31105, L/Cpl. Cooper J. B Coy; 24834, Pte. Nicholson W. D Coy; 201900, Pte. Freeman W. D Coy; 202043, L/Cpl. Peaker W. B Coy; 27757, Pte. Symington A. Att. 29th Div H.Q.	
"	26th October		Close Order Drill & Specialist Training. Baths. Notification received of the a/m awards:- Bar to M.Bs of Major C.H. CRAWSHAW M.C., M.C. of Lieut A.W. WYLIE; Bar to M.M., 21871, L/Cpl. BELL C.M.H. A Coy; M.M., 202327, Sgt. ELLIS F. B Coy, 10257, L/Cpl. STORGEON R. C Coy, 41637, Pte. COOKE E. D Coy, 24986, Pte. McCONNELL T. B Coy, 13465, Pte. BELL R. A Coy; 24166, Pte. LITTLE D. A Coy, 30936, Pte. KING H. D Coy; 12157, Pte. BROWN T. D Coy, 284831, Pte. CROUGHAN J. B Coy, 33596, Pte. McKENZIE W. B Coy, 20164, L/Cpl. HUDSON T.H. A Coy, 27879, Cpl. RAESIDE H. D Coy, 15860, L/Cpl. JONES R. A Coy, 27222, L/Cpl. HALE J. D Coy, 16376, L/Cpl. PORTER J.L. B Coy, 17190, Pte. SYLES J. A Coy, 10742, L/Cpl. STEWART J.H. D Coy, 10946, Cpl. DORAN J. B Coy. I.O.R. Sick, none.	

Army Form C. 2118.

WAR DIARY
or
INTELLIGENCE SUMMARY.
(Erase heading not required.)

Ref. Map Sheet 36 (Belgium & France).

Place	Date	Hour	Summary of Events and Information	Remarks and references to Appendices
HARLEBEKE	27th October		Battalion paraded at 0725 & marched via STACEGHEM, COURTRAI, & HELBEKE to Billets in the MOUSCRON Area (at TOURCOING). 13 O.R. sick evac.	
MOUSCRON AREA	28th October		Battalion paraded at 0853 & marched via TOURCOING, MOUVEAUX & WAINBRECHIES, to Billets in the Reghem at STATION ST. ANDRE. 5 O.R. sick evac. M/O Capt. A.W. WYLIE to F.A. Sick.	
ST. ANDRE	29th October		Companies at disposal of O.C. Coys for Kit Inspection & Close Order Drill. Battalion addressed by the S.O.C. 87th Bde. 10 O.R. sick evac.	
"	30th October		Companies at disposal at O.C. Coys. Close Order Drill. Commanding Officer's Parade for Ceremonial Drill. Major C.H. CRAWSHAW M.C. to U.K. for 6 mths tour of duty. Captain C.H.V. CRICHTON-BROWNE, a/Adjutant, resumed duties of Second in Command. Captain F. DALE M.C. appointed a/Adjutant. Lieut. D.C. BULLEN-SMITH M.C. joined for duty. 3 O.R. sick evac.	

Army Form C. 2118.

332

WAR DIARY
or
INTELLIGENCE SUMMARY.

(Erase heading not required.)

Instructions regarding War Diaries and Intelligence Summaries are contained in F. S. Regs., Part II. and the Staff Manual respectively. Title pages will be prepared in manuscript.

Place	Date	Hour	Summary of Events and Information	Remarks and references to Appendices
ST. ANDRE.	31st October		Brigade Ceremonial Parade (rehearsal). Draft of 35 O.R. joined.	

Dictated by

[signed] Captain,
Adjutant
1st [illegible]

OPERATIONS OF 87th INFANTRY BRIGADE
From 28th September, 1918 to 15th October, 1918.

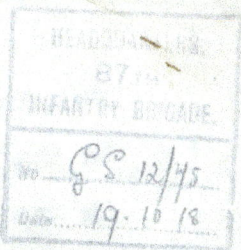

September 28th. On the 28th September, all preparations for the attack having been made, zero hour was fixed for 5.30 a.m. At 5.30 a.m. the 2nd S.W.B. jumped off under our barrage and the German reply to our barrage was weak. The Brigade went over in the following order: 2nd S.W.B. attacking, 1st Border Regt. in support and the 1st K.O.S.B. in reserve. The 1st K.O.S.B. crossed our old front line at 5.55 a.m. just behind Brigade Headquarters, and the 2nd S.W.B. gained their first objective, the JACKDAW SWITCH PLANK ROAD, by 6.30 a.m. with very little resistance. At this point the 1st Border Regt. leapfrogged over the 2nd S.W.B. and continued the advance, having as their objective the high ground at STIRLING CASTLE. This objective was gained by the 1st Border Regt. by 7.35 a.m., and Headquarters of the 1st Border Regt. were established in JACKDAW TUNNELS, the Battalion having passed over the crest and making good the forward slope.

Thus the first objective of the 87th Infantry Brigade was gained well up to time.

On this line the 1st K.O.S.B. leapfrogged the 1st Border Regt. and moved on for their objective, TOWER HAMLETS. TOWER HAMLETS was reached by the 1st K.O.S.B. at 9.40 a.m., and they pushed through nearly to GHELUVELT, capturing an enemy battery.

The resistance, which was not very great, was chiefly from machine guns, and the different regiments having gained valuable experience in the method of dealing with pill-boxes and machine guns in the advance from OUTTERSTEENE, were able to deal efficiently with any centres of resistance which attempted to hold them up.

Many prisoners and much material, including artillery, was captured, but owing to the rapid advance it was impossible to deal with prisoners or material, and thus neither were counted.

After the 1st K.O.S.B. had taken TOWER HAMLETS the 89th Infantry Brigade pushed through astride the MENIN ROAD, and the

87th Infantry Brigade arranged to guard their right flank, owing to the left Brigade of the right Division not having advanced at th same rate as the 87th Infantry Brigade. The 2nd S.W.B. went forward to fill the gap between TOWER HAMLETS and the right of the 88th Infantry Brigade. Two Coys. of 1st K.O.S.B. were also sent up to support this movement.

By nightfall the 2nd S.W.B. had reached a general line G.35.b.9.5. - G.35.b.3.0. - G.35.d.8.0. - P.5.a.5.7. - J.35.c.0.0. Brigade Headquarters were established at GLASS HOUSES, J.28.b.1.5.

September 29th. Orders having been received from the 29th Division for the 88th Infantry Brigade to push on towards MENIN, the 2nd S.W.B., with two Coys. of 1st K.O.S.B. attached, were ordered to move in conjunction and guard the right flank. The enemy put up a stiff fight during the whole of the day, and from prisoners it was found that he had put in new troops to hold the KRUISEECKE high ground. During the day the left Brigade of the right Division not having moved forward from ZANDVOORDE, the Germans tried to turn the right flank of the Brigade. This was noticed, and the situation dealt with by placing the two Coys. of the 1st K.O.S.B. to guard the right flank of the 2nd S.W.B. During the whole of the day the resistance from KRUISEECKE high ground was considerable, and the whole slope of the hill was swept by hostile machine gun fire. Stokes Mortars were used to silence the machine guns, and in spite of the resistance of the enemy some progress was made. However, towards mid-day and during the afternoon the enemy shelled the ridge with field guns at very close range, and also with guns of heavy calibre.

By nightfall the 2nd S.W.B. had gained the following line on the crest of the hill: J.36.c.5.8. - J.36.c.8.5. - J.36.c.5.2. - P.6.a.3.2. - P.5.a.95.15. - J.35.c.0.0.

After nightfall the 2nd S.W.B. and the two Coys. 1st K.O.S.B. attached were relieved by the 1st Border Regt. plus the remaining two Coys. of the 1st K.O.S.B.

Brigade Headquarters remained at J.28.b.1.5.

3.

September 30th. Relief complete was reported by 4.30 a.m. Patrols having been sent out by the 1st Border Regt. resulted in a message being received at 6.40 a.m. to the effect that it was suspected that the enemy had withdrawn. The 1st Border Regt. was immediately ordered to follow up. This they did, leaving the two attached Coys. of the 1st K.O.S.B. to guard their right flank on the KRUISEECKE high ground. Progress was made over the KRUISEECKE high ground and little opposition was found until the troops got over the crest and on to the forward slope, where the resistance of the enemy suddenly stiffened. He had disposed his machine guns in depth in the pill-boxes back to the GHELUWE Switch Line.

It was reported that the 88th Infantry Brigade had reached GHELUWE and so in spite of considerable opposition the 1st Border Regt. pushed on to keep touch with them. Eventually the Regiment found itself to be in advance of troops on either flank, but maintained its position under cross fire of machine guns from both flanks.

The general line reached at nightfall was: Q.2.c.0.3. - down the road to farm in Q.8.b. - and due West to Q.8.a.1.2.

This position had not been attained without loss, and casualties in this operation were rather severe. However, the position was maintained during the night and all of next day. During the evening of the 30th orders were received that the boundaries of the Division had been altered, and that during the night a Brigade of the 41st Division would pass through and thus relieve the 1st Border Regt. when the 87th Brigade would then come into Divisional reserve.

Brigade Headquarters moved to J.35.c.8.0. during the day.

October 1st. No relief appeared for the 1st Border Regt. during the night, and daylight found them still hanging on to the precarious position into which they had advanced the day before.

However, they received orders to maintain this position until relieved.

At 6.30 a.m. it was found that the advance Brigade of the 41st Division was marching on to WERVICQ. They were turned and sent in the right direction over AMERICA CORNER to the 1st Border Regt. Owing to the heavy Artillery fire and machine gun fire, and the fact that WERVICQ had not been taken, the Brigade of the 41st Division was unable to go forward and relieve the 1st Border Regt. A few men of this Brigade did manage to reach the 1st Border Regt. and at nightfall the whole Brigade moved forward, and the 1st Borders were withdrawn into huts in P.5.a. and J.35.c.

Brigade Headquarters remained at J.35.c.8.0.

October 2nd. The whole Brigade was in rest, and spent the majority of the day in sleeping off the effects of three days very hard fighting.

Orders were received during the day to take over the line on the Divisional front from the 86th and 88th Brigades. The 2nd S.W.B. and 1st K.O.S.B. were ordered forward to effect this relief, a most difficult task with such short notice. The 1st Border Regt. was too exhausted to move.

October 3rd. Relief was completed at 3 a.m. but was not very satisfactory owing to the fluid state in which the posts had been left owing to the attack on GHELUWE. During the whole of the day the front was organised and the exact dispositions were located.

The only post which had been handed over in GHELUWE itself was a Coy. Headquarters at fork road in Q.4.d.3.2. During the morning the enemy brought up some heavy Minenwerfers and shelled this Coy. H.Q. out.

The line now ran as follows: Q.10.a.3.7. - Q.4.c.6.1. - Q.4.c.5.3. - Q.5.b.3.1. - K.33.d.8.2. - K.34.c.8.6. - K.34.d.0.9. - K.34.d.5.0. - K.34.b.0.1. - K.35.a.7.7. - K.29.d.1.5. - with a post at K.29.d.0.7., this later being in liaison with 36th Division,

Orders were received for the front to be handed over to the 124th Infantry Brigade.

October 4th. Relief was completed by 3 a.m., and Battalions moved back to positions they had occupied before going into the line on the night of the 2nd.

At 2 p.m. the Brigade moved out from the KRUISEECKE area to WESTHOEK. Battalions marched independently, and all arrived without incident into the new area.

October 5th. The whole day was spent at WESTHOEK in reorganising and cleaning up.

During the night the area was badly bombed, but no casualties occurred.

October 6th. WESTHOEK. - Warning Order was received that the Brigade may have to go forward again and Officers spent the day reconnoitring the ways across the high ground to BECELAERE and NOORDENHOEK.

Orders were received for the relief of the 87th Infantry Brigade by the 88th Infantry Brigade.

October 7th. 88th Infantry Brigade moved into WESTHOEK during the morning thus relieving the 87th Infantry Brigade in support.

During the afternoon the Brigade moved into YPRES and became brigade in reserve.

October 8th. Day spent in YPRES in reorganising.

October 9th. Brigade was inspected by II Corps Commander during the morning.

Orders were issued for the relief of the 86th Infantry Brigade in the WESTHOEK area.

October 10th. Brigade moved during the afternoon into WESTHOEK area in relief of 86th Infantry Brigade.

Orders were issued for the relief of the 88th Infantry

Brigade on the Divisional Front on night 11/12th.

October 11th.   During the morning, the 2nd S.W.B. and 1st K.O.S.B. moved over the ridge to KEIBURG where they were given a hot meal.

The 1st Border Regt. moved from BECELAERE to POTTERIZBURG during the afternoon relieving the reserve Battalion of the 88th Infantry Brigade.

Guides met the 2nd S.W.B. and 1st K.O.S.B. at 5 p.m. at KEIBURG from whence those Battalions went into the line. Relief was reported complete by 11 p.m.

The 2nd S.W.B. was in the line in LEDEGHEM on the left and the 1st K.O.S.B. on the right.

Brigade Headquarters moved to K.6.o.3.5.

October 12th.   During the early hours of the morning the enemy put down very heavy counter preparation. The day was generally quiet except for some scattered shelling.

At 23.00, 300 gas projectors were put on to LEDEGHEM, and in reply the enemy put down a very heavy barrage of H.E. and gas.

Orders were issued for the relief of 87th Infantry Brigade by 86th and 88th Infantry Brigades on night 13/14th October.

October 13th.   Again during the early hours of the morning the enemy put down a very heavy counter preparation. The day was fairly quiet except again for harassing fire.

The relief was satisfactorily completed by 23.00 and the Brigade moved back into its assembly positions.

The Brigade was dispersed as follows ready for the attack on the 14th. 2nd S.W.B. in trench from K.11.b.5.7. to K.5.d.4.5.
1st K.O.S.B. in shell slits and consolidated shell holes in K.11.a. and b.
1st Border Regt. in trench from K.11.d.5.8. to K.11.b.5.8.
Brigade Headquarters remained at K.6.o.3.5.

Here in the assembly positions the units were given hot food and all preparations were ready for the Brigade to go forward in reserve the next day.

October 14th.   Zero hour was fixed 5.35 a.m. Just prior to Zero

SECRET

Operation Order No.
by
Major G.H. CRAWSHAW MC
Commanding 1/KOSB

Copy No.

Reference. Sheets 28 N.E. and 29 N.W. 1/20000

I. On a day to be known as "J" day and at an hour to be known as "H" hour - the 29 Div: in conjunction with the 9th Div on the North and the 26 Div on the S will attack.

II. The 86 and 88 Bodes will attack on the 29th Divl Front - the 87 Inf Bde being in Divisional Reserve.

III. D Coy 29 Bn M.G.C. will be attached to the Bde.

IV. The Divisional Front will be covered by the following Artillery
  29 D.A + 2 18 pounder batteries.
  2 Bdes R.G.A less two heavy batteries
  1 Siege Battery R.G.A

V. The barrage will fall at H - 3 minutes on a line approx. 200 yds in advance of the forming up posn of the Infantry
At H hour barrage lifts and advances 100 yds every 2 minutes to a line about 250 yds E of light Railway in L3 and L9 a.p. where it will halt until H+45
At H+45 minutes the barrage will again lift and advance about 1500 yds at the same rate until H+73 minutes on which line it will rest until H+87
At H+87 minutes the barrage will commence to advance a further 1500 x at the same pace until H+115 min where it will rest till H+132 minutes
After this hour any Artillery support

still within range, will be given lines W J which no fire is to be put down.

These lines will be 600 & 9000 yds from orig inf starting line and the times of ceasing fire W J these lines will be H + 126' and H + 156'.

VI. ~~The H will advance on a bearing of~~
~~105°T from St Georges Bogh~~ ~~as far as~~
~~Bogh~~ N
Compass bearings as per attached Table

VII Companies will move in following order,
in diamond formation of platoons. 300 yds between Coys

A   .·. D
B   .·. A
C   .·. B
HQ   .·. C
T.M Section

Coy, Adj - Runners with Brigadier in rear of 1 Border Regt.

VIII 2/Lt Slade M.C. who will carry a white flag, will be responsible for direction. Three scouts will be attached to HQ of 1/Border Regt.
Remainder scouts with 2/Lt Slade in advance of the Bn. ~~Lt Slade will carry a white flag~~
Companies will be responsible for keeping touch with the Coy in front.

IX Each Coy will have 1 pair pigeons. These will be carried as soon as ready.

X Orders re move to Assembly posns will be issued as soon as possible.

SECRET. Copy No..........

1st.Batt.The K.O.S.B. - ORDER No. 73.

REF.MAPS, GERMANY 2L & 2K. 12th.DECEMBER,1918.

1. The 87th.Infantry Brigade Group will continue its march to-morrow through COLOGNE and cross the RHINE via the HOHENZOLLERN BRIDGE. The Battalion will be Billeted in BERG GLADBACH.

2. Routine to-morrow will be as follows:-
   REVEILLE - 0530. BREAKFAST - 0730.
   DINNER - On arrival in Billets.
   Remainder of Routine as for to-day.

3. The Battalion will parade ready to pass the Starting Point at 0930. Platoons will parade at 0845 and Company Parade will be at 0915.

   Starting Point - X-Roads immediately North of present Billet.

   Order of March - Band,H.Q.,C,D,A,B,Coys.

   Dress - Marching Order. Waterproof Sheets & Leather Jerkins in the Packs. Steel Helmets on back of Packs.

   10 yards distance will be maintained between Companies and 20 yards distance between Battalions. After clearing HOHENZOLLERN BRIDGE normal distances will be assumed when possible.

4. ROUTE - HOHENZOLLERN BRIDGE-DEUTZ-MULHEIM STR.-DANZIER STR.--BERG GLADBACH STR.-DELLBRUCK.

5. The Saluting Point will be at the West end of the HOHENZOLLERN BRIDGE. The Army Commander or the G.O.C.Division will take the Salute. The Band of the Battalion will wheel to the left opposite the Army Commander and counter march to form up facing him, playing the Regimental March whilst counter marching and whilst the Battn. is passing. They will join behind the Battalion and will cease to play on doing so, but will strike up again when 300 yards past the Saluting Point. They will resume their position at the head of the Battalion as opportunity offers.

   All ranks are warned to look the Army Commander straight in the face.

6. The Transport will be Brigaded and march in rear of the Bde. in the following order:-Bde.H.Q-S.W.B-K.O.S.B.-BORDER REGT. All cookers will march at the head of Brigade Transport in the above order. Company Lewis Gun Limbers only will follow in rear of Companies.

7. Blankets(rolled in bundles of ten),and greatcoats(rolled in bundles of five),securely tied & properly labelled,will be at the Qr.Mr. Stores by 0630,and Officers'Kits by 0730.
   Company Mess Boxes will be collected at 0800,the Mess Cart to be at H.Q.Mess at 0815.

8. The Billeting Party under Major J.B.W.PENNYMAN will parade at Battn. H.Q. at 0715. Bicycles will be taken.

9. The first 10 minutes halt from 0950 to 1000 will not be observed.

10. All Lorries will either clear the HOHENZOLLERN BRIDGE by 0800 or move in rear of the whole Division in which case they will not reach the Bridge before 1600.

11. The usual certificates re cleanliness of Billets will be handed to the Adjutant before marching off.

12. The Regtl.Police,F.P.Prisoners,and soldiers in arrest,will march in rear of the Battalion under the Orderly Officer.

8 Copies issued at 2330.
Copies to H.Q.,Coys,Qr.Mr., (SD) F.DALE,Captain,
T.O.,& R.S.M. A/Adjutant,1st.Batt.The K.O.S.B.

Army Form C. 2118.

WAR DIARY
or
INTELLIGENCE SUMMARY.
(Erase heading not required.)

NOVEMBER 1918

Reference Map. Sheet 36 (Belgium France.)

Place	Date	Hour	Summary of Events and Information	Remarks and references to Appendices
ST. ANDRÉ	1st November		Battalion Ceremonial Parade. Shickshot Jumping. Lecture to Battalion by Medical Officer. 4 O.R. Sick evac.	
"	2nd November		Brigade inspection in Ceremonial Drill by Lieut. General H.d.B. de Lisle K.C.B. Commdg. XVth. Corps. Draft of 5 O.R. joined. 1 O.R. Sick evac. To Base unfit. 3 O.R.	
"	3rd November		Divine Service. Lt. Colonel Wilkinson D.S.O. assumed command of the Bde. during absence of Brigadier General. 1 O.R. rej. wounded. 1 O.R. Sick evac. Lieut. G.L. BROWN M.C. to U.K. Sick.	
"	4th November		Specialist Training. Saluting & Sword Drill; Musketry; Close order Drill & Field work. Draft of 5 O.R. joined. 3 O.R. Sick evac. 1 O.R. to U.K. for Temp Commission.	

Army Form C. 2118.

WAR DIARY
or
INTELLIGENCE SUMMARY.
(Erase heading not required.)

Instructions regarding War Diaries and Intelligence Summaries are contained in F.S. Regs., Part II. and the Staff Manual respectively. Title pages will be prepared in manuscript.

Place	Date	Hour	Summary of Events and Information	Remarks and references to Appendices
ST ANDRÉ	5th November		Specialist Training. Remainder of Coys. at Midroad of O.C. Coys. Inspection of S.B. Res. Sports & Amusements Committee formed. Draft of 3 O.R. joined.	Ref. Map. Sheet 37.
"	6th November		Training as for 5th inst. Intimation received of the following awards:— 10475, C.S.M. R.H. SMITH M.M., & 241606, Pte. D. LITTLE M.M. 'A' Coy; Bar to M.M.; 29458, L/Sgt. MIXON J. 'B' Coy; 241362, L/C. H. THOMPSON 'B' Coy; 22226, Pte. H. BOWIE 'A' Coy; 41043, Pte. T. SUMMERS 'C' Coy, the M.M. Inter-Platoon Football Competition instituted. Draft of 3 O.R. joined. 1 O.R. sick evac. 1 O.R. to U.K. for Temp. Commission.	
"	7th November		Battalion paraded at 09.30 & marched via WAMBRECHIES & BONDUES to Billets in TOURCOING. Battalion in Billets at 13.10. Intimation received of the award of the D.C.M. to the following:— 8178, C.S.M. TURNBULL 'D' Coy; 41807, L/C. D. CRANSTON 'D' Coy; 27714, Pte. J. MILLIGAN 'B' Coy; 12411, Pte. A. McELWRATH 'C' Coy, & 10332, L/C. FERGUSON J. 'C' Coy. Draft of 4 O.R. joined.	
TOURCOING	8th November		Battalion paraded at 08.45 & marched via TOM BROEK & BREDA to Billets in the Support Area. Battalion in Billets about 13.30. Information received	Ref. Map Sheet 29.

Ref. Map. Sheet 29

Place	Date	Hour	Summary of Events and Information	Remarks and references to Appendices
SUPPORT AREA	9th November		that the enemy were retiring all along our front, & Bde. ordered to follow up 88th. Bde. as Bdn. in Support. Capt. E.K. RYAN M.O. to hospital sick. 1st. Lieut. F.M. SMITH M.C. U.S.A. joined for duty as M.O.	
"			Battalion at half hours notice. Battalion paraded at 1400 & marched to Billets in the Area O.33.b. & O.34.a. b & c. Battalion in Billets at 1730. Lt. Colonel WILKINSON D.S.O. rejoined from Bde. 1 O.R. sick evac. Intimation received of the following awards:- Bar to D.C.M., C.S.M. H.B. TURNBULL D Coy; 201776, L/Cpl. RUSH J.H. C Coy; 19250, Sgt. COTTON J.A. C Coy; & 20727, L/Cpl. PAXTON W, D Coy the D.C.M. 1 O.R. sick evac.	
"	10th November		Battalion paraded at 0800 & marched to Billets about D.Q. central (on the outskirts of CELLES). Battalion in Billets about 1115. Intimation received of award of M.C. to a/Capt. R.D. SMITH & a/Lieut. G.F. McVEAN; & D.C.M. to 20r. 21871, L/Cpl. BELL C. M.M. A Coy. 2 O.R. rej sick.	
CELLES	11th November		Battalion under orders to move forward in direction of LESSINES in support of the 88th. Bde. While Battalion was on parade ready to move off official notification was received that an armistice had been signed & that hostilities would cease at 1100. Orders for move cancelled & Battn. instructed to work on the	

Army Form C. 2118.

WAR DIARY
or
INTELLIGENCE SUMMARY.
(Erase heading not required.)

Instructions regarding War Diaries and Intelligence Summaries are contained in F. S. Regs., Part II. and the Staff Manual respectively. Title pages will be prepared in manuscript.

Place	Date	Hour	Summary of Events and Information	Remarks and references to Appendices
CELLES	12th November		Improvement of the roads in the vicinity of the village. 1.O.R. Rifle Exh.	
			Companies at disposal of O.C. Coys. for Inspections, cleaning ups, etc. Inspection of Billets by the Commdg. Officer. 'A' Coy. working on cleaning up roads. Casualties Nil.	
"	13th November		Orders received in the early morning that the Division was to be concentrated in an Area East of a line at 30/S.16.c & 38/A.24.c. Battalion paraded at 1100 & marched via ARC-AINIERES & AINIERES to Billets in the vicinity of ST. SAUVEUR. Battalion in Billets at 1630.	Ref. Map Sheet 37.
ST. SAUVEUR	14th November		Battalion paraded at 0700 & marched to Billets on the outskirts of GHOY. Battalion in Billets at 1400. Information received that the Division would almost certainly be part of the Army of Occupation & would be prepared for a 12 days' march to a station in German territory. 3 O.R. sick rmc.	Ref. Maps Sheets 29, 30, 37.
"	15th November		Divine Service. Rifle Inspections. Company Drill. Criminal, cleaning equipment. 9/Lieut. A.R. FORREST. 3/1 Royal Scots joined for duty. Draft of 154 O.R. joined.	

Army Form C. 2118.

WAR DIARY
or
INTELLIGENCE SUMMARY.

(Erase heading not required.)

Place	Date	Hour	Summary of Events and Information	Remarks and references to Appendices
ST. SAUVEUR	16th November		Companies at disposal of O.C. Coys. 1st Lt. F.M. SMITH M.C. U.S.A. rejoined 88th F.A. Capt. A.A. WILSON R.A.M.C. joined for duty vice M.O. 10 R. Sick one. 1 O.R. inj. Self. 7 O.R. to Base unfit.	
"	17th November		Bde. ordered to take over the area of the 229th. Infy. Bde. comprising the Right (Ref. Ops. Sheets 30&38) Bde. area of the new Divisional Area. Battalion paraded at 0900 & marched via LESSINES to Billets in STOQUOI, 6 miles, taking over from the 16th. Battn. DEVON REGT. Battalion in Billets at 1130. Draft of 12 O.R. joined. 1 O.R. Rein. 226 Emp. Coy. 10 R. Sick one.	
STOQUOI	18th November		57th. Bde. ordered to advance in the first echelon on the Right of the 29th. Division, with a Canadian Division on the Right & the 86th. Bde. on the Left, the advance to be covered by cavalry advancing one day's march ahead. The Bde. marched to the line of the Road from SOIGNIES to ENGHIEN between HORRUES & MARIE BOIS, both inclusive. A halt of 2 days to be made on this line. The Battalion paraded at 0910 & marched to Billets near SOIGNIES. Battalion in Billets at HAUT BOIS 1400. 3 O.R. Sick one.	Ref. Maps Sheet 38.

Army Form C. 2118.

WAR DIARY
or
INTELLIGENCE SUMMARY.
(Erase heading not required.)

Place	Date	Hour	Summary of Events and Information	Remarks and references to Appendices
SOIGNIES AREA	19th November		Decided to move Battalion to better & more convenient Billets in the village of PETIT ROEULX-LES-BRAINE about a kilometre away. Companies moved independently commencing about 1400. Battalion in Billets by 1500. 2/Lieut. A.W. WYLIE M.C. Evacuated Sick. Strength: 30 O.R. Sick one.	Ref Map BRUSSELS 6 1/100,000.
PETIT ROEULX-LES-BRAINE	20th November		Companies at disposal of O.C. Coys for training. 30 O.R. Sick one.	
"	21st November		The Bn. continued its march, the 1st K.R.R.C. providing the Advance Guard. The Bn. marched at 0945 & marched via BRAINE-LES-COMTES & VIRGINAL SANNE to billets on the outskirts of ITTRE. Progress delayed somewhat through some of the other units of the Bde. being late. The column halted in the square at ITTRE to admit of a public welcome being accorded the Troops by the inhabitants. Battalion in Billets at 1530 hrs. Billets rather hurriedly constructed. Casualties Nil.	Ref Map BRUSSELS N.W.1/50.
ITTRE	22nd November		Companies at disposal of O.C. Coys. for cleaning up, inspections, etc. 11 men per Coy. under Capt. R.D. SMITH M.C. took part in	

Army Form C. 2118.

WAR DIARY
or
INTELLIGENCE SUMMARY.
(Erase heading not required.)

Instructions regarding War Diaries and Intelligence Summaries are contained in F. S. Regs., Part II. and the Staff Manual respectively. Title pages will be prepared in manuscript.

Ref. Map. BRUSSELS 6
1/100,000.

Place	Date	Hour	Summary of Events and Information	Remarks and references to Appendices
ITTRE	22nd November		ceremonial entry of King of the Belgians into BRUSSELS. Major J.B.W. PENNYMAN 2/ K.O.S.B. joined for duty as Second in Command.	
			The Bde. continued its march. The Battalion paraded at 0910 & marched via LILLOIS, WITTERZEE & GENAPPE to Billets at BOUSVAL. Battalion in Billets at 1400. Casualties NIL.	
BOUSVAL	24th November		Battalion paraded at 0930 & marched via BEAURIEUX to Billets in WAHAIN ST. PAUL. Battalion in Billets at 1500. Lieut. A.W. WYLIE M.C. rejoined from wounded (Gas). Lieut. R.R. HOGARTH, Lieut. A McDONALD, & 2/Lieut. D.J. CRACKER. Scouts joined for duty.	
"	25th November		Bde. ordered to take our whole of Divisional front. Battalion paraded at 1055 & marched via SART-LEZ-WAHAIN to Billets in ORBAIS (distance about 5 miles). Battalion in Billets at 1345. 1 O.R. sick evacuated.	

Army Form C. 2118.

WAR DIARY
or
INTELLIGENCE SUMMARY.
(Erase heading not required.)

Reference Maps - BRUSSELS, MARCHE, & LIEGE.

Place	Date	Hour	Summary of Events and Information	Remarks and references to Appendices
ORBAIS	26th November		Battalion resting & cleaning up. Ceremonial Drill & L.G. Training. Party of Officers & O.R. visited Brussels by motor lorry. 11 O.R. sick evac.	
"	27th November		Battalion paraded at 0810 & marched via PERWEZ HAMBRAINE, and FORVILLE to Billets in BIERWART. Battalion in Billets at 1410. Battalion inspected on the march by General PLUMER G.O.C. Second Army & complimented by him on the turnout & good marching. 1 O.R. sick evac.	
BIERWART	28th November		Battalion paraded at 0915 & marched via WANZE & HUY to Billets in ROUSÉ = OUTRELOUX FERRE & villages near ETRÉE. Dinners on the march. Battalion in Billets at 1645. 3 O.R. sick evac.	
FERRE	29th November		Battalion paraded at 0830 & marched via STREE, TINLOT, FRAITURE & ANTHISNES to Billets in MONT. Battalion in Billets at about 1500. Casualties - Nil.	

Army Form C. 2118.

WAR DIARY
or
INTELLIGENCE SUMMARY.
(Erase heading not required.)

Place	Date	Hour	Summary of Events and Information	Remarks and references to Appendices
MONT.	30th November.		Battalion under orders to continue the march to LA REID in the LA CREIZE area. About 0645 the march was cancelled & Companies were placed at disposal of O.C. Companies for cleaning up etc. About 1000 Division issued instructions for the march to be proceeded with no previously ordered. The Battalion paraded at 1030 & marched via COMBLAIN-AU-PONT and AYWAILLE. Battalion in billets in LA REID at 1700. Casualties - Nil.	Ref. Map Sheet MARCHE 9.

Dictated by

[signature]
W/Adj. 10728923
Captain

Battle Instructions.   SECRET.

(1) Contact Aeroplanes

(a) Attacking troops will carry — Red Ground Flares.
Tin Discs — American Cloth & Box Respirator for the purpose of communicating with Contact aeroplanes.

(b) Contact aeroplanes will be marked by TWO BLACK RECTANGULAR FLAGS attached to and projecting from the lower plane on each side of the fuselage and each contact plane will also have a TRAILING STREAMER.
All troops will be taught how to recognise a contact aeroplane.

(c) The contact aeroplane will call for signals from the attacking troops by sounding a KLAXON HORN and dropping WHITE LIGHTS.

(2) COUNTER ATTACK AEROPLANE

A counter attack aeroplane will be in the air in 2 lifts hourly from zero + 1 hour and will give warning of hostile counter attack by dropping a RED PARACHUTE VERY LIGHT.

(3) WOUNDED

It has been noticed that walking wounded almost invariably arrive at R.A.P.s without arms or equipment.
Company, Platoon & Section Commanders must see that walking wounded in all cases take their arms and equipment to the R.A.P. where a dump will be formed.

(4) PRISONERS OF WAR

will be taken to Advd. Div. H.Q. K.7.c.4.8. where they will be taken over by the A.P.M.

(5) Bivouac & FORWARD AREAS

As an advance when any territory conquered from the enemy is likely to be attended by the spread of lowdegree disease in animals care must be taken with regard to watering & feeding of animals and occupation of buildings

(a) Water troughs or mangers used by enemy will be avoided.
If of wood - destroyed - iron or concrete cleaned or disinfected

(b) Special arrangements should be made for watering - canvas buckets - ground sheets etc being used
There is little danger in running streams.

(c) Stabling will not be occupied by horses until inspected by the veterinary authorities and certified free from danger.

(d) Any forage left behind by the enemy should be treated with suspicion

(e) Sudden deaths of animals should be reported to Vet. authorities immediately

(7) Medical Arrangements

R.A.P.   K 12 b 2.3.
Cou Stowes   NEIBERG. aw S5 B.0.1.

ADS   K 11 b 6.5.

Corps MDS.   Prison Ypres.

Walking wounded St. Kenworks "

Entraining point –   WATERDAMHOEK E 15 d 5.0.
for Stretcher cases
& walking wounded
            horses for w.w. K 7 c 5.8
2 squads   S.Bs allotted to R RAPs

Gassed cases   to M.D.S.

All slightly gassed & NYDG cases to 88 F.A at
Dw. Rest St =   Sheet 27 E 9 d central

ADS will be at BARAKKEN L 10 d 9.9
    as soon as condition permits

M.DS. will be at DADIZEELE as
    soon as condition permit

Battle Instructions.

(4) Each man will carry 1 days rations
+ [strikethrough] — [strikethrough] rounds — one
     on him
hand grenade — 2 sand bags.

Mules carrying S.A.A. ammunition —
each carrying 27 shovels & 6 picks
will move in rear of the batt'n

KOSB

Centre of general
~~General~~ line of advance will be

Mary's Bridge (over the Wulfdambeek)
Northern edge of Cork Copse (1000 yds)
Northern edge of Sovereign Wood (1000 yds)
Barn Fork (1500 yds)
Salines (2300 yds)
Railway Line (near Chapel) (2700 yds)
Queinne Aerodrome (2600 yds)

Magnetic Bearings

1st taken at MARY'S Bridge — 105°
2nd " " Beek of Woes crossing — 104°
    Railway at L 11 d 7.3 — 110°
3rd Road running N & S on SALINES — 104°

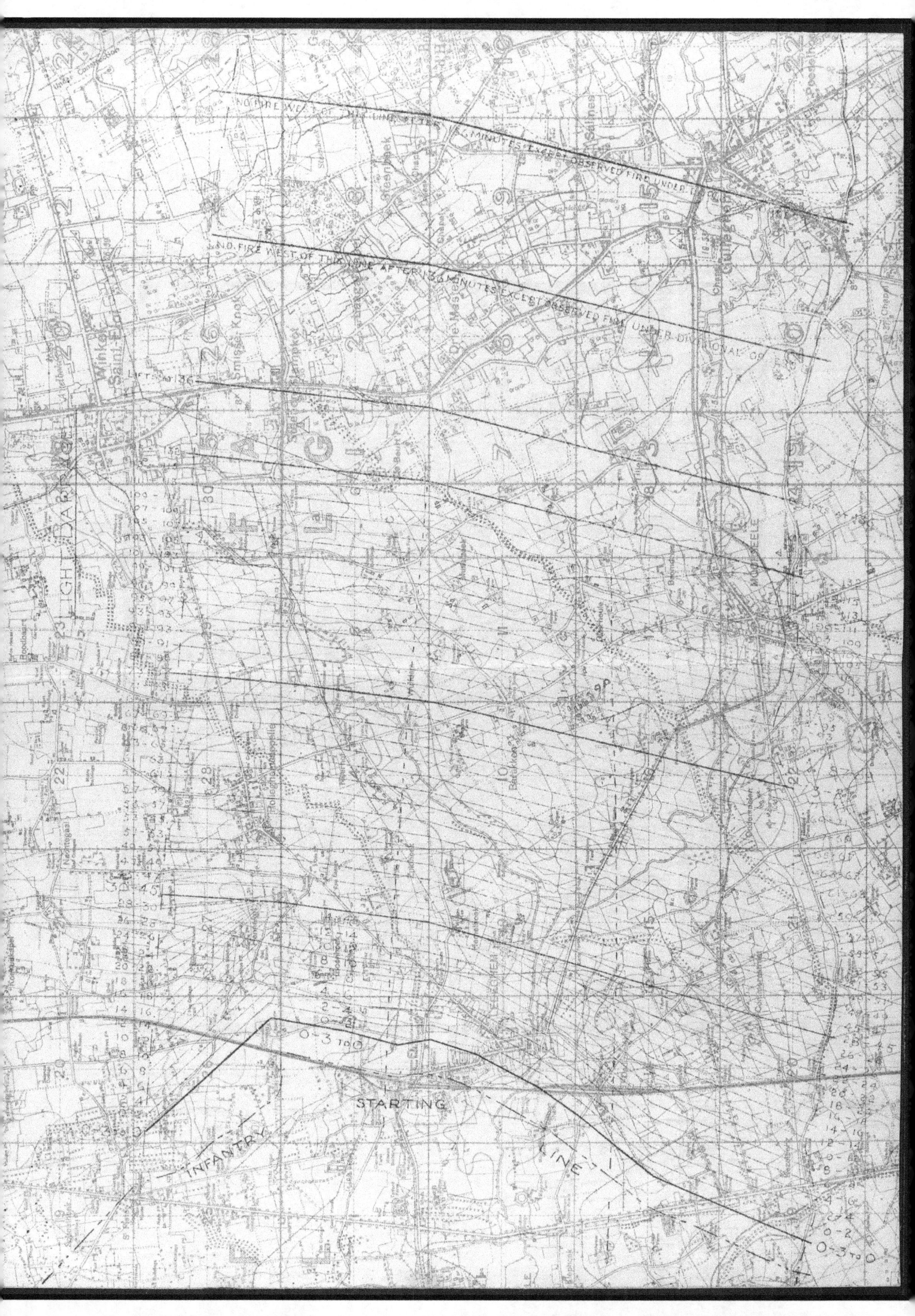

SECRET

Herewith war diary
for month ended 31/1/48.

Serial 42

Lt. Colonel
COMMANDING 1st BN. THE BORDER REGT.

Volume No. 53
Army Form C. 2118.

WAR DIARY
or
INTELLIGENCE SUMMARY.
(Erase heading not required.)

1/KOSB Vol 33

Title pages DECEMBER 1918.

Place	Date	Hour	Summary of Events and Information	Remarks and references to Appendices
LA REID	1st December		The Bde. continued its march to Rhineland. The Battalion paraded at 09.20 & marched via SPA to billets in outlying villages of FRANCORCHAMPS, 2 kilometres from the frontier. Battalion in Billets at 13.00. 1 O.R. rejoined from hospital.	Ref. Reft. MARCHE 9
FRANCORCHAMPS	2nd December		Companies at disposal of O.C. Coys. for cleaning up, inspection, repair of boots, etc. Orders for move of Bde. received but cancelled later. 4 O.R. sick week.	"
"	3rd December		Companies at disposal of O.C. Coys for inspections, General Drill etc. Casualties - Nil.	
"	4th December		The Bde. continued its march & crossed the Frontier into Germany on this date. The 87th Bde. led by the 1/K.O.S.B. was the first Bde. of the Division to enter enemy country. The Battalion, under the command of Major T.B.W. PENNYMAN, paraded at 06.30 & reached the Frontier Post at 08.40. The Pipe Band halted at the boundary & the Battalion marched into German territory to the	Ref. Reft. MARCHE 9 GERMANY IN.

Army Form C. 2118.

WAR DIARY
or
INTELLIGENCE SUMMARY.
(Erase heading not required.)

Place	Date	Hour	Summary of Events and Information	Remarks and references to Appendices
			Return of the Regtl March. Battalion proceeded via BURNENVILLE, MALMEDY, WEISMES, & JANNER to Billets in WEYWERTZ. Battalion in Billets at 1515. Inhabitants were more curious than antagonistic. Orders issued for all civilians to be in their houses between the hours of 1700 & 0600. Kept the Burgomaster & the Curé, Officiers & O.R. ordered to carry arms on proceeding from Billets. 20 O.R. Sick was.	
WEYWERTZ 5th December.			Battalion paraded at 0800 & marched via NIDRUM – ELSENBORN – KALTERHERBERG Ref. M.sh to Billets in the town of MONTJOIE. MONTJOIE reached about 1300 but Battalion did not get into Billets until 1400 on account of some confusion in & A. no to apportionment. 30 R. Sick was.	GERMANY IM & IA
MONTJOIE 6th December.			Battalion paraded at 0800 & marched via INGENBROICH – SIMMERATH – STRAUCH – (Ref. M.sh SCHMIDT – HARSCHEIDT and NIDEGGEN to Billets in THUM. Battalion in Billets at 1650. Casualties - Nil.	GERMANY IL
THUM 7th December			Battalion paraded at 1055 & marched via FROITZHEIM – VETTWEISS & (Ref. M.sh GLADBACH to Billets in MÜDDERSHEIM. Battn. detailed to furnish Advance Guard for Bde-formed of A & C Corps. Battalion in Billets at 1015. Lt. Colonel W.T. WILKINSON D.S.O. rejoined from leave. 8 O.R. Sick was.	GERMANY IL

Army Form C. 2118.

WAR DIARY
or
INTELLIGENCE SUMMARY.
(Erase heading not required.)

Instructions regarding War Diaries and Intelligence Summaries are contained in F. S. Regs., Part II. and the Staff Manual respectively. Title pages will be prepared in manuscript.

Place	Date	Hour	Summary of Events and Information	Remarks and references to Appendices
MUDDERSHEIM	8th December		Battalion paraded at 0900 & marched via GLADBACH - ERP - LECHENICH & DIRMERZHEIN to Billets in GYMNICH. Battalion in Billets at 1410. Official intimation received of award of French Croix de Guerre à l'ordre Division to Lt. Colonel W.T. WILKINSON D.S.O. & the French Croix de Guerre à l'ordre Regiment to 9584 WRSM. STEVENSON P.D.C.M. 8 O.R. 5th Bn. Cmd.	Ref. Map of GERMANY 1L & 2L
GYMNICH	9th December		Battalion paraded at 0725 & marched via TURNICH - NODRETH - FRECHEN & HIND to Billets in the KRIEL Area of COLOGNE. Battn. halted 15 kilos from destination for dinner. Battalion in Billets at 1400 & housed in large German Military Hospital in LINDEN BERGER ALLEE. 2 O.R. Sick Evac.	Ref. Map of GERMANY 1L & 2L
KRIEL AREA	10th December		Battalion commenced preparation for Ceremonial March through COLOGNE. Lecture to Officers & N.C.Os on "Looting" etc. by the Commanding Officer. Battalion at Baths. 3 O.R. Sick Evac.	
KRIEL AREA	11th December		Work same as for 10th inst. except that 2 hours Ceremonial Drill was carried out. 2 O.R. Sick Evac. 3 O.R. rejoined from Sick.	

346

Army Form C. 2118.

WAR DIARY
or
INTELLIGENCE SUMMARY.
(Erase heading not required.)

Instructions regarding War Diaries and Intelligence Summaries are contained in F. S. Regs., Part II. and the Staff Manual respectively. Title pages will be prepared in manuscript.

Place	Date	Hour	Summary of Events and Information	Remarks and references to Appendices
KREFELD	12th December		New clothing & boots issued & fitted. A Inspection parade for Divisional Commander. Complete Transport inspected by the Commanding Officer. 2 O.R. Sick Evac.	
KREFELD	13th December		Battalion paraded for Divisional March at 0900. Being unable to march with 57th Bde. the middle Bn. of the Divisional Column, with bayonets fixed, the Column marched via the City square NEUMARKT, past the Cathedral & thence to the city end of the HOHENZOLLERN BRIDGE where The Corps Commander Lt. Gen. Sir C.W. JACOB K.C.B. took the Salute. Battalion crossed the RHINE at 1030, the Bank playing the Regtl. March as the Battn. marched over the Bridge. Battalion in Billets at 51035 G=D 34H (Sqm.1) 0930 establishments of M.O. (see H.Q.S. Order No. 73 at 12/12/18 attached). Capt. L.H. INGRAM-JOHNSON takes on R.I. C.C.S. & joins in command of Machine Guns on 14th inst. 2 Lt. AT HAMILTON # Bde. as Bde. Transport Officer.	By Wire GER.H.Q. 2 L & 2 K.
BERG GLADBACH	14th December		Brigade expected to move to finish destination but were one postponed for 24 hours. Companies not disposed of O.B. lays for cleaning up, inspection of arms & Lewis Guns carried out. Lewis Guns inspected by Asst. Adjutant (Capt. E.W. AGAR). 3 O.R. rejoined Sick.	
"	15th December		Battalion paraded at 0930 & marched via ODENTHAL–GLOBUSCH–BLECHER & KAPTERN HERBERG to Billets in town of BURSCHEID. Battalion in Billets.	By Wire G.S. GER H.Q. 2 L & 2 K

Army Form C. 2118.

WAR DIARY
or
INTELLIGENCE SUMMARY.
(Erase heading not required.)

Instructions regarding War Diaries and Intelligence Summaries are contained in F. S. Regs., Part II. and the Staff Manual respectively. Title pages will be prepared in manuscript.

Place	Date	Hour	Summary of Events and Information	Remarks and references to Appendices
		at 1230.	Cavalleria N12.	
BURSCHEID	16th December		Battalion paraded at 1030 & marched via HAGEN to Billets in BURS- first destination. Battalion in Billets at 1330. First 15 Battalion Billet in BURG Castle. 3.O.R. dich one. Lieuts BULLEN-SMITH M.C. + R.R.MACBRYAN & 3.O.R. to U.K. to bring Battn. Colours.	Bn. Ref. S.S.Y.N.ss. 28.
BURG CASTLE	17th December		The village of BURG understood to be Battalion's final destination. Companies at disposal of O.C. Coys. for cleaning up, inspections + Ceremonial drill. Battalion Officers' Mess inaugurated. Orders issued as to Bounds. The control of the civilian population, & demeanour to be observed by troops towards the German people. 7.O.R. dich one.	
"	18th December		Companies at disposal of O. C. Coys. for Guard Drill, Ceremonial, Handling of Arms & marching past in Line & in "fours". Battalion bathed at unopened Rgtl. Baths. Start made with the Army scheme of Refresher Courses for Tradesmen at Army Workshops. 3.O.R. rejoined from Sick.	

D. D. & L., London. E.C.
(N001) Wt. W17711M2031 750,000 5/17 Sch. 52 Forms C2. 6/14

Army Form C. 2118.

WAR DIARY
or
INTELLIGENCE SUMMARY.
(Erase heading not required.)

Place	Date	Hour	Summary of Events and Information	Remarks and references to Appendices
BURG CASTLE	19th December		Companies at disposal of O.o.C Coys. for Ceremonial & Guard Drill. Lecture to the Battalion by the Commanding Officer. C Coy moved from the Castle to Billets in the Village of Burg. 4 O.R. sick evac.	
"	20th December		Companies at disposal of O.o.C Coys. for Ceremonial & Guard Drill. 2Lt. A.R FORREST, 3/Bn Lento appointed Battn. Signalling Officer. Lieut. A. BROWN & Lieut. D. ARMSTRONG returned from 6 mths Tour of duty in U.K. Draft of 91 O.R. joined.	
"	21st December		Companies at disposal of O.o.C Coys. for Guard Drill, etc. All Signallers under the Signalling Officer for training. Orders issued that troops would disperse with carrying rifles or wearing full Order within the Billeting Area. 3 O.R. Sick evac. 1 O.R. rejoined Sick.	

Army Form C. 2118.

WAR DIARY
or
INTELLIGENCE SUMMARY.
(Erase heading not required.)

Instructions regarding War Diaries and Intelligence Summaries are contained in F. S. Regs., Part II. and the Staff Manual respectively. Title pages will be prepared in manuscript.

Place	Date	Hour	Summary of Events and Information	Remarks and references to Appendices
BURG CASTLE	22nd December		Sunday - Church Parades. Battalion bathed. 2 O.R. sick one.	
"	23rd December		Company Route Marches. Guard Drill. 9/Lieut. T. W. RENWICK, 5/K.O.S.B. to U.K. sick. 5 O.R. sick one.	
"	24th December		Lieut. Colonel W.T. WILKINSON, D.S.O., assumed temporary command of 88th Infy. Bde. and Major J.B.W. PENNYMAN temporary command of the Battalion. Companies at disposal of O.C. Companies for Ceremonial & Guard Drill, etc. Battalion paid out. Programme drawn up for Battalion New Year's Day Sports. 6 O.R. proceeded. Sgts. Mess formed. Casualties - Nil.	
"	Christmas Day		HOLIDAY. As it was anticipated that the special fare for the Battalion New Year Dinner would arrive before Xmas it was decided to have the dinner on Xmas Day instead of New Year's Day. Unfortunately the special food did not arrive so instead Xmas Dinner was possible. Voluntary Church Service was held in the morning & a Battalion Concert in ye Evng.	

350

Army Form C. 2118.

WAR DIARY
or
INTELLIGENCE SUMMARY.
(Erase heading not required.)

Instructions regarding War Diaries and Intelligence Summaries are contained in F. S. Regs., Part II. and the Staff Manual respectively. Title pages will be prepared in manuscript.

Place	Date	Hour	Summary of Events and Information	Remarks and references to Appendices
			in the evening.	
			Official intimation received of the award of the Military Cross to the late Captain C.H.W. CRICHTON-BROWNE, 3/K.O.S.B. Postings holding troops to enter COLOGNE & BONN received. 2 Guardsmen struck off 1 O.R. sick one. 2 O.R. rejoined from sick.	
BURG CASTLE	26th December		Companies at disposal of O.o.C. Coys. for Squad & Ceremonial Drill. All Lts. & Clks. under the R.S.M. for instruction in Guard Duties. 2 O.R. sick one.	
"	27th December		Company Route Marches. Education Classes commenced under direction of Lieut. D.A. KEIR, Shorthand, Book-keeping, languages etc., etc. 2 O.R. sick one. 1 O.R. rejoined sick.	
"	28th December		Companies at disposal of O.o.C. Coys. Commanding Officer's inspection of Billets. Work at Demobilization began. 50 O.R. sent home (all Miners with the exception of one Demobilizer & one Long Service man) - 45 to DUDDINGSTON Dispersal Station & 5 to Shorncliffe Dispersal Station. 2 O.R. sick one. 4 O.R. rejoined sick.	

Army Form C. 2118.

WAR DIARY
or
INTELLIGENCE SUMMARY.
(Erase heading not required.)

Instructions regarding War Diaries and Intelligence Summaries are contained in F. S. Regs., Part II. and the Staff Manual respectively. Title pages will be prepared in manuscript.

Place	Date	Hour	Summary of Events and Information	Remarks and references to Appendices
BURG CASTLE	29th December		Sunday. 2 O.R. to U.K. for Demobilisation.	
"	30th December		Companies at disposal of O.C. Companies for Musketry & Ceremonial Drill. 2 O.R. to U.K. for Demobilisation.	
"	31st December		Tactical Exercises by Platoon Commanders. - "The Platoon in the Attack". Battalion held ant. & A.R. to U.K. for Demobilisation work. The following were amongst the guests of the officers of the Battalion at dinner:- Major-General CAYLEY C.M.G. Commdg 24th. Division, with several members of his Staff; Brigadier-General JACKSON C.M.G. D.S.O. Commdg. 87th Bde; etc, etc. 1 O.R. sick evac.	

Dictated by
[signature] Captain
Adjt. 1/KOSB

SOUTHERN (LATE 29TH) DIV
87TH INFY BDE

1ST BN K. O. S. B.
JAN - APR 1919

To UK

WAR DIARY or INTELLIGENCE SUMMARY

Army Form C. 2118.

JANUARY 1919

1 KOSB

Place	Date	Hour	Summary of Events and Information	Remarks and references to Appendices
BURG CASTLE	1st January		NEW YEAR'S DAY. HOLIDAY. With the exception of Pudding Beer the special fare for the New Year's Dinner was not forward & in spite of all efforts the dinner fell somewhat short of that of former years. Battalion Sports were held on a field above the Castle. The Pipe Band & Survival Brass Band were in attendance. A prize of £5 subscribed by the Officers for the Company securing the most Points was won by "B" Coy being second, "A" Coy third, & "D" Coy last. Cinema show in "A" Coys Billet in the evening. Casualties NIL.	
"	2nd January		Companies at disposal of Co. C. Comps. Battalion Drill. 13 O.R. to U.K. for Demobilization. 2/Lieut. R.C. SLADE M.C. 3/K.O.S.B. joined for duty. 10 R. sick enne. 1 O.R. rejoined sick.	Jan – Apr 1919
"	3rd January		Battalion Route March. Lieut. W. BARNARD M.C. rejoined from 6 months Tour of duty at home. 6 O.R. to U.K. for Demobilization.	

Army Form C. 2118.
363

WAR DIARY
or
INTELLIGENCE SUMMARY.
(Erase heading not required.)

Instructions regarding War Diaries and Intelligence Summaries are contained in F. S. Regs., Part II and the Staff Manual respectively. Title pages will be prepared in manuscript.

Place	Date	Hour	Summary of Events and Information	Remarks and references to Appendices
BURG CASTLE	4th Jan.		Companies at disposal of O.C. Coys. Inspection of Billets by the Commanding Officer. Duties connected in connection with Shorts promoted by the Division. Advance Party arrived from Berwick with the Batln Colours. 3 O.R. to U.K. for Demobilisation.	
	5th Jan.		Divine Service. Regtl. Censorship of Letters & Postcards dispensed with. 2 O.R. sick wme. 30 R. to U.K. for Demobilisation.	
	6th Jan.		Companies at disposal of O.C. Coys. for Musketing Drill, Ceremonial & Physical Training. "A" Coy. at firing practice on Rifle Range. 5 O.R. sick wme.	
"	7th Jan.		Training as for 6th. "D" Coy. on the Rifle Range. Lieut. C.C. ROBERTSON, High. Lye. Bn. joined for duty. Draft of 44 O.R. joined. 10 O.R. reported sick.	

Army Form C. 2118.
354

WAR DIARY
or
INTELLIGENCE SUMMARY.
(Erase heading not required.)

Instructions regarding War Diaries and Intelligence Summaries are contained in F. S. Regs., Part II and the Staff Manual respectively. Title pages will be prepared in manuscript.

Place	Date	Hour	Summary of Events and Information	Remarks and references to Appendices
BURG CASTLE	8th Jan.		Practice Ceremonial Parade for visit of Divisional Commander.	
			1.O.R. sick one.	
"	9th Jan.		Coys. at disposal of Co. C. Coys. for practicing Position of Attention, Handling of Arms & Marching past in Line. "C" Coy. at firing practice on Rifle Range.	
			1.O.R. sick one. 2.O.R. spinal.	
"	10th Jan.		Training as for 9th inst. 2.O.R. sick one. 7.O.R. to U.K. for demobilization. Visit to E.D.V.S. paid.	
"	11th Jan.		Practice Ceremonial Parade for visit of Divisional Commander. Played 1st Border Regt. at Hockey & won 7–2. 6.O.R. sick one. 10.O.R. joined from base. 1.O.R. rejoined sick & 1.O.R. from Batt. H.Q.	

Army Form C. 2118.
355

WAR DIARY
or
INTELLIGENCE SUMMARY.
(Erase heading not required.)

Place	Date	Hour	Summary of Events and Information	Remarks and references to Appendices
BURG CASTLE	12th Jan.		Sunday. 10.O.R. to V.R. for Demobilization. 5 O.R. reported sick.	
"	13th Jan.		Corps. at disposal of O.C. Coys. for General Drill & Handling of Arms etc. 12.O.R. to V.R. for Demobilization. 1 O.R. joined from Base.	
"	14th Jan.		Practice in General Drill. 21 O.R. to V.R. for Demobilization. 30 R. joined from Base + 2 from Leave.	
"	15th Jan.		Battalion inspected by Major General CAYLEY C.V.O. Commdg. 29th. Actg. the Inspection the General presented the returns of decorations awarded Officers + O.R. of the Battn. Following the Parade the General inspected the Regtl. Institutes + Billets of the Battn. + expressed himself as highly satisfied. 1 O.R. sick rec'd. 2 O.R. reported sick.	
"	16th Jan.		Companies at disposal of O.C. Coys for Musketry & Physical Training. 30 R. sick evac.	

Army Form C. 2118.

WAR DIARY
or
INTELLIGENCE SUMMARY.
(Erase heading not required.)

Instructions regarding War Diaries and Intelligence Summaries are contained in F. S. Regs., Part II. and the Staff Manual respectively. Title pages will be prepared in manuscript.

Place	Date	Hour	Summary of Events and Information	Remarks and references to Appendices
BURG CASTLE	17th Jan.		Training as for 16th inst. Q.O.R. re-enlisted for 4 years. Information received of the award of the Belgian Croix de Guerre to A/Capt. D. SLOAN; Lieut. H.A. HENRY, 240753, C.S.M. WILSON M.M. "B" Coy; 201748, Cpl. RUSH, T. D.C.M., "C" Coy; 10796, A/Sgt. DARCY W. "D" Coy; & 12002, Cpl. HIBBERT J. (att. T.M. Bty.). In LONDON GAZETTE dated 11/1/14 the following awards were published:— T. Capt. E.W.T. AGAR M.C.; 9115, Sgt. MICHIE W. "A" Coy. D.C.M.; 8126, Dvr. Trooper W. McKENZIE & 10615, 2/Cpl. ALFORD J. "B" Coy. "MENTION". N.K.I.N.C. to Ouistrieuse Service failed. 2/L.R. joined from Base & 1 from hospital.	
"	18th Jan.		Voluntary Parade ordered but cancelled owing to bad weather. Indoor instruction substituted. Lecture to the Battalion on "Demobilisation" by the Comdg. Officers. 1 O.R. re-enlisted for 4 years. 1 O.R. to U.K. for Demobilisation.	
"	19th Jan.		Divine Service. 1 O.R. to U.K. for Demobilisation. 1 O.R. Sick leave. 1 O.R. sick from Base & 1 from Hospital.	

(A9759) Wt W3358/P260 600,000. 12/17. D. D. & L. Sch. 53a. Forms/C118/13

Army Form C. 2118.

357

WAR DIARY
or
INTELLIGENCE SUMMARY.
(Erase heading not required.)

Instructions regarding War Diaries and Intelligence Summaries are contained in F. S. Regs., Part II and the Staff Manual respectively. Title pages will be prepared in manuscript.

Place	Date	Hour	Summary of Events and Information	Remarks and references to Appendices
BURG CASTLE	20th Jan.		Coys. at disposal of O.C.Corps. for Handling of Amn. Musketry, etc. 2.O.R. sick evac. U.K. rejoined sick.	
"	21st Jan.		Conferences at disposal of O.C.Corps. 1.O.R. rejoined sick.	
"	22nd Jan.		Conferences at disposal of O.C.Corps. 1.O.R. sick evac.	
"	23rd Jan.		Conferences at disposal of O.C.Corps. N.C.Os.Class started under this Appt. 9. The R.S.M. 2.O.R. rejoined sick.	
"	27th Jan.		Conferences at disposal of O.C.Corps. 1.O.R. Sick evac. I.O.R. To U.K. for demobilization.	

Army Form C. 2118.

WAR DIARY
or
INTELLIGENCE SUMMARY.
(Erase heading not required.)

Place	Date	Hour	Summary of Events and Information	Remarks and references to Appendices
BURG CASTLE	25th Jan		Battalion Route March as strong as possible. C.O. & U.K. for Demobilisation.	
"	26th Jan		Divine Services. O.C. & U.K. for Demobilisation. O.C. Sick was. 10 O.R. temporal to the F.C.	
"	27th Jan		Companies at disposal of Co. O. Conference. Battalion photographed by official Army Photographer Marseilles No.	
"	28th Jan		Companies at disposal of Co. C. Companies. Marseilles No.	
"	29th Jan		Battalion Route March as strong as possible. 2/Lieut. W.C. SELLAR to U.K. for Demobilisation. 10 O.R.s U.K. for Demobilisation.	

Army Form C. 2118.

WAR DIARY
or
INTELLIGENCE SUMMARY.
(Erase heading not required.)

Instructions regarding War Diaries and Intelligence Summaries are contained in F. S. Regs., Part II and the Staff Manual respectively. Title pages will be prepared in manuscript.

Place	Date	Hour	Summary of Events and Information	Remarks and references to Appendices
BLR CASTLE	30th June		Companies at disposal of Co. C. Companies. Company Guards discontinued. 3.B.B. sick none.	
"	31st June		Companies at disposal of Co. C. Companies. Lecture by Major NAETH on "German East Africa". 3.B.B. sick none.	
			Detail by Milligan Captain July 1922 3.B.B	

WAR DIARY or INTELLIGENCE SUMMARY

Army Form C. 2118.

Vol 38

Place	Date	Hour	Summary of Events and Information	Remarks and references to Appendices
Bihucourt	1st February		Guard Mounting Display for all Officers + N.C.Os Commanding Officers Inspection of Billets. Companies at disposal of Co. Cdrs during remainder of forenoon. 13 O.R.'s & 2 for duty sent to 1.C.R. reported from 87th I.W. Bn. 1.C.R. reported from 87th I.W. Bn.	
"	2nd February		Divine Services. 1.C.R. Reinforcement of 13 on section in 1.C.R.	
"	3rd February		Companies at disposal of Co. Cdrs. 2 Lieut. W.C. Brown struck off strength on being sent to hospital. 1.C.R. T.H.L. to Hospital sick. 1 N.C.O. reported sick.	
"	4th February		Companies at disposal of Co. Cdrs. 1 O.R. sick etc.	

Army Form C. 2118.

WAR DIARY
or
INTELLIGENCE SUMMARY.
(Erase heading not required.)

Instructions regarding War Diaries and Intelligence Summaries are contained in F. S. Regs., Part II. and the Staff Manual respectively. Title pages will be prepared in manuscript.

Place	Date	Hour	Summary of Events and Information	Remarks and references to Appendices
BURG CASTLE	5th February		C.O's Parade ordered but cancelled on account of weather. Route march substituted. Lecture by Dr. E.L. HATZFELD on "to Circumnavigate the World". 2C.R. Sick one.	
"	6th February		Conference at disposal of de L. Corps. 2nd Lieut. T.C. HOWIE to U.K. sick. 1 O.R. To U.K. for Demobilization	
"	7th February		Conference at disposal of Div 8 temporarily but 8 & M.G.Batty's sent a Comm to U.K. for Demobilization. 10R Sick one.	
"	8th February		Conference at disposal of de L. Corps. Cavalry Officers lectures to Brdn. to day. 1 Captain of other Bomb'rs also Lieut. G.E. de JEAN M.C. to U.K. on leave. 1 O.R. to hospital sick. 1 other Rank to U.K. sick. 2 S+T.H.O.S.B. on S.O.	
"	9th February		Divine Service. 10R Sick one. 1 OR reported sick	

(A972) Wt W3251/369 80000 12/17 D D & L. Sch. 53a. Forms/C2118/13.

362

Army Form C. 2118.

WAR DIARY
or
INTELLIGENCE SUMMARY.
(Erase heading not required.)

Instructions regarding War Diaries and Intelligence Summaries are contained in F. S. Regs., Part II. and the Staff Manual respectively. Title pages will be prepared in manuscript.

Place	Date	Hour	Summary of Events and Information	Remarks and references to Appendices
BURG CASTLE	10th February		Companies at disposal of Co. Cmdr. 'A' Coy. on Rifle Range. 'B' R. Rush Lane.	
			3 O.R. Evacuated in U.K. 1 O.R. to U.K. for Demobilization. 2 O.R. reported sick.	
"	11th February		B Coy on Rifle Range. Lecture by Chaplain. Capt. J. Evans to 'A' & 'C' Coys. on the History of 8 R.Q. CASTLE. D Coy at disposal of Co. Cmdr.	
			1 O.R. reported sick	
"	12th February		Battalion route march under Lieut. G.E.M. THWAITES M.C.	
			2 O.R. to U.K. for Demobilization.	
	13th February		A Coy - D Coy - Musketry C Coy - on Rifle Range. Lecture to B & D Coys on the History of Burg Castle.	
			1 U.R. Sick evac.	
	14th February		Companies at disposal of Co. Cmdr. B Coy - Medical Inspection.	
			2 O.R. Sick evac.	

WAR DIARY
or
INTELLIGENCE SUMMARY.
(Erase heading not required.)

Army Form C. 2118.

Instructions regarding War Diaries and Intelligence Summaries are contained in F. S. Regs., Part II. and the Staff Manual respectively. Title pages will be prepared in manuscript.

Place	Date	Hour	Summary of Events and Information	Remarks and references to Appendices
BUSTO CASTLE	15th February		Preliminary conference at Bishop of No. 6 Corps. Conveying Officers' Instructions at Bristo. Draft of 3 O.R. joined. 10 O.R. reported sick.	
"	16th February		Routine duties. 1 O.R. searchlight to U.K.	
"	17th February		Conference at Bristo to Coveying Officers. D'Bryen Ofle Range. Lt. D.C. BURDEN SMITH M.C. to U.K. as Reg. Officer for Leave Party. 10 O.R. joined.	
"	18th February		Conference at Bishop. No. 6 Conference. "B" Coy. on Rifle Range. Lieut. R.R.M. BRYAN to U.K. as Reg. Officer for Leave Party. 3 O.R. searchlight U.K.	
"	19th February		Agstant Ranche on duty to travell for Agge Bay. B Coy. on range. The best of weather, continues more & more, the Castle. T/Lt. F.W. TATAR M.C. to U.K. as Reg. Officer for Leave Party. 10 O.R. from U.K. 12 O.R. sick conv.	

Army Form C. 2118.

WAR DIARY
or
INTELLIGENCE SUMMARY.
(Erase heading not required.)

Instructions regarding War Diaries and Intelligence Summaries are contained in F. S. Regs., Part II. and the Staff Manual respectively. Title pages will be prepared in manuscript.

Place	Date	Hour	Summary of Events and Information	Remarks and references to Appendices
BULG OESTLE	20th February		Conference at midday at Bn. C. Coys. Billy. Coys allotted to D. Coy. Wiring Letion to Battalion by Lt. Smithson South in in Press. "B" Coy carried out the dangerous nearly from the doubtful mortality of the guns. Lieut A. v. Dixon D. of Scott went to Hospital I.K. in hurry "Hornsell" To drive by G.O.C.	
"	21st February		Conference at midday at Bn. C. Infantry Coys. in Range at Lucca. Gun Practice. Lt. Lacer, Chamlet, Hamishe, in Command of Sp. Tournament by 3 and 4 Pl. Battalion concert Party gave performance in A Coys. billet. 2.O.R. Sick evac.	
"	22nd February		Conference at midday of Cl. Coys. "B" Coy wiring. Officers & Sergeants Locus Hostel Quart. Masters & gooks dinners 5 goats. Casualties - nil.	
"	23rd February		Divine Serice. 1. O.R. Sick evac. 1. O.R. reyound Sick.	

Army Form C. 2118.

WAR DIARY
or
INTELLIGENCE SUMMARY.
(Erase heading not required.)

Instructions regarding War Diaries and Intelligence Summaries are contained in F. S. Regs., Part II. and the Staff Manual respectively. Title pages will be prepared in manuscript.

Place	Date	Hour	Summary of Events and Information	Remarks and references to Appendices
BURG CASTEL	24th February		Conference at entrainment H.Q. C. Coy. B Coy. Diary. D Coy. on Duty. Three spare wagons allotted to C Coy. Battn. Train met 1st R.W. on 2nd Bound of Divisional Reserve at Boxy at about 1-1 after noon. Time 10 R. Sick 202. 2W R. report sick. 2 C.R. report from 8/7th T.M. Bty.	
"	25th February		Conference at departure of C. Coy. B Coy. arrived. Winnal Dumps allotted to D. Coy. 11 Coy. moves to C Coy. formed Ghubiq report 2W R. W. R. at Buigesfraw D. Pinad 2 wife with an 30 devices sent 3 C.R. Sick one.	
"	26th February		Conference at departure of C Coy. D Coy. on Leave in Rest B.'s place. B Coy. on Reaf in town. Ghurs Coy. allotted to C Coy. O Coy. Rugby match versus Yeomanry at Batln. transport lost 4 tries to nil. Result in 12th Hussars Beach Coy. 2W R. Spotlight on Coue.	

Army Form C. 2118.

WAR DIARY
or
INTELLIGENCE SUMMARY.
(Erase heading not required.)

Place	Date	Hour	Summary of Events and Information	Remarks and references to Appendices
BHQ CSSH	27th February		Batteries at disposal of C.R.A. Bgd. D'Coy. Wiring Ruyaulcourt. To B'Coy Hz L.G. Practice. B'Coy reported at the Gymnasium. 10.R Sick case. 10.R. reported sick. 3 O.R. excused for Duty.	
"	28th February		Companies at disposal of the C.R.A. Bgd. D'Coy. Wiring Ruyaulcourt. B'Coy H.Q. L.G. Practice. Lt. Col. J.P. Barth Cmm R.E. at HQ & R.E. Bathed in try bath. Piping with gas. 11 gas 2O.R. Sick wire. 1O.R. reported sick.	

Signed
[signature]
Lt. Col.
Commanding
3rd Bn [?]

DA
GHQ
3rd ECHELON

Herewith WAR DIARY of 1st. Batt. Th. K.O.S. Borderers for month of March 1919 & for 2 days of April 1919. Volume No. 56.

This completes Battalion's war record to date of cadre's arrival in U.K.

Please acknowledge.

3/4/19.

Captain
Adjt. for Lt. Colonel
Commdg. 1/KOSB

Army Form C. 2118.

WAR DIARY
or
INTELLIGENCE SUMMARY.
(Erase heading not required.)

MARCH - 1917.

WO.39/UCloud

Place	Date	Hour	Summary of Events and Information	Remarks and references to Appendices
BURG CASTLE	1st March		Battalion Route March as strong as possible under Capt. SLOAN. 2/O.R. Light cases. M.O. to O.C. left investigating.	
"	2nd March		Church Parades. Battalion met 1st Border Regt. at HILGEN in 3rd round of Divisional Football Tournament & won by 3 goals to 1. 2/O.R. Light cases.	
"	3rd March		Companies at disposal of O.C. Companies. D' Coy. continued Wiring. C' Coy. at Lewis Gun Practice. 2/O.R. Light cases. M.R. admitted hospital 4/O.R. still on list.	
"	4th March		Companies at disposal of O.C. Companies. 'D' Coy. Wiring. 'B' Coy. at Rifle Grenade Practice. Battn. met 2/Hants at BERG GLADBACH in the semi-final of Divisional Football Tournament & won by 3 goals to 2 after Extra Time. M.R. discharged returned to lists in U.K.	

Army Form C. 2118.

WAR DIARY
or
INTELLIGENCE SUMMARY.
(Erase heading not required.)

Instructions regarding War Diaries and Intelligence Summaries are contained in F. S. Regs., Part II and the Staff Manual respectively. Title pages will be prepared in manuscript.

Place	Date	Hour	Summary of Events and Information	Remarks and references to Appendices
BURG CASTLE	5th March.		Companies at disposal of O.C. Companies. C & D Coys. Wiring. B Coy. at grenade practice. 3 O.R. sick. W.c.c.	
"	6th March.		Companies at disposal of O.C. Companies. C & D Coys. Wiring. B Coy. at Lewis Gun & Rifle Grenade Practice. 2/Lieut. E. HUNTER W.Y. Regt attd. left on leave to U.K. 16 O.R.s. left attd. to U.K. 2 O.R. to Military Prison ROUEN. 1 O.R. rejoined from hospital.	
"	7th March.		Companies at disposal of O.C. Companies. B & D Coys. Wiring. 2 O.R. sick. W.c.c.	
"	8th March.		Battalion Medical Inspection. Lecture by Lt. KIRTLAND on Burns the Poet. Casualties - Nil.	

Army Form C. 2118.

WAR DIARY
INTELLIGENCE SUMMARY.
(Erase heading not required.)

Instructions regarding War Diaries and Intelligence Summaries are contained in F.S. Regs., Part II. and the Staff Manual respectively. Title pages will be prepared in manuscript.

Place	Date	Hour	Summary of Events and Information	Remarks and references to Appendices
BURG GASTEL	9th March		Church Parade. Battalion played 1st. Lanco. at BERG GLADBACH in the final of the Divisional Tournament & lost by 4 goals to 1. 2 U.S. Leave.	
"	10th March		B, C & D Coys. Congratulatory message from Brigadier with regard to smart turn-out of Bn. 10 A.R. rejoined from hospital. No leave to U.K. 3 Leave proceeded U.K. on re-enlistment leave.	
"	11th March		B, C & D Coys. Military U.R. rejoined from hospital.	
"	12th March		B, C & D Coys. Training. 1 O.R. rejoined Bn. 1 O.R. rejoined Bn.	

364

WAR DIARY
INTELLIGENCE SUMMARY.
(Erase heading not required.)

Army Form C. 2118.

370

Place	Date	Hour	Summary of Events and Information	Remarks and references to Appendices
BURG CASTLE	13th March		"B" & "D" Coys. History, Education classes terminated in view of immediate reduction to cadre strength. Groups of "intensivs" officers & O.R.s announced. A/Capt. R. SLOAN & 2/Lieut. R.C. SPADE M.C. with 111 O.R.s proceeded to join 1/5th K.R.R.s. A/Capt. R.D. SMITH M.C.; 2/Lieuts. A.W. WYLIE M.C. & D.M. OGILVIE; & 2/Lieuts. R. KENNEY & J.H. BRUCE transferred (on paper) to 1/5th K.R.R.s.	
"	14th March		Companies at disposal of O.C. Coys. A Coy of the 52nd DEVONS arrived & took over the outpost duties of A Coy & 1 Platoon of C Coy. 1 O.R. reported sick.	
"	15th March		The remainder of the 52nd DEVONS arrived & the process of "handing over" commenced. Lieut. J. MARTIN M.C. & 2/Lieuts. D.F. CLACHER & G.B. McKENZIE & 107 O.R.s proceeded to U.K. for Demobilization.	
"	16th March		Divine service. Lieut. D. DONLEY & 2/Lieut. A.R. FORREST & 50 O.R.s proceeded to U.K. for Demobilization. 2/Lieut. A.G. STOREY & 40 O.R.s.	

Army Form C. 2118.

WAR DIARY
or
INTELLIGENCE SUMMARY.
(Erase heading not required.)

Instructions regarding War Diaries and Intelligence Summaries are contained in F. S. Regs., Part II and the Staff Manual respectively. Title pages will be prepared in manuscript.

Place	Date	Hour	Summary of Events and Information	Remarks and references to Appendices
			Demobilised whilst on U.K. leave Major G.I.N. TOWNLEY M.C., Lieut. McNICOL, BERNARD, ARMSTRONG, HIGGINS & MORGAN & 197 O.Rs. Proc. to 1/5 K.R.R.B	
BURG CASTEL	17th March		The remainder of the Battalion proceeded by motor lorry to MULHEIM. Billeted in a School in the centre of the town. 5 O.R. sick evacuated.	
MULHEIM	18th March		Cleaning up & settling into Billets. Casualties NIL.	
"	19th March		Rifle Inspection. Capt. C.C. ROBERTSON & Capt. D.L. KEIR & 19 O.Rs. proceeded to U.K. for demobilization. Lt. Colonel W.T. WILKINSON D.S.O. rejoined from duty as G.O.C. 88th Bde.	
"	20th March		Rifle Inspection. Casualties - NIL.	
"	21st March		Battalion paraded at 0900 for inspection. 13 O.Rs. to U.K. for demobilization.	

Army Form C. 2118.

WAR DIARY
or
INTELLIGENCE SUMMARY.

(Erase heading not required.)

Instructions regarding War Diaries and Intelligence Summaries are contained in F. S. Regs., Part II. and the Staff Manual respectively. Title pages will be prepared in manuscript.

Place	Date	Hour	Summary of Events and Information	Remarks and references to Appendices
MULHEIM.	22nd March.		Baths. All Demobilization Carys etc. instructed on account of strikes in U.K.	
"	23rd March.		Rifle Inspection. Casualties - Nil.	
"	24th March.		Battalion paraded at 0900 for inspection. Information received that normal movements for Leave & Demobilization were resumed.	
"	25th March.		Rifle Inspection. Casualties - Nil.	
"	26th March.		Battalion paraded at 0900 for Inspection. Lieut. H.A. HENRY, & Lieut. A.E. HAMILTON & 7 O.R. to U.K. for Demobilization.	

Army Form C. 2118.

WAR DIARY
or
INTELLIGENCE SUMMARY.
(Erase heading not required.)

Instructions regarding War Diaries and Intelligence Summaries are contained in F. S. Regs., Part II and the Staff Manual respectively. Title pages will be prepared in manuscript.

Place	Date	Hour	Summary of Events and Information	Remarks and references to Appendices
MOLHEIM	27th March		Rifle Inspection. 6 O.R. to U.K. for Demobilization. Notified that probable date of departure of Cadre for U.K. was 29th March.	
"	28th March		Rifle Inspection. 56 O.R. to U.K. for Demobilization. 2 O.Rs. Transferred to 115th K.O.S.B.	
"	29th/31st March		Cadre left in motor lorries at 0800 & entrained at COLOGNE Train Station for DUNKIRK at 0900. Route to DUNKIRK area VERVIERS, HUY, NAMUR, LILLE & HERRIS. Train halted at LILLE for about 7 hours. Arrived at DUNKIRK at 0600 on 31st. Detrained & proceeded to No 1 Camp. Cadre bathed & disinfected & transferred to No 2 Camp.	
DUNKIRK	1st April		Awaiting orders to proceed to U.K.	

Army Form C. 2118.

WAR DIARY
INTELLIGENCE SUMMARY.
(Erase heading not required.)

Place	Date	Hour	Summary of Events and Information	Remarks and references to Appendices
DUNKIRK	2nd April		Embarked on S.S. ANTRIM at 1230. Sailed at 1305 & arrived at DUNKIRK at 1630. Entrained for ALDERSHOT at 1620 & arrived in Barracks at ALDERSHOT about 2300. At Greenock Entire relieved at Station by His Excellency Murray G.C.E Albrecht Cormont. The Entire consisted of Lieut. W.T. WILKINSON D.S.O. (Comdg. Officer), Major. T.S.W. PENNYMAN (2nd in command), Capt. G. DALE McOLYMONT, Lieut. G.B. MS., AA & ST. BGE., Capt. R.A. MORETON, Lieut. D.T. HUMS WHN & 2Lieut. JSIMPSON, Together with 51 other Ranks. Officers in charge of Entire were Lieut. HOLMES & 2Lieut. SIMPSON. Dictated by [signed] Captain O/C 1st Bn. The KRRB	

www.ingramcontent.com/pod-product-compliance
Lightning Source LLC
Chambersburg PA
CBHW081435300426
44108CB00016BA/2371